Practitioners Perspectives on Contemporary Supply Chain Management Issues

The Danish Supply Chain Panel 2012-2016

Practitioners Perspectives on Contemporary Supply Chain Management Issues

The Danish Supply Chain Panel
2012-2016

University Press of Southern Denmark

© University Press of Southern Denmark and the authors

Copies from this book are only allowed according to agreement between Copy-dan and the Ministry of Education.

Edited by Jan Stentoft
ISBN 978-87-91070-91-4

Published by
University of Southern Denmark
Department of Entrepreneurship and Relationship Management
Universitetsparken 1
DK-6000 Kolding
Phone: +45 65 50 14 02
Web: www.sdu.dk/ier

Layout and print Specialtrykkeriet Arco

Danish Purchasing and Logistics Forum – DILF – is the largest member association in Denmark for people working with procurement and logistics. In total these people comprise a professional network of about 2000 members. Founded in 1962 DILF make a point of being an unpolitical, not-for-profit based association with nation-wide coverage. The aim is to help improve the professional standard in purchasing and logistics in the private and public sector.

To my wife Mona Stentoft

Contents

Preface 9
Introduction 11

Section 1 – Panel articles in 2016
Big data applications in sourcing processes 23
Total cost of ownership: A strategic important tool 32
Do you have the right supply chain talent on board? 42
Increased expectations of using disruptive technologies
   in supply chains 52

Section 2 – Panel articles in 2015
Supply chain executives and net working capital:
   An untapped potential 65
Business process outsourcing is driven by needs for increased
   flexibility and cost reductions. 76
Strategic awareness of supply chain complexity and firm
   performance: The missing link 84
Few CEO's have a background in SCM 94
Effective inventory management is permanent job
   in a changeable world 104

Section 3 – Panel articles in 2014
Risk management in supply chains is considered important
   but resource allocation is difficult 115
Supply chain planning: An area with room for improvements 125
Sustainable sourcing: Supplier control or development 135
Social media in Danish supply chains:
   A top or pop phenomenon? 148

Section 4 – Panel articles in 2013

Supply chain innovation: About the ambidextrous dilemma
    in the supply chains 163
Danish companies practice with Sales & Operations Planning 176
The role of purchasing in open innovation:
    Fixed partners and flirts on new hunting grounds. 187
Organizational-wise the supply chain is a bag of mixed candies 199
Time-to-market: A cross-functional process with a
    gap between theory and practice 209

Section 5 – Panel articles in 2012

Working with sustainability is primarily driven by financial savings . 219
"Home knitted" approaches to measuring supply chain performance 227
Cost-focused supply chain innovation 238
Supply chain strategy is prioritized in top management. 248

About the contributors 259

Preface

This book focuses on a supply chain management (SCM) institution, *The Danish Supply Chain Panel* founded in 2011, in collaboration with a group of researchers from University of Southern Denmark and Danish Purchasing and Logistics Forum (DILF).

The panel conducts four to five surveys a year that are designed to take the industrial pulse in selected areas: Disruptive Technologies in Supply Chains, Business Process Outsourcing, Time-To-Market, etc. Based on the data collected, SDU researchers write a popular science article that both disseminates research and builds a bridge between the practical and academic worlds.

More specifically, the book comprises 22 articles from the period 2012-2016. These articles cover a wide spectrum of SCM-related issues and subjects. The hope is that the authors maintain this relevance and cadence, so that we can a look forward to a 2021 edition.

The book's positioning in the academic ranking– A, B, C, D, E – is unclear. However, based on the readability of the publication and its relevance, the book probably falls into the second half of Piercy's classification schema (Piercy, 2002). This makes it a relevant book, and worth reading because each article has significant content and is well-structured; making it easy to navigate. It is also well written and highly accessible – despite the fact that it is in English.

This is probably not the type of book to be read from end to end, but rather it is an inspirational read to be used to highlight certain topics that a reader might be interested in. Such an approach is likely to whet a reader's 'appetite' for further information on a topic.

The book is based on a great idea, contributes towards filling a gap in the SCM literature, and therefore can only be welcomed.

John Johansen, Professor, Aalborg University

Introduction

The idea to establish *The Danish Supply Chain Panel* came on our journey home from an international field study trip with M.Sc. students from University of Southern Denmark to Rio de Janeiro in Brazil in November 2010. During a stopover in Sau Paolo, I had a conversation with a former colleague about the need to continuously being close with industry since we both had practical industrial experience after our Ph.D. studies. After a period where the idea matured more, a contact was established to Danish Purchasing and Logistics Forum (DILF). A meeting was held in the spring 2011with CEO Søren Vammen, DILF and Marketing and Communication Manager Mie Holm Christensen, DILF about the idea and we agreed to start up such a panel from the calendar year 2012.

The core idea

Companies' supply chains account for an ever growing source of competitive advantages both through customer-oriented service and cost reduction initiatives. Leading companies have recognized that the supply chain must have the same strategic attention as product development and sales/marketing. The globalization of supply chains contribute to increased complexity and dynamics. This requires still increased skills to ensure change readiness in order to deal with conflicting objectives such as service levels and net working capital. There are no simple answers to the challenges that supply chain executives are facing. However, we can bring such challenges in the light, exchange ideas and viewpoints as a basis for own learning and improved decision making within this area. This is basically the idea with *The Danish Supply Chain Panel*.

The participants in *The Danish Supply Chain Panel* do receive annually four to five mini-surveys, each focusing on a specific practical and academic problem. Each survey consists of 10 to 15 questions. As a novelty in 2015, the mini-surveys started to be conducted in English to accommodate a request from the panel. This helped in recognizing the importance of international colleagues and partners and in turn it did lead to a larger audience.

The need for more practical relevant research

Universities all over the world have not evaded an increased output oriented performance management of the research efforts. This takes place through acknowledged ranked peer-reviewed academic journals leading to a still intensified debate concerning the pros and cons of such ranking systems and the metrics such as different types of rankings are being applied (Adler and Harzing, 2009; Lambert and Enz, 2015). Performance measures are important instruments for deans in evaluating their staffs for carrier advancement and to assess their performance in relation to other research institutions. Thus, people follow the incentives with more publications, but relevance does not automatically increase (Arlbjørn et al., 2008).

The ranking environment has both positive and negative effects however with a direction and strengths being much depended on the eyes that view. Among positive elements, the ranking might stimulate what is good quality and increase competition among journals, universities and business schools. On the contrary, this ranking culture has also created challenges for academic environments i.e. coerciveness to site journals (Wilhite and Fong, 2012); development of citation cartels among researchers (Franck, 1999), standardization of research regarding questions and methods (Arlbjørn et al., 2008); higher emphasis on quantity at the expense of quality (Davis, 2014) and the practical relevancy is downplayed to tailor themes, methods as well as theoretical perspectives to fulfill the needs through the academic journals gatekeepers (Bennis and O´Toole, 2005).

Alvesson and Gabriel (2013) summarize the positive side-effects of this development as:
- clearer procedures and rules
- standardization of work
- efficiency in the labor process
- smooth and predictable evaluation processes
- limited anxiety and worries associated with too much ambiguity and surprises.

Alvesson and Gabriel (2013) also point out some challenges to this development:
- limited imagination and creativity
- predictable and, at best, moderately interesting texts written in an impersonal, committee like style
- strong sub-specialization and exploitation of a narrow "core competence,"
- evaluation based on ticking off different boxes
- limited chances of unexpected, challenging, and surprising results and texts, as researchers feel constrained by different rules and standards for doing research.

Finally, Alvesson and Gabriel (2013) argue that articles in leading journals often score high on rigor while making incremental contribution; in other words, the articles fail to say something very novel or make a strong social impact.

Bennis and O'Toole (2005) state: "Nevertheless, a management professor who publishes rigorously executed studies in the highly quantitative *Administrative Science Quarterly* is considered a star, while an academic whose articles appear in the accessible pages of a professional review, which is much more likely to influence business practices, risks being denied tenure." Piercy (2002) has made an alternative and ironic explanation of the ranking system as:

A-journal: **A**lmost no-one reads this, and even fewer understand it. This must be one of the best journals in the world! We spy world-class irrelevance and must reward it!

B-journal: **B**ut, a few people might read this and understand it. This cannot be quite as good.

C-journal: **C**rowds of people read this regularly. So, it cannot be very prestigious then, national performance only at best!

D-journal: **D**ozens of people read this. Well that cannot rate very highly in academic terms at all.

E-journal: **E**verybody reads this. Oh, how very unpleasant – writing things that other people read, yuk! We must denigrate this as fast as possible, and penalize those who produce such things.

Schacht (2016) has covered this problem area in an article in the weekly magazine Mandag Morgen [Monday Morning] in August 2016 from which the following quotations are included to illustrate the problem area:

"Our Head of Department is not rewarded based on whether we do something that is practical relevant. She is measured on whether we can attract external funding and publish something that can yield more money. However, we should reward researchers to conduct international recognized research as well as reward their abilities to translate the results of the theoretical research into practice", Professor Per Vagn Freytag, University of Southern Denmark in Schacht (2016). [Translated from Danish to English].

"The current performance measures pull uneven. If I should publish much of the industry works in a research journal then I will consider the most prestigious research, it will be rejected since it is too practical and applicable. We are not against the ranking that exists today. However, there must be a balance. Right now it is tipped toward advantages for theoretical rather than practice relevant research. There is so much useful knowledge at the universities that never come out to the practical world (practice) because they are not rewarded to anchor research in practice" Professor Jan Stentoft, University of Southern Denmark in Schacht (2016). [Translated from Danish to English].

"I do agree that the focus is on publishing where you earn the highest points. It controls the way one plan his or her research and the dissemination. And these highest points will never increase the probability of research being read by the industry (practitioners), because it often is irrelevant for practice. However, one can publish upon it. What is worse is that we need to educate candidates about the industry, but when researchers and teachers have an obsession towards theory, then basic and common problem areas become theoretical topics that talented practitioners already know how to solve. This is not the right way to educate engineers who later will work in the industry." Professor John Johansen, Aalborg University in Schacht (2016). [Translated from Danish to English].

As discussed by Stentoft and Rajkumar (2017) using the work by Van de Ven and Johnson (2006), practical relevance in SCM research must be related to both relevance in the research questions (a problem of knowledge production) and relevance in communication with practice (a problem of knowledge transfer). In order to fulfill such objectives one must interact with practice. Otherwise we run the risk of losing the taste of practice sitting in ivory towers eating candy with wrapping! Still it is important to remember that researchers should not become practitioners, but are ought to have capabilities that make them capable to communicate with practitioners. The central issue here is that, it is difficult to communicate the alternatives of implementing research if you do not know the outset of practicability! (Arlbjørn et al., 2008).

Recently researchers within SCM and operations Management have begun discussion about the need for more practical relevant research and concrete solutions to create more relevancy (Lambert and Enz, 2015; Tang, 2016; Toffel, 2016). *The Danish Supply Chain Panel* can be seen as a supplement to existing approaches to secure relevancy in knowledge production and knowledge transfer.

Evaluation of The Danish Supply Chain Panel

In January 2017, members of *The Danish Supply Chain Panel* were asked to evaluate their participation in the panel. The main purpose of this evaluation was to get insights into their motivations for attending the panel and to learn what works and can be improved. As a result, 50 useable respondents came of this survey. 90% of the respondents reported seniorities with the practice of purchasing, logistics or SCM and of more than 10 years. Then, 80% of the respondents are working in companies with more than 100 employees, 62% are working in manufacturing companies, 16% in retail and few respondents are from transport and consultant companies.

Some examples of comments the respondents provided in an open question about their motives for being part of *The Danish Supply Chain Panel*.

- Contribute to shared knowledge of status and needs for the industry
- Share my knowledge and experience
- Get inspiration
- To be part of the survey and thereby both contribute AND follow how things move
- General interest in most of the topics chosen
- Because I hope that it will provide some insight
- Is it relevant to get an update on the supply chain focus in Denmark
- I was invited, and I think the panel is interesting, as well as I would like to support the network

- Feel an obligation to share knowledge in a business area of my concern, for the benefit of my company and other companies in general
- To see general topics from companies
- The future is about development and I can through my participation in *The Danish Supply Chain Panel* get business updates
- Enjoy to contribute and also read the survey results
- Through the panel it is possible to fuel/participate in dialog on specific SCM topics and also gain insights
- I do think it is very important to keep and expand a direct Integrated link between the operative industries and University of Southern Denmark
- The topics covered are relevant, and so are the analysis produced
- To share data which can be used to develop and share supply chain challenges among DILF members.
- To contribute with data for research and case studies on how supply chains are operating in Denmark, and how it can be improved to strengthen the Danish competitiveness.
- Working with a leading company within our industry I find it interesting to contribute with information to the studies of the challenges that Danish companies have concerning supply chain.
- To give something back to an organization [DILF] which I regard as the number 1 organization within Procurement in DK.

The respondents were also asked through which sources they gain new knowledge in this area. As evident from Figure 2, the topmost source for knowledge is through industrial networks (38%), followed by trade press

Figure 1: The panel members use of various sources of SCM knowledge

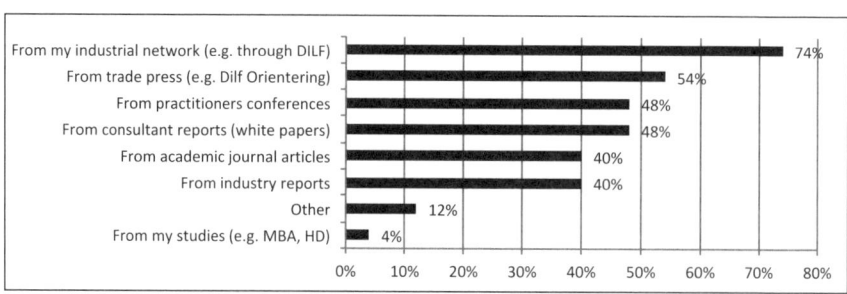

Source: Stentoft and Rajkumar (2017)

articles (27%), practitioner conferences (24%), consultant reports (24%), academic journals articles (20%), industry reports (20%), and so on.

The respondents have been asked to evaluate what they would like to have more of in the mini-surveys. In general, they are satisfied with comments like "they are appropriate as they are; they are fine and most of them are good and meaningful". Some have also raised good points as:
- More specific questions and surveys
- Learning about other companies
- More in depth analysis with supporting text
- Green logistics, ERP systems, digital logistics
- Innovation and use of planning tools
- Commercial aspects with impact on supply chain
- Warehousing and a focus on B2B
- Supply chain combined with APP's, internet applications, webpages
- Something about leading a procurement organization and develop successful ways of implementing some of the trends in the organization over time
- Within the field of Supplier Relationship Management and which tools are used, why and how within the area of
- Procurement and Category Management.
- Transport and production – potentially try and develop KPI for us to refer to – like % of turnover spend on logistic services etc.

In general the respondents are satisfied with the surveys, but they have also provided some inputs on what they find beneficial to have lesser of in the mini-surveys:
- Less broader topics where the generalization is a risk
- Graphs that are superficial
- Try not to get too theoretical
- Some of the surveys seem to be very "tool" oriented or "buzz-word" oriented and it is hard (for me) to decode
- The real value of the result
- Too broad or "week" questions, so interpretations can be wide
- Abstract topics, but again this is hard to define before you see the answers…
- Make shorter
- I would like to have few options in each question

INTRODUCTION

A common pattern among the mini-surveys from 2012 til 2016

Looking across all mini-surveys conducted between 2012 and 2016 reveals a common type of result in the surveys. Whatever the topic we have investigated, the respondents, in general, have answered that the importance of the specific topic are being evaluated with higher scores of importance than their scores for their actual work on it. This can both indicate a humble view of their own practice but also reveal the backlogs of developments of their supply chains. Another common finding among the mini-surveys is that the respondents in general have been asked about various barriers for working with a specific topic in focus. Here, the barrier "lack of time – too much focus on operation at the expense of development" appears every time among the top three listed barriers. One way to conclude, the companies need to be better in balancing operation and development tasks. Another reason for an imbalance between operation and development would be an excuse for escaping from their failures instead of sticking to the problems, outlining plans for improvements and then demonstrating execution skill.

The articles in this book

This book contains 22 articles that have been published between the year 2012 and 2016. The articles cover a variety of SCM issues that still exists and offer relevant messages. However, for some of the mini-surveys, practitioners might have moved their practice, nevertheless; the core challenge within each topic is believed still being relevant. Thus, while reading the articles, please bear in mind about the time when the data was collected and do also try to evaluate how well your company's practice is within the areas.

Thank you

Being able to run *The Danish Supply Chain Panel* would never have been possible without the great administrative work completed by DILF staff. The division of roles is that the researchers are developing the questions for the mini-surveys, DILF maintain the member list, set-up the questionnaire in SurveyXact, manage the data collection process and distribute the results to the researchers who then analyze the data and write practitioner-oriented articles based on the findings. DILF again is responsible for doing the layout of the articles and get them published. Furthermore, thanks to all current and past panel members. Without your answers to all the mini-surveys, we would not have had the raw material to make the various articles as presented in this book. From an academic perspective many "interest hours" have been spend to run this panel both from DILF and the researchers. Then, thanks to all the co-contributors of articles presented here: Ole Stegmann Mikkelsen, Thomas Johnsen, Morten Munkgaard Møller, Jesper Kronborg Jensen, Morten Brinch and Antony Paulraj. A special thank is given to Christopher Rajkumar who has managed to language proof this entire manuscript. The book is published with financial support from the Department of Entrepreneurship and Relationship at University of Southern Denmark, which I also owe a great thank you for this contribution. As a department with strong emphasis on applied science I truly acknowledge that there is a continued focus on practical relevance both in terms of knowledge production and knowledge transfer.

Happy reading!

Kolding, June 2017
Jan Stentoft
Professor in Supply Chain Management

References

Adler, N.J. and Harzing, A-W. (2009), "When knowledge wins: transcending the sense and nonsense of academic rankings", *Academy of Management Learning & Education*, Vol. 8 No. 1, pp. 72-95.

Alvesson, M. and Gabriel, Y. (2013), "Beyond formulaic research: in praise of greater diversity in organizational research and publications", *Academy of Management Learning & Education*, Vol. 12 No. 2, pp. 245-263.

Arlbjørn, J.S., Freytag, P.V. and Damgaard, T. (2008), "The beauty of measurement", *European Business Review*, Vol. 20 No. 2, pp. 112-127.

Bennis, W.G. and O'Toole, J. (2005), "How business schools lost their way", *Harvard Business Review*, Vol. 83 No. 5, pp. 96-104.

Carter, C.R. (2008), "Knowledge production and knowledge transfer: closing the research-practice gap", *Journal of Supply Chain Management*, Vol. 44 No. 2, pp. 78-82.

Davis, G.F. (2014), "Editorial essay: Why do we still have journals?", *Administrative Science Quarterly*, Vol. 59 No. 2, pp. 193-201.

Franck, G. (1999), "Scientific communication--a vanity fair?", *Science*, Vol. 286 No. 5437, pp. 53-55.

Lambert, D.M. and Enz, M.G. (2015), "We must find the courage to change", *Journal of Business Logistics*, Vol. 36 No. 1, pp. 9-17.

Piercy, N.F. (2002), "Research in marketing: teasing with trivia or risking relevance?", *European Journal of Marketing*, Vol. 36 No. 3, pp. 350-363.

Schacht, M.K. (2016), "Forskere: Teorivældet udsulter virksomhedsnær forskning" [Researchers: Theory might starve practical relevant research], *Mandag Morgen*, August 22, 2016. https://www.mm.dk/forskere-teorivaeldet-udsulter-virksomhedsnaer-forskning/, Accessed April 30, 2017.

Stentoft, J. and Rajkumar, C. (2017), "Balancing theoretical and practical relevance in supply chain management research", paper presented at the *29th Annual NOFOMA conference* in Lund, Sweden, June 8-9, 2017.

Tang, C.S. (2016), "OM forum—making OM research more relevant: "why?" and "how?", *Manufacturing & Service Operations Management*, Vol. 18 No. 2, pp. 178-183.

Toffel, M.W. (2016), "Enhancing practical relevance of research", *Production and Operations Management*, Vol. 25 No. 9, pp. 1493-1505.

Van de Ven, A.H. and Johnson, P.E. (2006), "Knowledge for theory and practice", *Academy of Management Review*, Vol. 31 No. 4, pp. 802-821.

Wilhite, A.W. and Fong, E.A. (2012), "Coercive citation in academic publishing", *Science*, Vol. 335 No. 6068, pp. 542-543.

Section 1 – Panel articles in 2016

Big data applications in sourcing processes[1]

By: Jan Stentoft, Ole Stegmann Mikkelsen and Morten Brinch

Introduction

The emerging possibilities of integrating data, systems and analytic techniques, as well as the increased computer power, makes companies strive for capturing new strategic and economic gains for better competitiveness. Here, big data and business analytics are terms for data-driven processes that receive increasingly interest by companies and its managers as a mean to achieve fast, precise, informed and better decision-making. In supply chain management big data applications can be deployed in sourcing, manufacturing, service, logistic, planning and return processes (Brinch et al., 2017). A well-known example is Facebook, who's micro-segmentation in marketing processes automatically targets individual persons based on their online behavior, and also Facebooks capability for face recognitions by using machine learning techniques. Thus, much can be learnt and improved by utilizing the vast and various amount of fast-moving data available. The concept and understanding of big data could for some be rather confused, but from a company perspective big data can be viewed as "a holistic approach to manage, process and analyze 5 Vs (i.e., volume, variety, velocity, veracity and value) in order to create actionable insights for sustained value delivery, measuring performance and establishing competitive advantages" (Fosso Wamba et al., 2015).

The sourcing department and procurement processes have received less attention towards big data compared to e.g. service, planning and logistics. Though, just as any other process, the application of big data for sourcing

---

[1] This article is reproduced from Stentoft, J., Mikkelsen, O.S. and Brinch, M. (2016), "Big data applications in sourcing processes", *DILF Orientering*, Vol. 53 No. 4, pp. 38-42.

purposes is also important for developing data-driven companies, where supply and demand are to be aligned. The goal of utilizing big data and its analytic techniques is to develop better decision-making models and processes, at both strategic and operational levels (Wang et al., 2016). For strategic purposes, the use of big data in supplier relationship management may generate better financial performance, minimize operations cost and improve their suppliers' performance. A possible application is to evaluate and select suppliers, where big data enables industry benchmarks and customized metrics for each supplier. Also, big data and new data sources can increase the validity of predicting supply disruptions which identifies the sources of uncertainty, which is in turn considered while selecting suppliers. Another strategic application is to evaluate spend profiles, procurement processes and future demand and, thereby, align company and sourcing strategy. For operational purposes, big data can be implemented in existing procurement processes to enhance day-to-day decision-making. In general, the key is to provide decision-makers with accurate, data-based analysis for major decisions and sourcing issues. Two key applications are managing supply risk and managing supplier performance. By monitoring external data (e.g. public available news and social media) on the supplier database, the sourcing department could be constantly updated on supplier and market developments, which may perhaps be utilized to quickly identify potential risks and, hence, contingency plans can be implemented in adequate time to avoid any supply issues. Supplier performance can be evaluated by consolidating a large range of supplier data across companies, which can influence sourcing channel options. For example, Amazon uses analytics to determine whether joint replenishment, coordinated replenishment or single sourcing would be the optimal decision (Sanders, 2016). Also, the performance assessment on suppliers can potentially increase the bargaining power when negotiating with suppliers.

The opportunities of collecting and utilizing big data and business analytics for sourcing purposes are present. This mini survey will shed light on big data from a sourcing perspective and will focus on the potentials, the use of various data and analytics, expected benefits and the barriers that hinders big data from being implemented in sourcing processes. One of the prime intentions is to understand, to which extent big data is implemented in various functions within the companies. The results of this question are depicted in Figure 1.

Figure 1: The extent to which big data analytics is implemented in various company functions

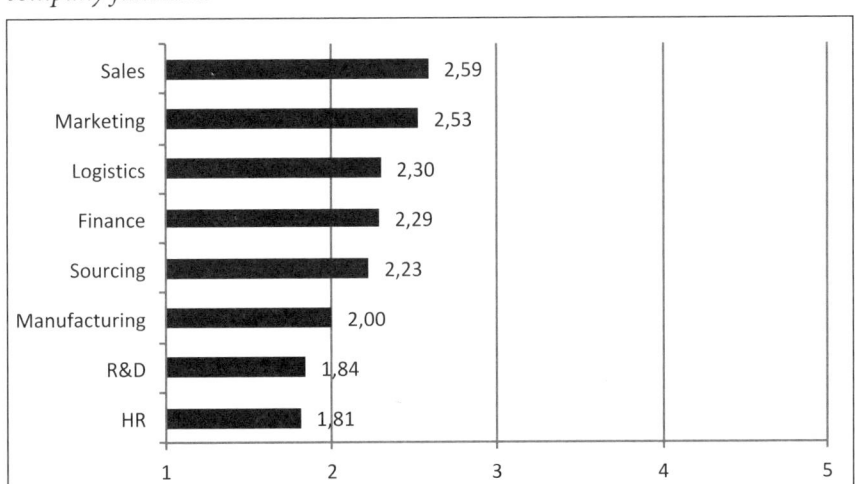

Based on a 5 point Likert scale, it appears from Figure 1 that big data is only to a limited degree implemented within the companies participated in this survey. These data is based on the respondents (supply chain executives) perception of their companies' big data applications within the above mentioned functions. Hence, the results might be biased. However, with regards to sales and marketing, it is undoubtedly in front as expected due to a strong customer focus, on the other hand, sourcing positions itself somewhere in the middle. There seems to be a great business potential for sourcing functions to further explore how big data applications could improve decision making. R&D and HR evidently are the functions with the lowest level of implementation when it comes to big data.

Even though sourcing on average only to a limited degree has implemented big data, we further wanted to dig into how many companies actually do work with big data in their sourcing department. These responses are depicted in Figure 2.

As shown in Figure 2, approximately only one third (34%) of the respondents operates with big data in their sourcing department. Even though 19% is planning to work with big data in the sourcing department; the figure also shows that another one third (33%) of the respondents are not working with big data nor planning to do it. Furthermore, another 14%

Figure 2: Does your sourcing department operate with big data?

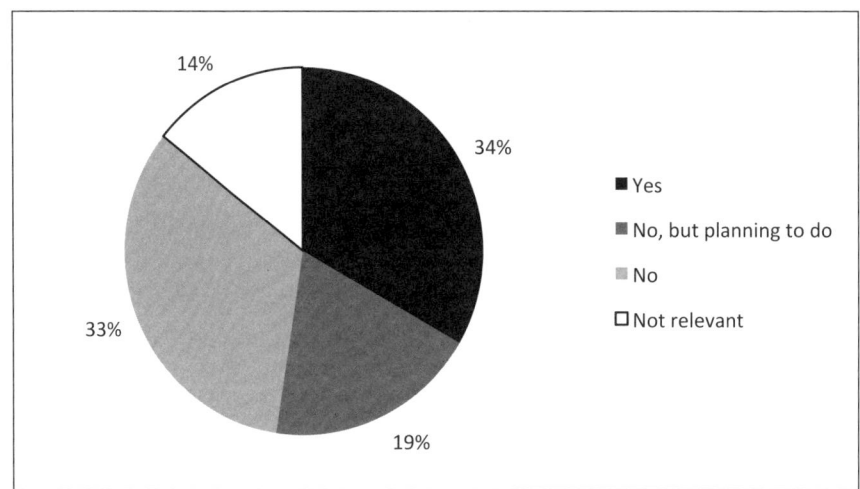

of the companies claiming that big data in the sourcing department is not relevant for them, we see that approximately one half (47%) of the companies has no intention to use big data in connection to their sourcing. Later in this article, we present some reasons that might explain this relative high absence of big data mindset.

The rest of the analysis is based solely on the 34% who have answered that they operate with big data in their sourcing department.

Strategic emphasis on big data

In the next question we ask, those companies who uses big data in their sourcing department, whether the company has a strategic emphasis on big data analytics in the sourcing department. The answers to this question appear from Figure 3.

As appears from Figure 3, half of the companies (50%) who operate with big data in their sourcing department have a strategic emphasis on the big data analytics in the sourcing department. Also, 36% has to some extent a strategic emphasis. Interestingly the numbers show that 14% of companies working with big data in the sourcing department only have a low degree of strategic emphasis on big data analytics. There seems to be a task in the sourcing departments concerned with analyses and discussions about the

Figure 3: To which extend is there a strategic emphasis on big data analytics in the sourcing department?

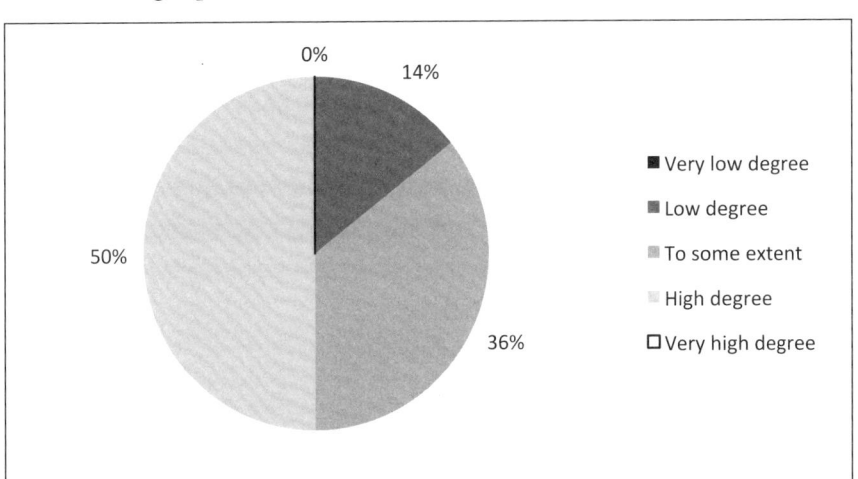

strategic value of the potential of big data and how this should take place. We take a deeper look on this in the next section.

Better sourcing decisions through big data analytics

In the following we seek to understand how big data may support better sourcing decisions. First, we have asked the respondents, what big data characteristics they perceive as being valuable for better sourcing decision. This is shown in Figure 4. We further wanted to know what types of analytics are perceived of value for sourcing decisions in the companies. This is shown in Figure 5.

As it appears from Figure 4, half or more than half of the companies finds most of the big data characteristics of value for better sourcing decisions. Only utilization of various data formats and the utilization of unstructured data stands out as perceived lesser valuable characteristics than the rest with only 14% each.

The data in Figure 5 clearly shows, with an average of 3.93 out of five, that the respondents perceive prescriptive analytics by far is the most valuable to impact decisions in sourcing for the better. However, also descriptive (3.64) and predictive analytics (3.57) are perceived valuable for better

Figure 4: Big data characteristics perceived valuable for better sourcing decisions (several marks allowed)

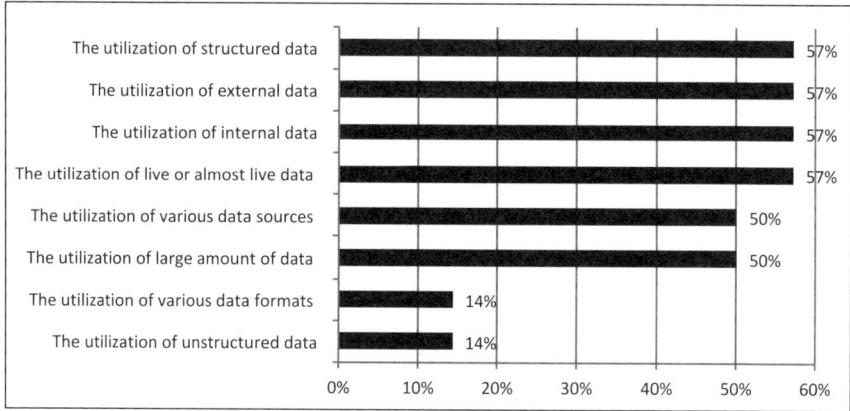

Figure 5: To which extend is the following type of analytics valuable for better sourcing decisions?

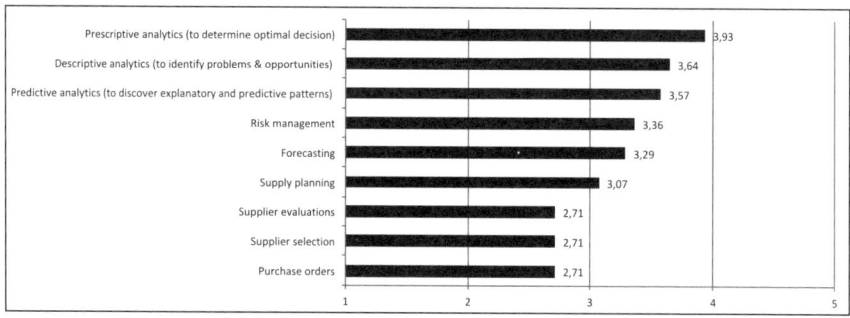

sourcing decisions. Risk management, forecasting and supply planning are to a lesser extent perceived valuable. In the bottom, we find supplier evaluations & selection together with purchase orders, each perceived with a value of only 2.71. One way to interpret the figures is that respondents perceive traditional sourcing tasks such as supplier evaluation & selection, issuing purchasing orders etc. as rather structured and known processes and activities that may not be further enriched by applying big data analytics. On the other hand, more unstructured and unknown tasks such as identifying problems and opportunities, discovering explanatory and predictive patterns and, hence, be able to determine the optimal solution, may profit well from implementing big data to support the analysis.

Current benefits of big data analytics and further potential

We are also interested in understanding what companies perceive as current benefits and future potential of implementing big data analytics. The answers to this question are shown in Figure 6 below.

Figure 6 reveals some interesting results. First, we observe that on top of current benefits we find process improvements, followed by increased decision support for purchasing and lower overall sourcing cost. Process improvements are likewise perceived in the top on future potential of implementing big data analytics. At the same time, process improvements is the only topic mentioned of which current benefits is ranked higher than perceived future potential. This result indicates that process improvements initiatives might have reached a saturation point, at least in this survey. For the rest of the topics in Figure 6 there seems to be a gap between current obtained benefits and the perceived potential of big data analytics in sourcing, however, to a varied degree. Especially the topics improved supplier performance, increased product quality, enhanced supplier risk management, reduced delivery time and increased supplier integration seem to offer large future potential compared to perceived current benefits. We find only minor gaps for the topics such as increased decision support, lower overall sourcing costs, lower prices, better bargaining position and better sourcing options.

Figure 6: Actual benefits and future potential of implementing big data analytics

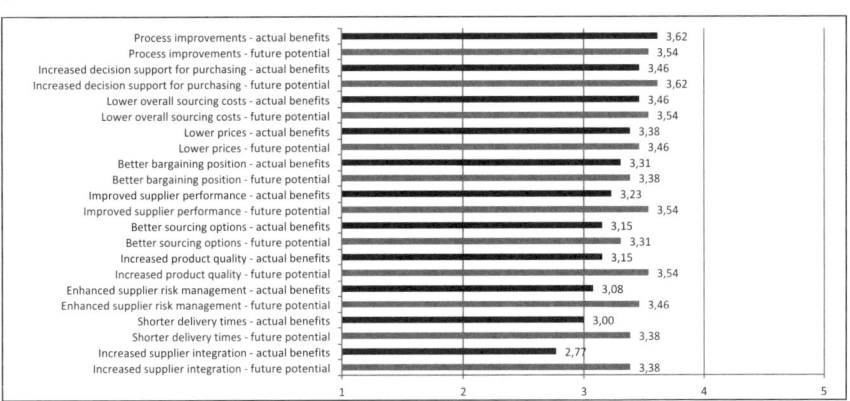

Note: Actual benefits display the respondents perception of the benefits achieved with big data whereas the future potential indicate the scope for further developments

Barriers for implementing big data analytics in sourcing processes

As in previous surveys from *The Danish Supply Chain Panel* we have asked about the perceived barriers. For this survey on big data analytics in sourcing processes the barriers of implementing are depicted in Figure 7.

As it appears from Figure 7, it is especially the lack of systems integration and time which companies perceive as hinders for working with big data analytics in their sourcing processes, both pointed at by 36% of respondents. The two are closely followed by lack of external data (33 %) and missing strategic emphasis (31%). Compared to other surveys conducted with *The Danish Supply Chain Panel*, lack of management support and lack of capabilities are not to the same magnitude, even though not low, perceived as barriers when working with big data analysis in sourcing processes. One quarter of the companies still struggle with lack of both internal data and

Figure 7: Perceived barriers for implementing big data analytics in sourcing processes

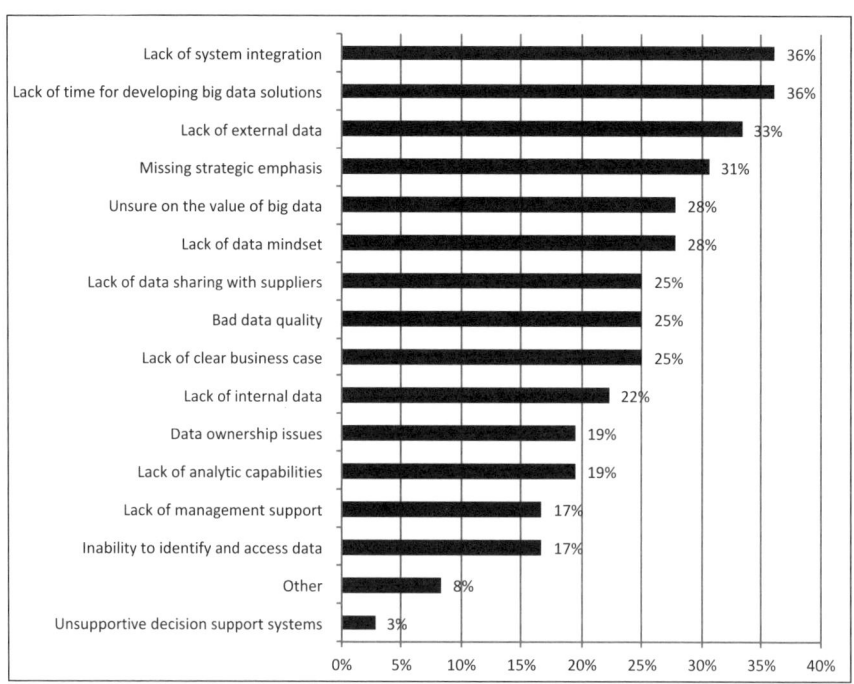

data quality and also a lack of a clear business case. The latter corresponds with 28% of the companies being unsure of the value of big data and data mind-set. Hence, there seems to be a challenge in the companies to get the data right and available and not least to understand the value of access to correct data for steering the company.

Conclusion

This mini-survey completed by *The Danish Supply Chain Panel* has set out to explore the practical and potential application of big data in a sourcing context. The results reveal that few companies are approaching big data from a strategic sourcing perspective. Compared with sales, marketing and logistics the sourcing function apply big data to a lower degree. It seems that big data is most applied in customer oriented events that leave an untapped potential in the sourcing area. Big data is one of several disruptive technologies in the supply chain. Supply chain executives must take such technologies serious in order to design competitive supply chains for the future (Stentoft and Mikkelsen, 2016). We hope this mini-survey can stimulate that this important topic is being discussed and prioritized on the top management agenda.

References

Brinch, M., Stentoft, J. and Jensen, J.K. (2017), "Big data and its applications in supply chain management: Findings from a Delphi Study", *Hawaii International Conference on System Sciences (HICSS-50)*, January 4-7.

Fosso Wamba, S., Akter, S., Edwards, A., Chopin, G. and Gnanzou, D. (2015), "How 'big data' can make big impact: Findings from a systematic review and a longitudinal case study", *International Journal of Production Economics*, Vol. 165, pp. 234–246.

Sanders, N.R. (2016), "How to use big data to drive your supply chain", *California Management Review*, Vol. 58 No. 3, pp. 26–48.

Stentoft, J. and Mikkelsen, O. S. (2016), "Increased expectations of using disruptive technologies in supply chains", *DILF Orientering*, Vol. 53 No 1, pp. 36-41.

Wang, G., Gunasekaran, A., Ngai, E.W.T. and Papadopoulos, T. (2016), "Big data analytics in logistics and supply chain management: Certain investigations for research and applications", *International Journal of Production Economics*, Vol. 176, pp. 98–110.

Total cost of ownership:
A strategic important tool[1]

By: Jan Stentoft and Ole Stegmann Mikkelsen

Introduction

The cost management tool Total Cost of Ownership (TCO) is a concept that is focused on the development of a deeper understanding of the true cost associated with trading with a supplier about a given product or service (Ellram, 1994). It is an effective way of tracking the hidden indirect costs associated with supplier transactions. The relevance of the concepts is high since purchasing costs in many firms can be as high as 80% of the total production costs (Cousins et al., 2008, p. 75). Thus, the purchasing functions are becoming more strategically important and relevant (Cousins and Spekman, 2003) where managers to a higher degree focus on the many indirect costs and life-cycle costs besides the actual prices of goods and services from suppliers. It is vital for companies to be able to track and control this large cost pool, as it represents a large portion of the total manufacturing costs (Zachariassen and Arlbjørn, 2011). Furthermore, TCO plays an important role in supplier selection and evaluation, and as an aid for strategic cost decisions (Degraeve et al., 2000). Although literature has stressed the usefulness of TCO, it is still surprising to find that the use of TCO in industry seems to be limited (Feriin and Plank, 2002; Hurkens et al., 2006). The reasons for this might be that purchasing managers have little experience in applying TCO and value analyses (Wouters et al., 2005) and some managers fail to see the purchasing function as a strategic resource (Ellram and Siferd, 1998). This paper contains the results of mini-survey distributed among the members of *The Danish Supply Chain Panel*. First of all,

---

1 This article is reproduced from Stentoft, J. and Mikkelsen, O.S. (2016), "Total cost of ownership: A strategic important tool", *DILF Orientering*, Vol. 53 No. 3, pp. 36-41.

Figure 1: Is a TCO model in use in your company?

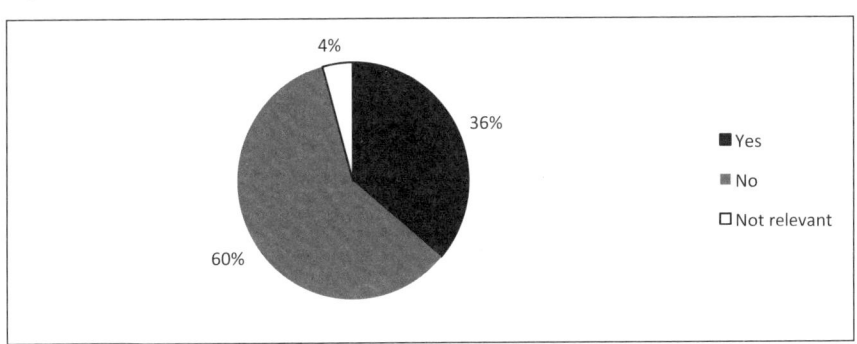

we wanted to find out if a TCO model is in place in the companies in this survey. The answers to this question emerge from Figure 1.

Figure 1 clearly shows that only 36% of the respondents have a TCO model in place in the company. Other 60% reports that they do not have a TCO model in place and the rest 4% reports that a TCO model is of no relevance for their company. By opening for the response that a TCO model is not relevant, we argue that the 60% who do not employ a TCO model is not because it's irrelevant, but merely that it is relevant, however lagging. It is surprising that 60% do not use a TCO model. However, to inquire this, we therefore asked the 60% about the perceived value of employing a TCO model in their company. The answers to this question are shown in Figure 2.

Figure 2: Would a TCO model be of value for your company?

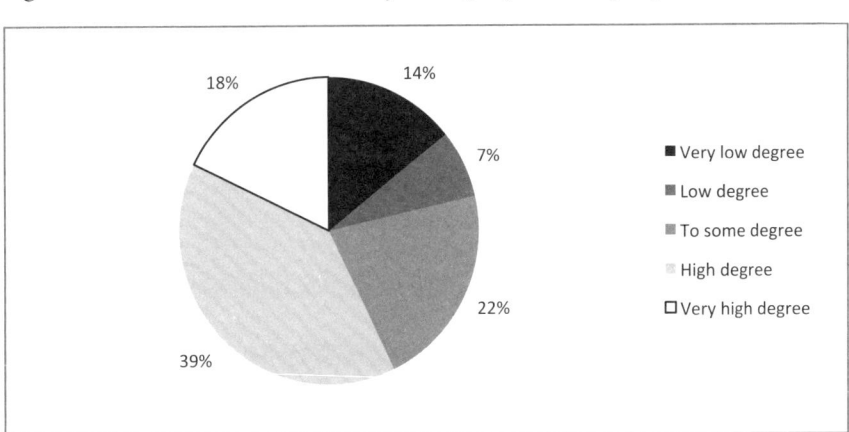

Figure 2 shows the results about the perception of the usefulness of implementing TCO, of those 60% respondents who have answered that they currently do not use a TCO model. As it appears, 57% finds to a very high or a high degree that a TCO model would be of value in their company. In other words, this correspond to that every third company (60% x 57%) in industry lacks a TCO model or framework for decision making even though they finds that it to a high or very high degree would be of value for them. This indicate a significant gap between 'as-is' and 'as-should-be'. In the other end, 25% does not see the value of a TCO model in their company (including the 4% answering irrelevant). In the middle 22%, of the 60%, finds that a TCO model would be of some value.

TCO implementations

Excluding those who have not implemented a TCO model, we now turn to those 36% respondents who have answered that they do work with a TCO model or framework for decision making. First of all, we are interested in, to what degree the models currently are implemented compared to the perceived 'ideal' degree of implementation. The answers originate from Figure 3.

The scale used to calculate the averages in Figure 3 range from 1 (very low degree) to 5 (very high degree). From Figure 3, it is evident that the actual implementation level lacks behind what is perceived as the 'ideal' degree TCO should be implemented in the responding companies.

We further wanted to investigate where the responsibility for TCO is anchored in the companies. As it is shown in Figure 4, the responsibility for TCO is very much anchored in finance or purchasing, with 35% and 29% of the respondent respectively.

Figure 3: TCO model implementation vs. 'ideal' level

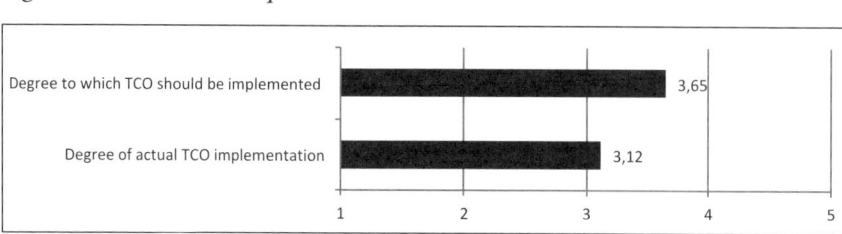

Figure 4: Where is the responsibility for TCO anchored in your organization?

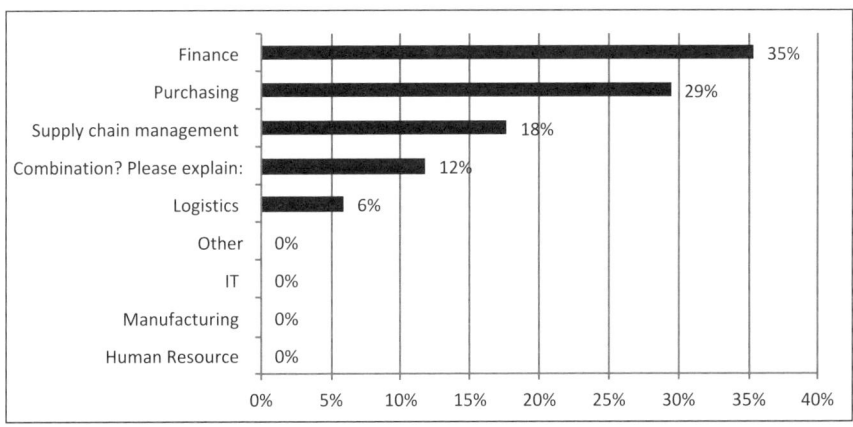

Interestingly, the responsibility is only to a lesser degree anchored in more cross-functional areas such as supply chain management function (18%) or a combination of different functions (12%). This is interesting since TCO is cross-functional in nature, and as one respondent replied "… it has to be a joint effort – not linked into one specific area only…", which we find it to be very true. However, this is only the case for 30% of the companies.

TCO and KPIs

We also wanted to know how well TCO is understood in the companies and if TCO is part of a defined key performance indicator (KPI) structure. The answers to these questions are shown in Figure 5.

As it is shown in Figure 5, the respondents' report that TCO is only to some extend understood among top management. That is quite interest-

Figure 5: Understanding of TCO and KPI structure

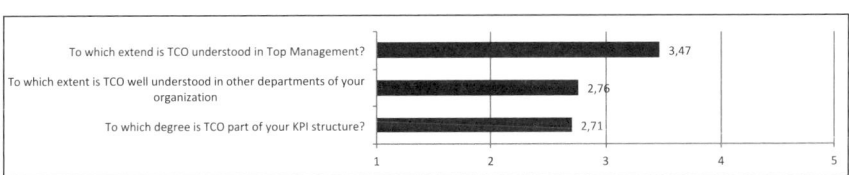

ing as 'only' 21% of the respondents, according to Figure 8, report that a challenge is lack of top management attention for TCO employment. In other words, it is not the will as such, but merely the competencies of top management that seems lacking. This indicates an interesting potential in 'training' top management about TCO and application hereof to support the decision making in the companies. The respondents further report a lack of understanding of TCO from colleagues in other departments. This correspond with that TCO to a rather low level is part of the KPI structure. It could be argued that if it is not part of the KPI structure, then there is a little incitement to work with, or try to understand, TCO as a framework for decision making. You get what you measure. What gets measured get done and get done can be rewarded. One might argue that as top management only to some degree understands TCO, this might be the reason for not having it as part of the KPI structure, because it is hard to measure something that is not understood.

TCO contents

After now having discussed the results in connection to the level of use, understanding and implementation, we now turn to the application of TCO. First, we want to look into the content elements of the applied TCO models. The answers to this are shown in Figure 6. We have separated the elements into different categories; negotiation related, delivery related, management related, service related, quality related and communication/administration related elements. Each of the elements were scaled from 1 to 5.

Not surprisingly, price is still the first and foremost used element in TCO models. For the negotiation related elements quality is also on the top of the list to be included in a TCO model. More surprisingly is it to see that impact on cash flow seem not so much used in TCO models, not least as many companies have a high focus on cash flow. Also low in use in TCO models is the inspection costs. This is interesting as quality is so high. However, maybe the high focus on quality leaves room for not focusing on inspection cost. Why inspect if quality is high? Also accept delivery is a highly used element in TCO models. It is interesting to see that the cost of relationship management (travel, meetings, time, etc.) is the least applied element in TCO models used. Not least as these costs may vary significantly if the collaboration partner is situated just outside the company door or

Figure 6: Content elements in the applied TCO model

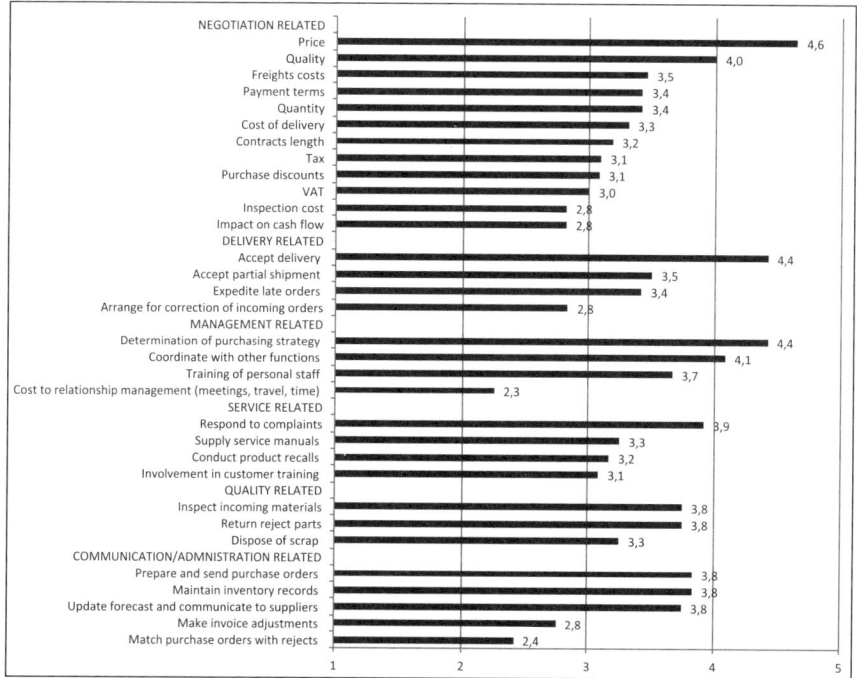

thousands of miles away, or if the relationship is an operational relation or a relationship with a strategic R&D partner.

TCO application purposes

From looking into the content of TCO, we now turn to the application of the models – what are TCO models used for in the companies. This is accounted for in Figure 7.

In answering this question, the respondents were allowed to provide several answers. As it appears TCO models are very much used for supplier selection. Surprisingly, TCO is on the contrary much lesser used for supplier evaluation/audits. Also TCO is much used for benchmark, and to a little lesser degree make or buy decisions and target costing purposes. It is interesting that TCO models are used by only 29% to allocate business to suppliers. This especially in the light, that TCO is highly used for supplier selection and benchmarking.

Figure 7: What is TCO used for?

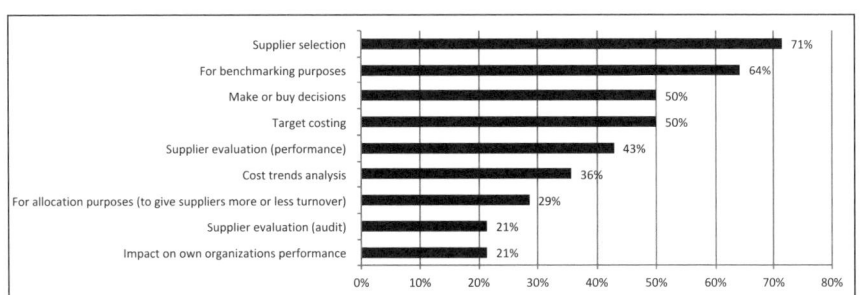

As with the other supply chain panel surveys, we also want to investigate what are perceived as the main challenges in working with TCO. The responds to this question is shown in Figure 8.

In other surveys of the supply chain panel we often see lack of resources as a major challenge. Interesting however, in this survey, lack of resources is listed 'only' as number nine challenge. Other issues are more challenging. As it appears from Figure 8, it is not only perceived challenging to identify the relevant cost elements to include into the TCO model (64%) but also getting the right data (57%). So not only is the relevance element of data important also the availability of data is hard to obtain. The first may be

Figure 8: Main challenges working with TCO

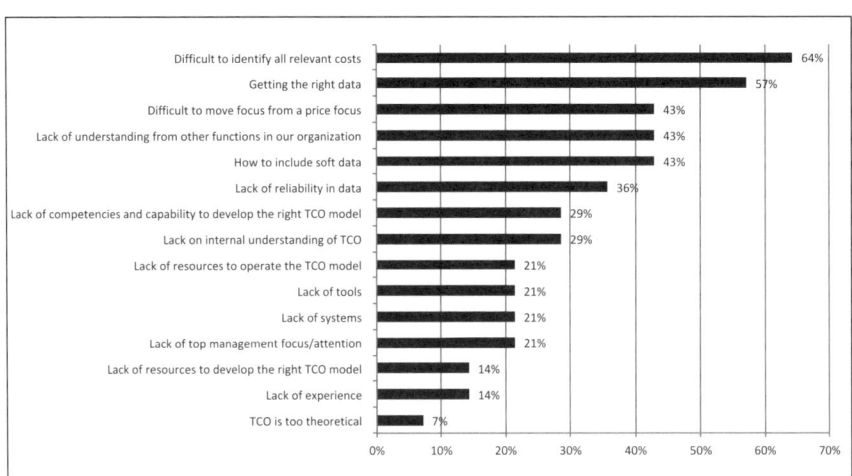

revealed by a cross-functional working group, who decides on a first TCO model version and then work forward from this. The latter may require a little more work as this is about having access to the right data both internally and externally. To support the chosen elements, companies may first have to construct a way of developing the missing data and afterward a procedure for collection and validation of the data.

As also shown in Figure 8, it is a challenge to move away from price focus. This is in line with the lack of TCO as part of KPI structure shown in Figure 5. If not in the KPI structure, why then worry about it? Also the lack of understanding from the other departments is recognized as a challenge. Again it corresponds with the findings in Figure 5 on the low level of understanding. Getting hold of soft data is in line with the challenge of getting the right data. Further, it is not only hard to get the right data, but also the reliability of data is perceived as a challenge in working with TCO.

Finally, we wanted to understand the challenges as seen from the perspective of those companies who do not work with TCO. We were curious about why not. The answers to this question are shown in Figure 9.

Again it is interesting to observe that lack of resource appears down the list (ranked number 11) as a challenge to work with TCO. In addition, other challenges are perceived as more prominent. We especially observe that lack of experience plays a role, as do lack of understanding TCO and lack of tools. For the first two, and lack of capabilities (no. 5) it is just to say that, like many other challenges, experience, understanding and capabilities comes with working with the task, here TCO modeling and implementation. By doing nothing one can be assured that no experience, understanding or capability will build up in the organization. So it is about getting

Figure 9: Main reasons for not working with TCO

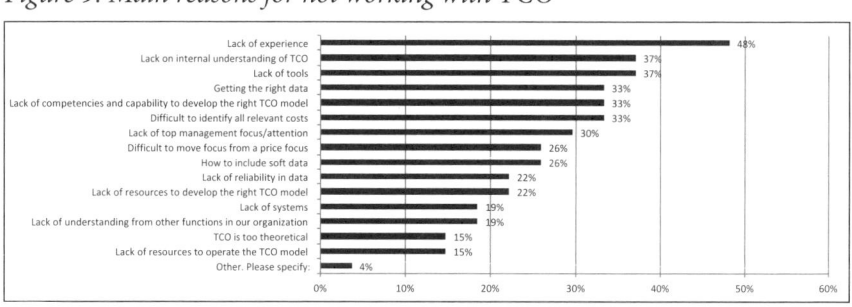

started, not least for that 1/3 of companies who, according to Figure 2, does not have a TCO model in place but perceive that it would be of high or very high value to the company.

Conclusion

This paper has set out to explore the usage of TCO among the members of *The Danish Supply Chain Panel*. In all, only 36% of the respondents report that they have implemented TCO in their companies. The responsibility for TCO is reported to be finance and the purchasing department. TCO is perceived as a strategic important tool for purchasing and finance but seems to be a secret for rest of the organization. The main purpose of working with TCO is reported to be in connection with supplier selection and benchmarking. The main challenges are listed to be the difficulty to identify all relevant costs and to get the right data. The respondents who have answered that their corporations do not operate with a TCO model list the top three reasons for this absence to be lack of experience, lack on internal understanding of TCO and lack of tools. Thus, there seems to be a potential for developing new courses in order to disseminate the knowledge of TCO in the Danish enterprises. We hope this short paper presenting the results of the mini-survey could stimulate a discussion on TCO in your organizations. Finally, we find it healthy to recognize that there are often many solutions to practical problems why it is beneficial to start with a pragmatic approach when beginning with TCO. We wish you good luck with TCO and hope you will share the knowledge of TCO in your organizations so the secret of TCO can be eliminated.

References

Cousins, P.D., Lamming, R.C., Lawson, B. and Squire, B. (2008), *Strategic Supply Management*, Pearson Education, Harlow.

Cousins, P.D. and Spekman, R. (2003), "Strategic supply and the management of inter- and intra-organisational relationships", *Journal of Purchasing & Supply Management*, Vol. 9 No. 1, pp. 19-29.

Degraeve, Z., Labro, E. and Roodhoft, F. (2000), "An evaluation of vendor selection models from a total cost of ownership perspective", *European Journal of Operational Research*, Vol. 125 No. 1, pp. 34-58.

Ellram, L.M. (1994), "A taxonomy of total cost of ownership models", *Journal of Business Logistics*, Vol. 15 No. 1, pp. 171-91.

Ellram, L.M. and Siferd, S.P. (1998), "Total cost of ownership: a key concept in strategic cost management decisions", *Journal of Business Logistics*, Vol. 19 No. 1, pp. 55-84.

Ferrin, B.G. and Plank, R.E. (2002), "Total cost of ownership models: an exploratory study", *Journal of Supply Chain Management*, Vol. 38, No. 8, pp. 18-63.

Hurkens, C., Valk, W. and Wynstra, F. (2006), "Total cost of ownership in the services industry: a case study", *Journal of Supply Chain Management*, Vol. 42 No. 1, pp. 27-37.

Wouters, M., Anderson, J.C. and Wynstra, F. (2005), "The adoption of total cost of ownership for sourcing decisions: a structural equations analysis", *Accounting, Organizations and Society*, Vol. 30 No. 2, pp. 167-91.

Zachariassen, F. and Arlbjørn, J.S. (2011), "Exploring a differentiated approach to total cost of ownership", *Industrial Management & Data Systems*, Vol. 111 No. 3, pp. 448-469.

Do you have the right supply chain talent on board?[1]

By: Jan Stentoft and Ole Stegmann Mikkelsen

Introduction

The race for the right supply chain is an ongoing phenomenon. The dynamic business environment continues to demand new skills in the supply chain to operate the supply chains most efficiently and to develop the supply chains to meet future requirements. This article is about talent management in supply chains. The right talent is related both to functional areas within the supply chain such as purchasing, warehousing, manufacturing and logistics as well as to integration such as business processes, relationship management and supply chain development. Supply chain managers can be seen as bridge builders. They join various business functions, from design, to production, to purchasing, to transportation with the goal of achieving target service levels at the lowest costs (Waller and Fawcett, 2014). Drivers for a stronger need on talent management are related to increased global competition that demand companies to operate more efficiently, rapid changes in technology that offer companies with the possibilities for technology driven supply chain innovations and the acknowledgement of supply chain management role to create competitiveness that extend the responsibility areas under supply chain management. For instance, Holcomb et al. (2015) report, "the talent squeeze comes as supply chain leaders face dramatically expanding responsibilities, where supply chain staff now are charged with overseeing the full span of logistical activities from sourcing to production planning to delivery and service".

Deloitte's third annual supply chain survey, conducted in the late 2014,

---

1 This article is reproduced from Stentoft, J. and Mikkelsen, O.S. (2016), "Do you have the right supply chain talent on board?", *DILF Orientering*, Vol. 53 No. 2, pp. 33-36.

highlighted the unease among supply chain executives over their organizations' performance in recruiting and developing talent (Marchese and Dollar, 2015). According to Langley and Capgemini Consulting (2015), the need for supply chain talent is massive. Their report based on a recent survey, clearly reports that nearly 50% of the respondents are already facing difficulty in finding or attracting talent, and the average hiring growth rate within the supply chain industry is expected to be higher than the average growth rate across other occupations (Langley and Capgemini Consulting, 2015, p. 5).

Supply chain management decisions significantly influence financial performance since firms expend up to 75% of their revenue on supply chain activities (Trent, 2004). Ellinger and Ellinger (2014) argue for a supply chain management talent shortfall which is further exacerbated by a lack of resources and strategic priority devoted to supply chain management. Estimated demand for supply chain professionals exceeds supply by a ratio of six to one (Ruamsook and Craighead, 2014). Thus, there are several relevant indications that focus on talent management within supply chain management perhaps is overlooked.

Therefore, we first asked *The Danish Supply Chain Panel* about their perceptions of their companies focus on talent management in general *vis a vis* talent management in supply chain management. Figure 1 shows 46% of the respondents do strongly agree or agree that they have a focus on talent management in general in their companies whereas 53% strongly agree or agree with a focus on talent management in supply chain management. Thus, despite the positive higher degree of focus on developing supply chain talent, there is no substantial difference between talent management in general and within supply chain management. The most surprising result of Figure 1 is actually that 54% and 47% do answer that they neither disagree nor agree, disagree or strongly disagree in that there is a strong enough focus on this issue in their company. It seems like there is a potential here that can be improved in order to avoid risks of losing the game for right supply chain talent.

However, one thing is to have a focus on talent management, another thing is whether we have the right people with the right talents in the supply chain to reach the strategic objectives. The respondents' perceptions on this issue are shown in Figure 2.

With approximately 89% agreeing or strongly agreeing, there seem to be

Figure 1: Strong enough focus on Talent Management

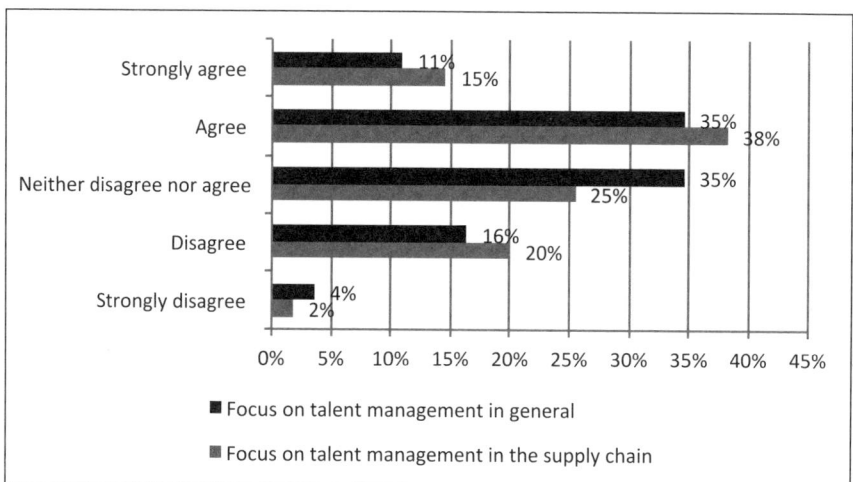

Figure 2: Need for the right talent and perceptions of the current level

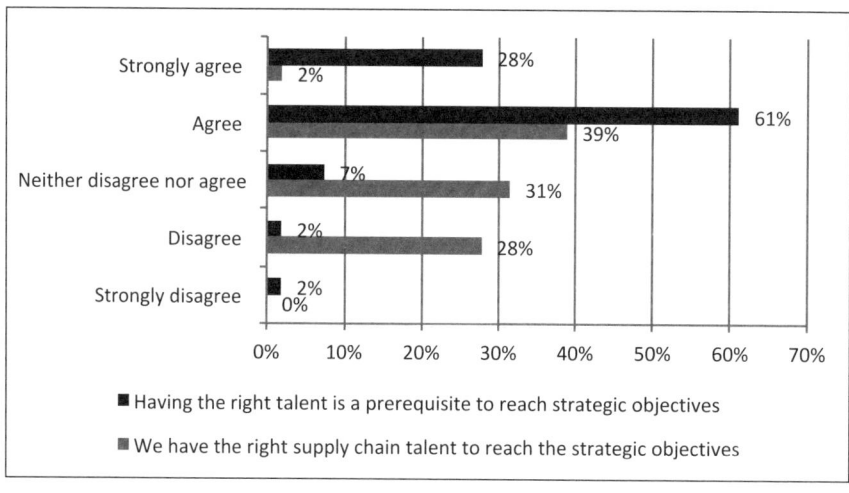

a high degree of consensus that having the right talent is a prerequisite to reach the strategic objectives. However, only nearly 41% agrees or strongly agrees that they have the right people with the right profiles in their supply chain. In addition, approximately 28% disagreeing that they have the right talent leaves a remarkable competence gap in the companies to fill in the future. The data shown in Figure 1, however, also indicate that close to half of the respondents perceive that their companies do not have the right level of focus on talent management within supply chain management. It is interesting to observe that close to 11% neither disagree, disagree or strongly disagree that the right people with the right talent is a prerequisite to reach the strategic goals. Consolidated this leaves the impression that some companies out there does not take talent management serious enough.

From the more top level questions above, we find it interesting to investigate what type of capabilities that companies request and find important in the supply chain and not least at what level they perceive them self to be at. The answers to this are shown in Figure 3 (results are averages scores on a 6 point Likert scale ranging from 0 (not needed) to 5 (strongly agree).

From Figure 3 it is observed that the respondents in general perceive their current level of capabilities to lack behind the importance for all the capabilities in question. The highest rankings on importance are Demand forecasting, Using optimization tools, Sales & Operations Planning (S&OP) and Supplier collaboration and Risk Analysis. Fortunately, these are perceived as well as being implemented at the highest levels. The high

Figure 3: Supply chain capabilities: Perceptions of importance and their current levels

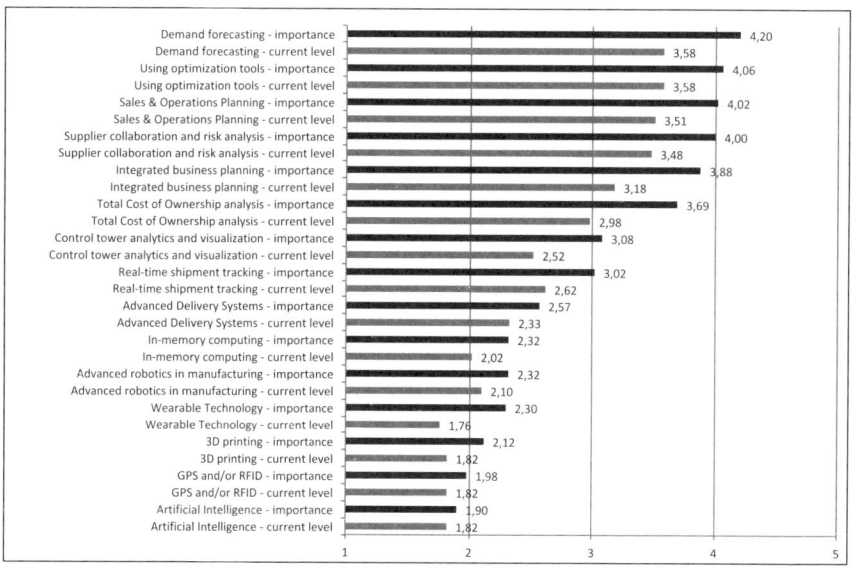

rank S&OP correspond well with a previous panel survey showing that more than 80% of respondents found S&OP as an important competitive parameter to a high or very high degree (Arlbjørn and Møller, 2013). Total Cost of Ownership (TCO) analysis is also in the top of the important capabilities. TCO will be explored further in a coming mini-survey here in 2016. 3D printing has been, and is, predicted to be one of the major disruptive technologies that will change the way supply chain operate (D'Aveni, 2015; Sasson and Johnson, 2016). It is therefore interesting that 3D printing is rated both relatively low not only in implementation of current stage, however also in importance. One could ask if this is an indication whether the companies asked are not aware of the potential supply chain impact of 3D printing, or if 3D printing is perceived as a fad that will soon disappear.

The respondents have also been asked about their perceptions of two different competence requirements in their supply chains, i.e. operation skills versus development skills. Figure 4 shows that 87% of the respondents do agree or strongly agree with the notion that they need more functional and operational skills in their supply chains. Then, 81% agree or strongly agree with that they need more development oriented staff in their supply chains. The results correspond with Figure 2, indicates competence backlog among the members of *The Danish Supply Chain Panel*.

Figure 4: Competence requirements

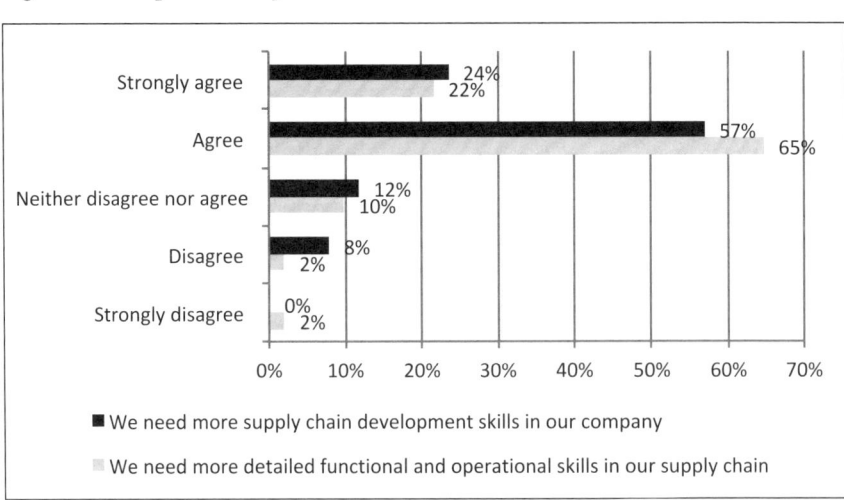

Figure 5: Perceived importance of supply chain competence areas

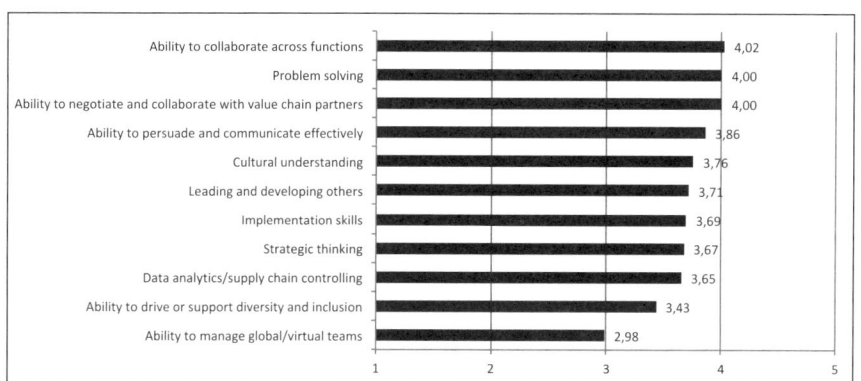

What competence areas do companies then perceive as important? The respondents answer to this question is shown in Figure 5.

As it appears from Figure 5 almost all the mentioned competences rank high in the perception of the respondents. Companies rate the ability to collaborate across functions highest. This is very much in line with previous panel surveys indicating that silo thinking still exists. As supply chain management is indeed a cross functional discipline, supply chain staff must have the ability to work cross functional. In the same vein companies highly value the ability to negotiate and collaborate with value chain partners. Hence internal and external collaboration competences are rated of high value. Correspondingly, problem solving is rated high. For the rest of the areas they are also rated rather high in perceived importance, indicating that the demands on the supply chain personnel profile are high.

We have also asked the supply chain panel about what obstacles the respondents perceive for getting the right supply chain talent on board. This could be either to get the right people on board, or to develop the competences of the current staff. The respondents' answers are shown in Figure 6.

It is interesting to observe that lack of budget for both hiring and investing in developing the right competences are perceived as the highest barriers. This is interesting especially when comparing to Figure 2, showing a high need for talent in the supply chain compared with a lack of the right current talent compared to the perceived need. The lack of budget is followed by a perceived lack of top management awareness. This is not

Figure 6: Perceived barriers of getting the right supply chain talent

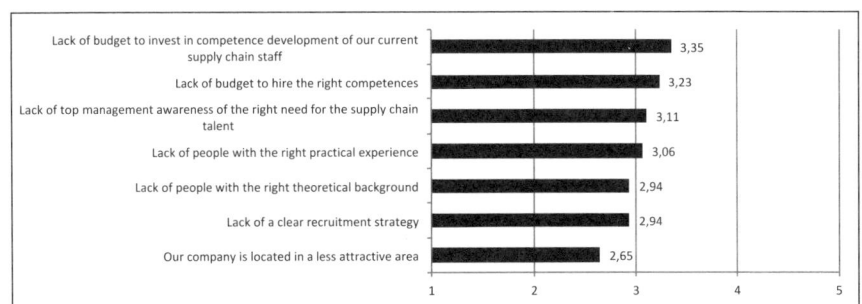

surprising, as budgets often travel together with top management awareness. Also lack of people with practical experience is perceived as a barrier. Hence, people with hands on experience of supply chain issues are in deficit.

In today's globalized business, the world is the market, and so is the pool of staff. Often we hear in the news that companies lack qualified candidates when they search for new staff. Therefore, we found it interesting to ask if companies are searching and recruiting supply chain staff outside the boarders of Denmark. The results are shown in Figure 7.

Figure 7: Degree to which staff is searched and recruited from outside Denmark

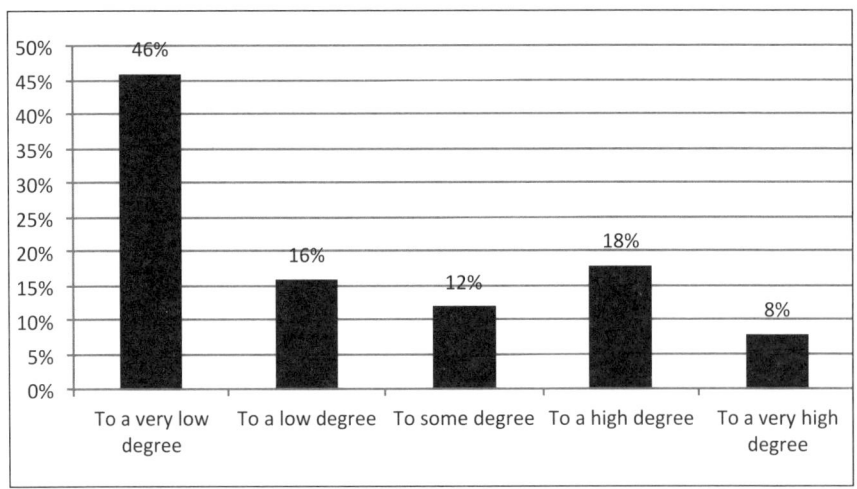

As shown in Figure 7, around one quarter of the responding companies have to a high or very high degree searched for and/or recruited outside Denmark, while 62% have to a low or very low degree. Hence, it indicates that there may be a lack in qualified potentials available in Denmark when it comes to supply chain staff. So, since some companies do look outside the borders for supply chain staff and that almost all the competence areas in Figure 5 are rated of high importance, one may ask if we have the right supply chain educations offered in Denmark to cover what is needed. Figure 8 displays the respondents answer on this question.

From Figure 8, it appears that 72 % of the respondents perceive that we do have to a high or very high degree the right supply chain education offered in Denmark. Then, 18% perceive that this is true to a certain degree, while only 10% think that this is not the case. Combined with that the perceived greatest barrier is lack of budget for competence development, and the need for the right talent (Figure 2) and skills (Figure 4) in the supply chain organization indicates that supply chain people need to be better at building the business case for investing in the development of the right people with the right competence profile.

Figure 8: Degree of perceptions of that the right supply chain educations are offered in Denmark

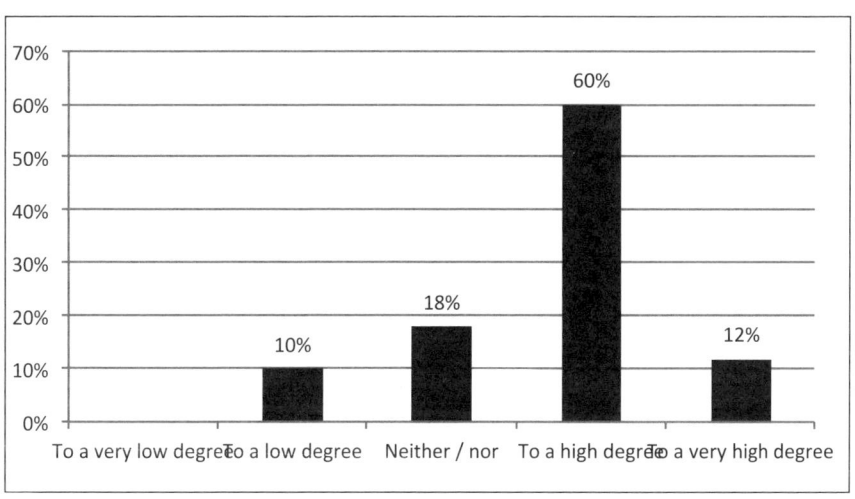

Conclusion

This mini-survey has focused on talent management in a supply chain management context. The mini-survey reveals that there is some focus on talent management among the respondents of *The Danish Supply Chain Panel*. Having the right talent on board is perceived as an important aspect to reach the strategic objectives. However, there is perception that the actual competence level is behind what is required. The three most importance supply chain capabilities are listed as being demand forecasting, using optimization tools and S&OP. In general, there is strong agreement among the respondents that their companies need injections of both operational and development oriented supply chain competences. The strongest barriers for getting the right supply chain is lack of budget to invest in competence development, lack of budget to hire the right competences and lack of top management awareness of the right talent.

Recent research advocates that the industry should also play a more active role in raising awareness and visibility about the supply chain field (Leon and Uddin, 2016). Such promotion efforts need to be seen as joint activities between higher industry and academia. We hope the article has presented findings that will stimulate discussions on this important topic in your company. For some this development is a jump start; others have been prepared for long time and approach talent management within supply chain management conscious strategic perspective. Welcome to the race!

References

Arlbjørn, J.S. and Møller, M.M. (2013), "Danske virksomheders S&OP-praksis", *Dilf Orientering*, Vol. 50 No. 5, pp. 16-20.

D'Aveni, R. (2015), "The 3-D printing revolution", *Harvard Business Review*, Vol. 93 No. 5, pp. 40-48.

Ellinger, A.E. and Ellinger, A.D. (2014), "Leveraging human resource development expertise to improve supply chain managers' skills and competencies", *European Journal of Training and Development*, Vol. 38, No. 1/2, pp. 118-135.

Holcomb, M., Krul, A. and Thomas, D. (2015), "Supply chain talent squeeze: How business & universities are collaborating to fill the gap", *Supply Chain Management Review*, Vol. 19 No. 4. pp. 10-18.

Langley, C.J. and Capgemini Consulting (2015), *2015 third-party logistics study: The State of Logistics Outsourcing*, Results and Findings of the 19th Annual Study.

Leon, S. and Uddin, N. (2016), "Finding supply chain talent: An outreach strategy", *Supply Chain Management: An International Journal*, Vol. 21 No. 1, pp. 20-44.

Marchese, K. and Dollar, B. (2015) *Supply Chain Talent of the Future Findings from the third annual supply chain survey*, Deloitte Consulting LLP.

Ruamsook, K. and Craighead, C. (2014), "A supply chain talent 'perfect storm?'", *Supply Chain Management Review*, Vol. 18 No. 1, pp. 12-17.

Sasson, A. and Johnson, J.C. (2016),"The 3D printing order: Variability, super-centers and supply chain reconfigurations", *International Journal of Physical Distribution & Logistics Management*, Vol. 46 No. 1, pp. 82 – 94.

Trent, R.J. (2004), "What everyone needs to know about SCM", *Supply Chain Management Review,* Vol. 8 No. 2, pp. 52-59.

Waller, M.A. and Fawcett, S.E. (2014), "Editorial: The SCM knowledge supply chain: Integrating world views to advance the discipline", *Journal of Business Logistics*, Vol. 35 No. 4, pp. 2

Increased expectations of using disruptive technologies in supply chains[1]

By: Jan Stentoft and Ole Stegmann Mikkelsen

Introduction

Globalization continues to be an important condition that requires consciousness of the companies and their supply chains. It also drives supply chain complexity, thereby presenting new challenges in maintaining the right level of operational costs, customer satisfaction, lead-times, inventory levels, etc. Complexity in the supply chain is characterized by internal manufacturing complexity as well as down-stream and up-stream complexities. Among others, shorter product life cycles, increasing product variety, increasing amount of suppliers and customers have increased the level of supply chain complexity (Bozarth et al., 2009). Excelling in supply chain management requires that the right data, information and knowledge are available in the right quality and at the right time. Information systems and organizational processes that focus on data quality are important in assisting SCM executives to make their supply chains competitive. Information technology is further a major component of making innovations in supply chains (Arlbjørn et al., 2011). This mini-survey is dedicated to justifying the use and potential of information technology in supply chain management. As with any other important issue in business, if top management does not understand the value and is not committed, then

---

[1] This article is reproduced from Stentoft, J. and Mikkelsen, O.S. (2016), "Increased expectations of using disruptive technologies in supply chains", *DILF Orientering*, Vol. 53 No. 1, pp. 36-41.

Figure 1: Does top management have a good understanding of IT's role in creating competitive advantage for our company?

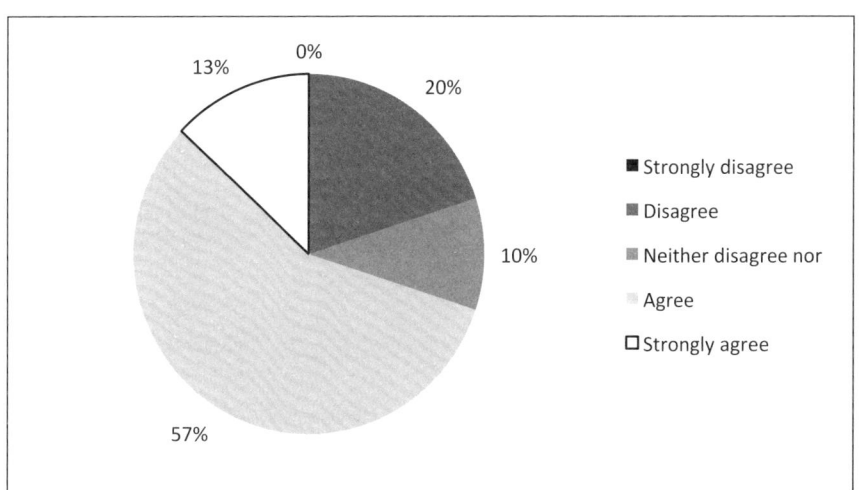

nothing will happen. Therefore, we started out with asking the respondents in *The Danish Supply Chain Panel* about their perceptions on how well top management understands the role of IT in creating competitive advantage for their company.

As it shows in Figure 1, 70% of the respondents either agree or strongly agree that top management has a good understanding of the role that IT can play in creating competitive advantage for their company. However, 20% indicated that they disagree while 10% indicated that they neither agree nor disagree. So every fifth company out there – according to the supply chain panel – has top management that has no understanding of the potential of IT in helping them in creating competitive advantage. One could safely conclude that the lack of understanding this link could be followed by the lack of commitment to invest resources in appropriate IT systems. Therefore, much potential for lifting such companies through IT may neither be addressed nor captured. A lack of such an IT focus can clearly drain the companies' competitiveness.

Next, we asked the respondents in *The Danish Supply Chain Panel* about the degree to which their ERP system supports the decision making process in their supply chains (see Figure 2).

As shown in Figure 2, 67% either agree or strongly agree that their ERP

Figure 2: Does your ERP system supports your decision making process in your supply chains?

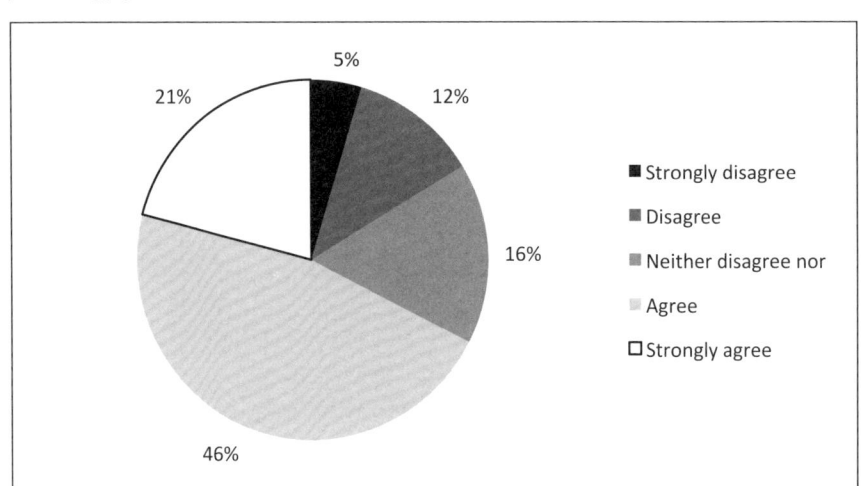

systems support their decision making processes in their supply chains. However, 17% of the respondents either disagree or strongly disagree. In other words, one of every sixth company has an ERP system which does not really support the decisions that are taken in their supply chain. This result indicates the need to initiate supply chain innovation projects (in terms of business processes, network structures with business partners and technology) in order to clarify the potential for business improvements. It can start with fact finding and AS-IS mapping of business processes and IT-systems landscapes (both formal systems and all the Excel spreadsheets). It also indicates a lack of an IT strategy that envisions how to achieve competitiveness through ERP-systems and other third party software.

Use of SCM software

Figure 3 shows the respondents' answers to the question about their perception of whether their company has the right IT solutions within different technical areas in order to manage their supply chains most efficiently. The respondents should choose among 5 different possible answers ranging from 1 "strongly disagree" to 5 "strongly agree". The results displayed in Figure 3 are thus averages of the respondents' answers.

Figure 3: Perceptions of having the right IT solutions within different technical areas in order to manage the supply chains most efficiently

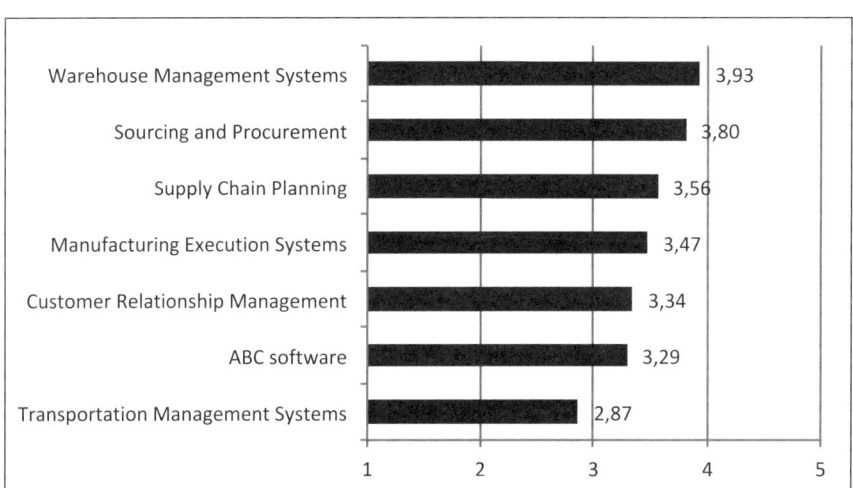

Interesting observations can be deducted from Figure 3. First of all, it appears that WMS and sourcing and procurement systems seem to be well covered in terms of having the right IT solutions. However, more surprisingly, it can be seen that in terms of customer relationship management systems, the companies perceive, to a far lesser extent, to have the right solution in place. As customers are those who ultimately 'pay the bills and the salaries', it is surprising that customers are not more in the focus, especially from an IT systems perspective. Furthermore, systems to assist staff conduct Pareto studies (e.g. ABC classifications of items and customers) also seems to be a possibility for further evaluation.

Data quality

While one thing is to have the right IT systems and the right IT tools to support the decision making process, another important thing is to secure the right quality of the data in the systems. In order to be able to make well-founded decisions and to run the daily operations efficiently, companies need data with good quality. However, previous surveys on the subject have shown that master data quality is not perceived to be in good shape as could be wished for (Haug and Arlbjørn, 2011; Schlichter et al., 2011).

Figure 4: Does your company have a high level of master data quality?

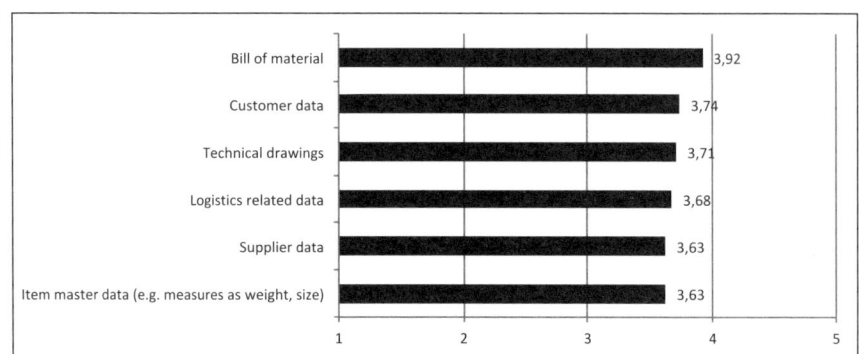

Therefore, it is interesting to ask the respondents about their perception on master data quality in their companies.

Figure 4 contains the respondents' perceptions of master data quality in various areas of the firms. An average on 3.92 is obtained from the respondents answering that their master data quality on their bills of materials is at the right level. The areas with the lowest averages are on the item master data and supplier data with an average on 3.63. In relation to these results, it is also interesting to understand what the respondents perceive as obstacles to obtain the right level of data quality. These answers appear in Figure 5.

As it appears from Figure 5, the lack of data control routines and lack of roles and responsibilities are considered as the most prevalent barriers for obtaining the right master data quality level. This is followed by the lack

Figure 5: Barriers for obtaining the right level of master data quality

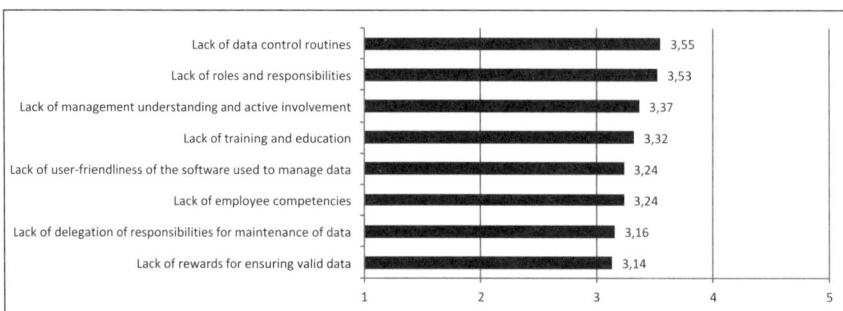

of understanding of this theme in the management teams. If management lacks involvement/commitment, it is not surprising that roles and responsibilities as well as the control routines are not in place. Lack of training and education, lack of user-friendly software, and the lack of employee competencies are also pointed out as potential barriers. Subsequently, the lack of delegated responsibilities for maintaining master data as well as lack of rewards for ensuring valid data is also considered as barriers. The answers shown in Figure 4 and 5 sketches a picture of barriers, to a large extent, can be handled by hiring one or more data stewards.

Big data and other disruptive technologies

One of the new and emerging focus areas in academia as well as business is the potential disruptive technologies emerging. One such technology is big data; it is important to know how to use it as potential for new business or as supportive for business decisions. However, there exists a wide range of different opinions on big data that is used in supply chains, wherein no unified definitions exist although there is a widespread acceptance that big data differs from data analytics through four Vs generally: Volume, Velocity, Variety and Veracity (Richey et al., 2014, p. 8). Big data is a new paradigm that combines these four V's (McAfee and Brynjolfsson, 2012). Volume is concerned with the total amount of data available. Velocity is related to the increasing speed of data. Variety refers to the multiple types of data that are created. Veracity is the changes in data that influences its usefulness. With this relatively new phenomenon, it is interesting to get some insights into how companies view the potential of big data and their actual use as a lever for better supply chain decisions.

As seen in Figure 6, 58% of the companies either agree or strongly agree that there is a high business potential in their companies in using big data. Only 7% disagree here. Approximately, one third of the companies neither disagree nor agree. None of the respondents answered that they strongly disagree about the business potential of big data. However, while one thing is to see the potential, another thing is to practice it. Therefore, we asked the panel about their use of big data in their supply chains. Please bear in mind that the use of big data might be higher in other areas of the companies than in the supply chain. Also, the very terminology of big data is quite

Figure 6: Big data has a high business potential in our company

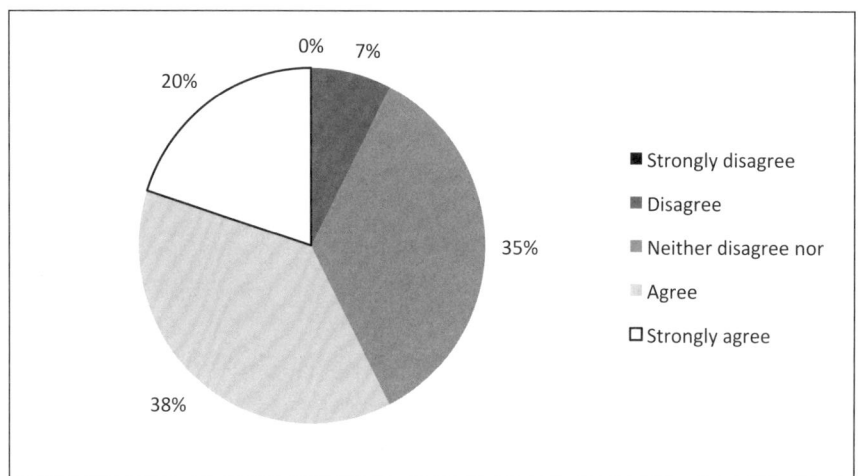

fuzzy. Therefore, some companies might actually work with big data, but might not call it big data.

As is seen in Figure 7, only 31% of the companies either agree or strongly agree that they use big data for better decisions. At the same time, more than half of the companies (54%) answer that they either disagree or

Figure 7: We are using big data in our supply chain in order to make better decisions

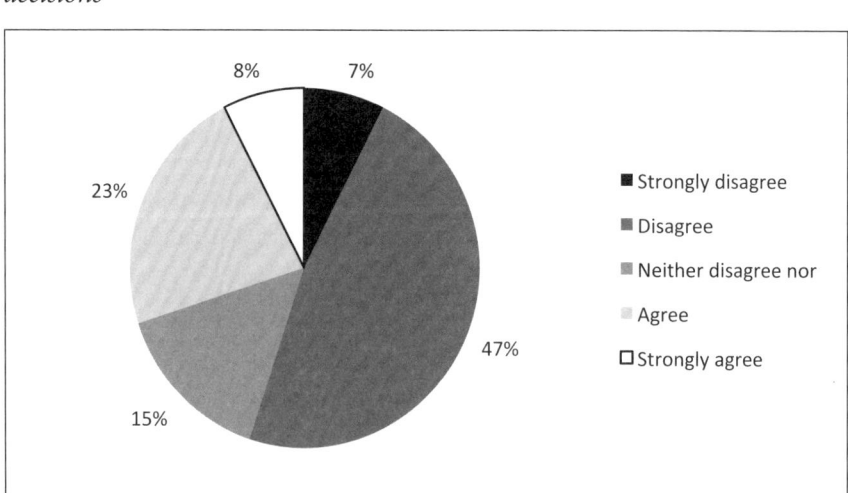

strongly disagree that they use big data for better decisions in their supply chain. So, when we compare the results shown in Figure 6 to those in Figure 7, it is clear that there is quite a gap between the potential of using big data and the actual use of big data.

Big data is, however, only one of several disruptive technologies discussed in various business media and academic journals. Other disruptive technologies discussed are for 3D printing, cloud technology and drones (see e.g. Manyika et al., 2013). Due to their nascent nature, we find it to be interesting to ask the panel about the perceived potential as well as the use of different disruptive technologies in supply chain design. The answers are illustrated in Figure 8.

As is seen in Figure 8, the use of all the mentioned disruptive technologies lag behind the perceived potential for their use in companies. But four technologies stand out – Mobile internet, automation of knowledge work, the internet of things and cloud technology are the technologies which are not only used the most by the companies, but are also perceived as entailing the most potential for use in supply chain design. On the next level, we observe 3D printing, autonomous vehicles, and, finally, drones coming in as last, both in use and in potential for use in the supply chain. All in all,

Figure 8: Disruptive technologies in use and its potential in supply chain design

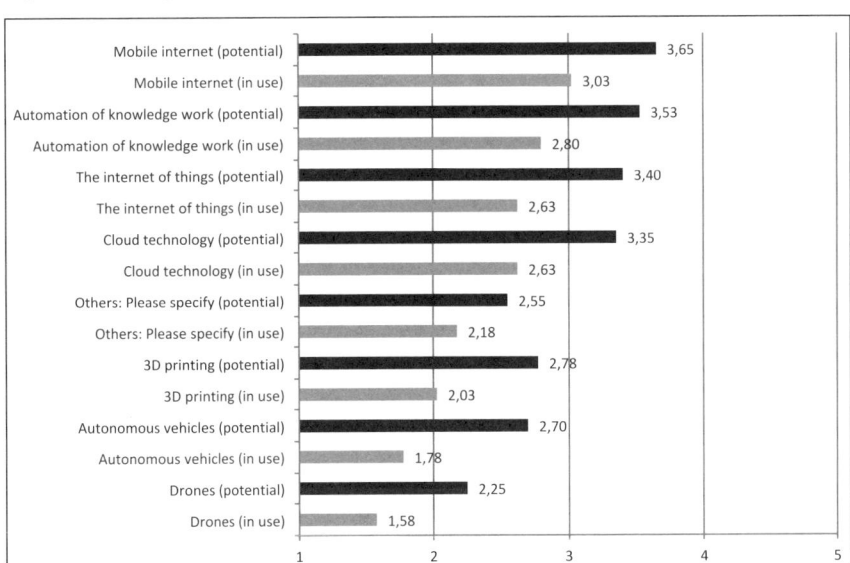

the answers call for Danish companies to focus more on the new and disruptive technologies to change the way they operate and run their supply chains. The answers in Figure 8 indicate a potential for improvement.

Barriers and challenges for implementing the right IT solutions

As a last question, we asked the respondents to indicate what they see as major challenges for implementing the right IT-solutions that support their supply chain strategy.

Figure 9 shows, not surprisingly, that focus on daily operations is, by far, the most challenging issue when it comes to implementing the right IT solutions to support the supply chain strategy (55%). This is a generally expressed issue that has been reported in most of the mini-surveys completed in *The Danish Supply Chain Panel*. Lack of internal competences as well as the lack of proper business cases (e.g. with a strong ROI) are also seen as major obstacles for implementing the right supply chain IT solutions. Additionally, as indicated by other mini-surveys, internal silo mentality is also mentioned as a significant obstacle. So, it still seems to be hard to work across internal functional boundaries. Under the other category, respondents included answers like "lack of full scale ERP solution that can handle the whole company from sourcing, production to financial with several legal entities that force us build stand-alone systems with linked interfaces" and "lack of capable ERP systems and lean IT processes".

Figure 9: Main challenges for implementing IT-solutions that supports the supply chain strategy

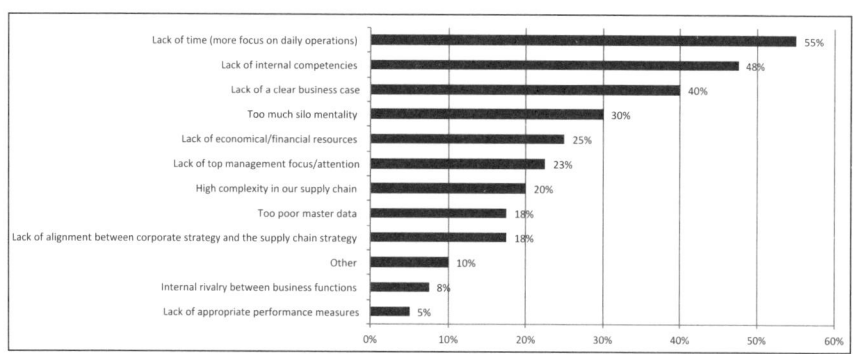

Conclusion

This mini-survey of *The Danish Supply Chain Panel* specifically focused on SCM and IT. Results from the mini-survey indicate that top management has a good understanding of IT's role in creating competitive advantages; however, with a large minority of top management lacking this understanding, the most widely used SCM software is WMS and sourcing and procurement systems, while CRM seems to be less prioritized. The most varied answers on master data quality are related to data quality of the item master with only 60% answering that they have the right level of quality, while more that 20% answering that there is a lack of good quality on the item masters. Lack of data control routines and the lack of roles and responsibilities are reported as the most dominant barriers for obtaining the right level of master data quality. Big data is, in general, seen as a technology with business potential. But there still seems to be a lot of work ahead to convey this message to practice. Other disruptive technologies that *The Danish Supply Chain Panel* consider to have potential in their supply chain designs are the mobile internet, automation of knowledge work, the internet of things and cloud technology. Finally, major challenges to implement IT-solutions that support supply chain strategies are the lack of time (more focus on daily operations), the lack of internal competences and the lack of a clear business case. Additionally, it seems that companies still struggle with cross functional collaboration. We hope that this little piece of work can stimulate discussions in organizations not only about these issues, but also on how to proceed to capture the potentials that exist.

References

Arlbjørn, J.S., de Haas, H. and Munksgaard, K.B. (2011), "Exploring supply chain innovation", *Logistics Research*, Vol. 3 No. 1, pp. 3–18.

Bozarth, C., Warsing, D.P., Flynn, B.B. and Flynn, E.J. (2009), "The impact of supply chain complexity on manufacturing plant performance", *Journal of Operations Management*, Vol. 27, pp. 78-93.

Haug, A. and Arlbjørn, J.S. (2011),"Barriers to master data quality", *Journal of Enterprise Information Management*, Vol. 24 No. 3, pp. 288-303.

Manyika, J., Chui, M., Bughin, J., Dobbs, R., Bisson, P. and Marrs, A. (2013) *Disruptive Technologies: Advances that will Transform Life, Business, and the Global Economy*, McKinsey Global Institute.

McAfee, A. and Brynjolfsson, E. (2012), "Big data: The management revolution", *Harvard Business Review*, Vol. 90 No. 10, pp. 61–68.

Richey, R.G., Morgan, T. R., Lindsey, K. K.,, Adams, F.G. and Autry, C.W. (2014), *Global Managerial Perceptions of Big Data Strategy in Supply Chain Management*, Council of Supply Chain Management Professionals.

Schlichter, J., Arlbjørn, J.S., Haug, A. and Zachariassen, F. (2011), *En analyse af stamdatakvaliteten i danske produktions virksomheder*, Institut for Entreprenørskab og Relationsledelse, Syddansk Universitet.

Section 2 – Panel articles in 2015

Supply chain executives and net working capital: An untapped potential[1]

By: Jan Stentoft and Ole Stegmann Mikkelsen

Introduction

One of the major benefits of a strong supply chain management mindset in practice is its recognition of its contribution to improving a company's cash flows. Supply chain management is about business and thereby also financials. This has led to the introduction of the term "supply chain finance" whereas one definition, among many, defines SCF as "an integrated approach that provides visibility and control over all cash-related processes within a supply chain" (Camerinelli, 2009). Applying a financial perspective to supply chain management (SCM) can improve both the requirement for short-term liquidity and also limit long-term financial burdens e.g. through collaboration not only between functions within a company but also between actors in the supply chain (Hofmann and Kotzab, 2010). Financial value can be improved by SCM using three generic levers of supply chain finance: 1) duration, 2) volume and 3) cost of capital (Gomm, 2010; Pfohl and Gomm, 2009). SCM executives have the possibility to affect all three levers. Financial requirements can be lowered by reducing the duration of the capital required (measured in days) and lowering the volume (amount of capital) needed. Finally, the cheaper the cost of capital (obtained using e.g. financial instruments), the higher financial value it creates. Supply chain executives must "speak the language" of both the

---

[1] This article is reproduced from Stentoft, J. and Mikkelsen, O.S. (2015), "Supply chain executives and net working capital: An untapped potential", *DILF Orientering*, Vol. 52 No. 4, pp. 46-51.

CEO and the CFO to communicate the impact of supply chain performance on financial indicators (Atkinson, 2008; Hoberg et al., 2015). The concept of net working capital might be such a language as it is a measure of both the company's efficiency and its short term financial health. The working capital is calculated by dividing current assets with current liabilities. If this calculation gives a value under 1, it indicates a negative working capital (liabilities are higher than the assets) and vice versa for values over 1. As shown in Figure 1, a little more than half of the respondents report that their companies to a very high degree or a high degree actively work with net working capital. 23% answer to some degree and 25% answer to a low degree or very low degree. It is surprising that only half of the respondents claim that they are working actively with net working capital. However, this survey does not tell how well they are working with this nor whether it is the right way to work with net working capital. There might be several reasons for the other 50% that have answered to some degree or low degree of a net working capital focus. It might well be an issue in their companies but they have not yet found the right formula to start up the process. It might also be the case that the companies' top management and/or SCM executives' conscious of net working capital is nowhere near adequate. Finally, there can be an acknowledgement that a stronger focus on net working capital is required but execution of such issues is absent due

Figure 1: Degree of working with net working capital

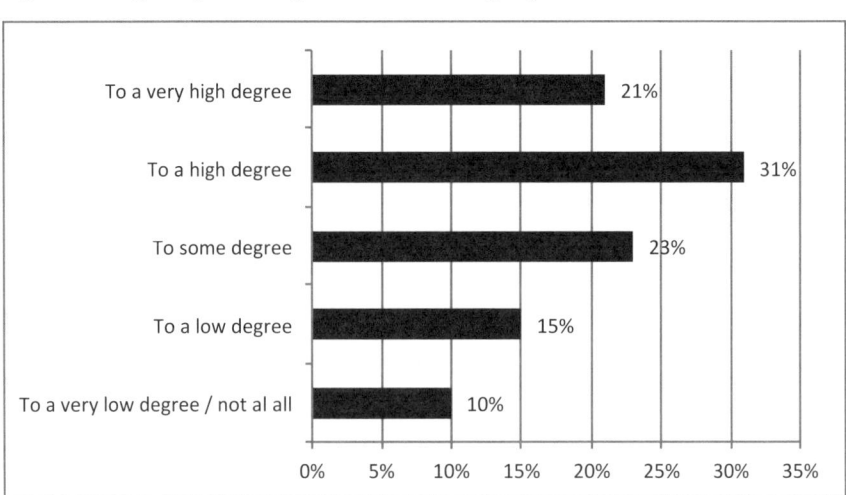

Figure 2: Net working capital being part of the overall performance management system

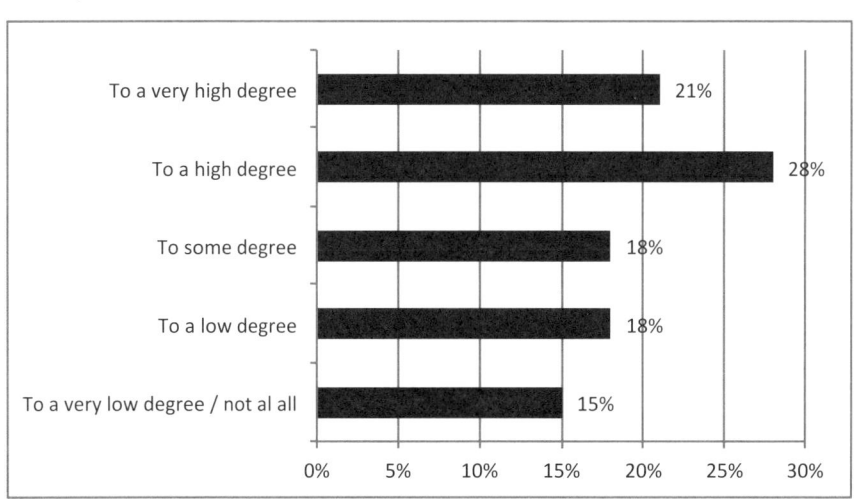

to lack of resources. Later in this article we will take a deeper look on some reported barriers of working with net working capital.

However, one thing is to actively work with net working capital. Another thing is if it is part of the performance management of the company. This is illustrated in Figure 2, which contains the respondents' replies regarding to which degree a net working capital focus is part of their overall performance management system. In general, the results here follow a similar pattern as to which degree they actually work with net working capital (cf. Figure 1); but with a lower percentage that answer to a very high degree and to a high degree (49%) against 53% that with the same degrees answered they work with net working capital. What gets measured gets done and what gets done can be rewarded. The results indicate that there is still some work to do in order to link the work with net working capital to the companies' overall performance management as a mean to get the right attention on this important theme.

Drivers for net working capital

The Danish Supply Chain Panel was also asked to evaluate what drives their companies to focus on net working capital. Figure 3 shows the respond-

Figure 3: Main drivers for working with net working capital

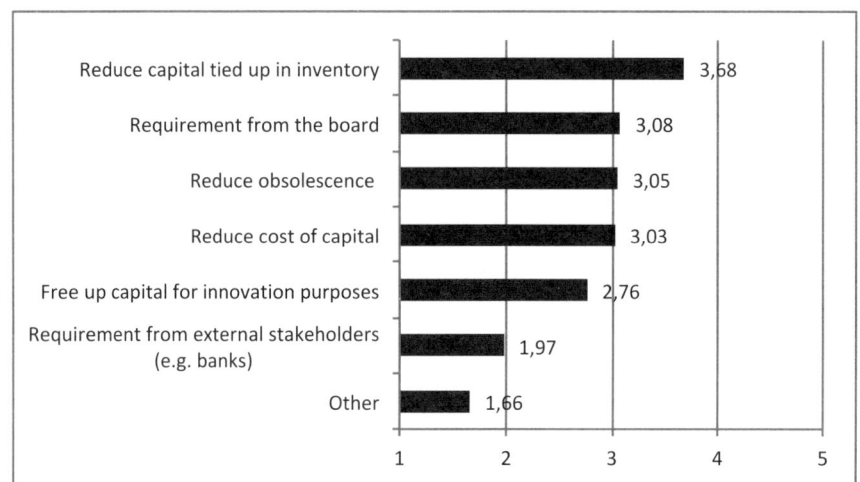

ents' answers regarding the drivers for working with net working capital in the companies. As is shown, the strongest drivers are internal, with focus on reducing capital tied up in inventory as the foremost driver with an average of 3.68 on a scale from 1 to 5. This is followed by demand from the board and reducing obsolescence and reducing cost of capital. Requirements from external stakeholders come in as last of the drivers, with an average of nearly 2. Other drivers mentioned are for example reducing trade debtor amounts and reduce management effort to manage large stocks. An interesting "other" driver mentioned is to improve supply chain processes, as net working capital is a very good KPI to measure process efficiency.

Using the supply chain as lever for improving net working capital

As mentioned above a KPI on net working capital is used to measure the efficiency of the supply chain processes of the company. Putting the question differently, we asked if companies work deliberately with restructuring of their supply chain to improve net working capital. The answers appear from Figure 4. As is seen, approximately 30% to a very high or high degree consciously work with supply chain restructuring to improve net working capital. However, as also is seen in Figure 4, approximately 30% work only

Figure 4: Consciously working with re-structuring of the supply chain as a lever for improved net working capital

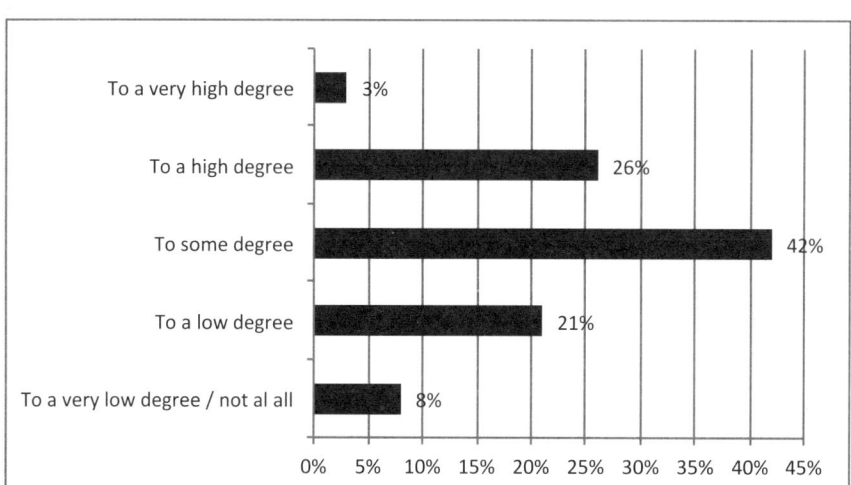

to a low degree or very low degree/not at all with supply chain restructuring as an approach to improve net working capital. 42% answer to some degree on the question. In other words, approximately up to 70% of the respondents do not see, or do not take full advantage, of the potential of the supply chain to improve net working capital.

Net working capital tools and potential

Various tools to improve net working capital may be used. Therefore the respondents were asked which tools are applied in the companies. The answers can be seen in Figure 5.

As appears from Figure 5, especially three tools are more applied among the respondents. On top is inventory management to reduce capital tied up in inventory. This is in line with the answers from Figure 3, reporting on the drivers of working with net working capital. Two other tools often used are increasing days of payable outstanding (DPO) and decreasing days of sales outstanding (DSO). Used alone both tools create a positive cash impact, while used simultaneously the two tools may even create a positive cash flow on discrete transactions. For example if a wholesaler's customers pay before suppliers are paid, a positive cash inflow is created from the

Figure 5: Applied tools to improve net working capital

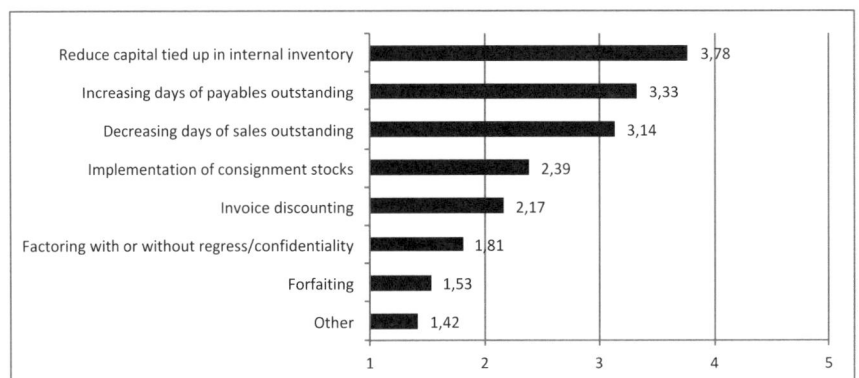

individual business enabling the wholesaler not to draw on the overdraft facility. Consignment stocks and invoice discounting are other tools used, while factoring and forfaiting are less used. Under "other" one respondent has answered alignment sales & sourcing – back to back on warranty, postponement, cancellation and return items.

However, one thing is what is being done, another thing is the (financial) potential to increase net working capital in the companies. The answers are illustrated in Figure 6, showing that approximately 40% perceive that there

Figure 6: Financial potential to increase net working capital

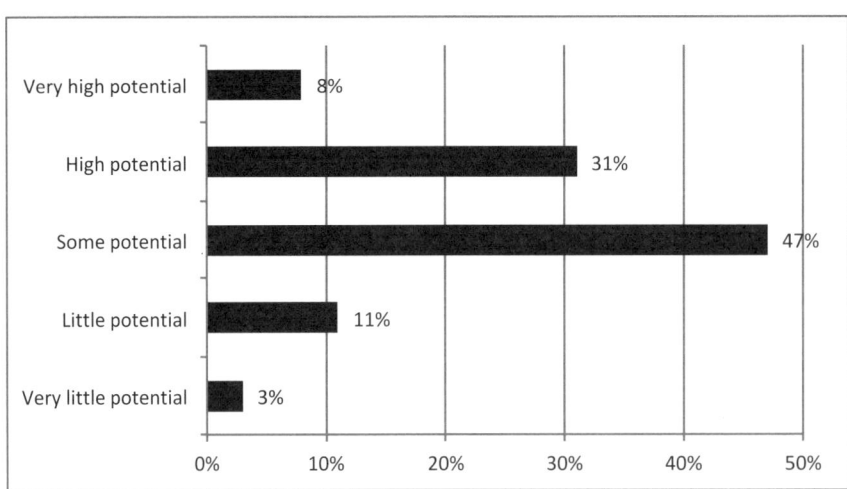

is a very high or high potential to increase the net working capital in their companies. So even though a little more than 50% to a very high or high degree work with net working capital (cf. Figure 1) there is still room for improvement according to the answers in Figure 6. Only 14% answer that there is nearly no potential for increasing the net working capital.

Competence development and anchoring of net working capital

Interesting is also to find out if the supply chain organization finds itself confident with working with net working capital. Asking if the supply chain organization of the companies needs to improve the competence level regarding supply chain finance returned the answers shown in Figure 7. As it appears, only 12% of the respondents are of the opinion that there is no need for competence improvement. No respondents think there is a very high need of competence development. Nearly 90% think to a high degree or some degree that there is need for competence development on supply chain finance in their supply chain organization. Seen together with the financial potential for increasing net working capital, these answers may indicate an untapped potential due to lacking competences.

Figure 7: Needs for improving the competence level regarding supply chain finance

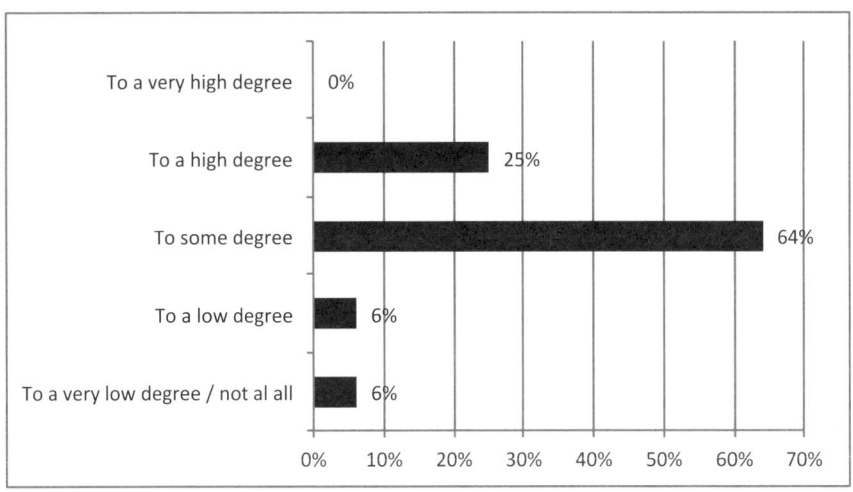

Figure 8: Responsibility for net working capital management (several marks allowed)

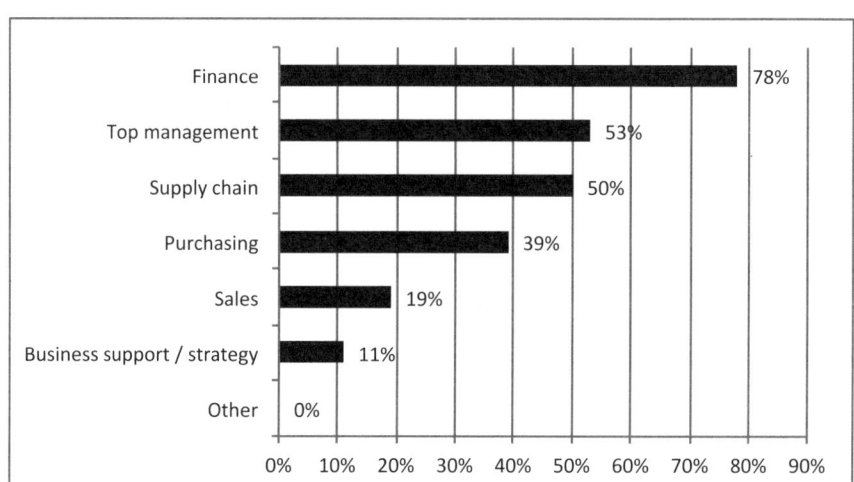

It is always interesting to look into an organization and see who has the responsibility and ownership of processes in a company. Not surprisingly the responsibility for net working capital is anchored mainly within the finance department in the companies. However, also top management and the supply chain have shares of responsibility for net working capital in the companies. Purchasing also bears some responsibility in some companies, while sales and business support/strategy to a minor degree bear responsibility.

Expectations on projects improving net working capital

Answers in Figure 1 showed that a little more than 50% of the companies actively work with net working capital to a very high or high degree. Figure 9 shows that net working capital is still on the agenda, as companies expect to further initiate projects. Only 8% expect not to initiate any projects on improving net working capital, while 14% expect to initiate a comprehensive amount of projects and 70% expect to initiate some projects.

Given that 25% of the respondents answered to a high degree that there is a need for improved competences in the supply chain organization on supply chain finances, one might expect that these companies rely on ex-

Figure 9: Expectations on initiating projects in the near future to improve net working capital management

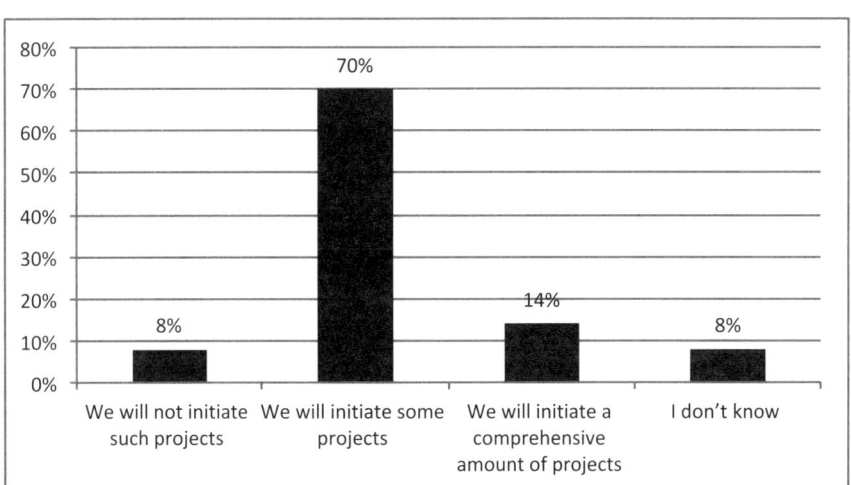

ternal resources when working with net working capital. As illustrated in Figure 10, 25% answer that they have some or a high dependence on external consulting assistance.

Respondents were lastly asked what the main challenges are in working with net working capital in their organizations. The answers appear in Figure 11. Silo mentality is by far perceived as the main challenge in working with net working capital (56% of the companies). This is in line with the results of other panel studies by *The Danish Supply Chain Panel*, indicating that the silo mentality is a major obstacle for improving the performance of many processes in many companies. Another major challenge is the focus on daily operation as mentioned by 39%. Coming in as third challenge we find lack of appropriate/conflicting performance metrics, which is in line with the silo mentality. Also respondents find that the understanding of the links from supply chain management over net working capital to company performance is a challenge. Together with the lack of competencies and clear tools and methods for working with net working capital, it draws a picture for further capturing the potentials in net working capital through dedicated training and education. However, as always data quality must be in place, which is also perceived as a challenge.

Figure 10: Dependence on external consulting assistance to work with net working capital management

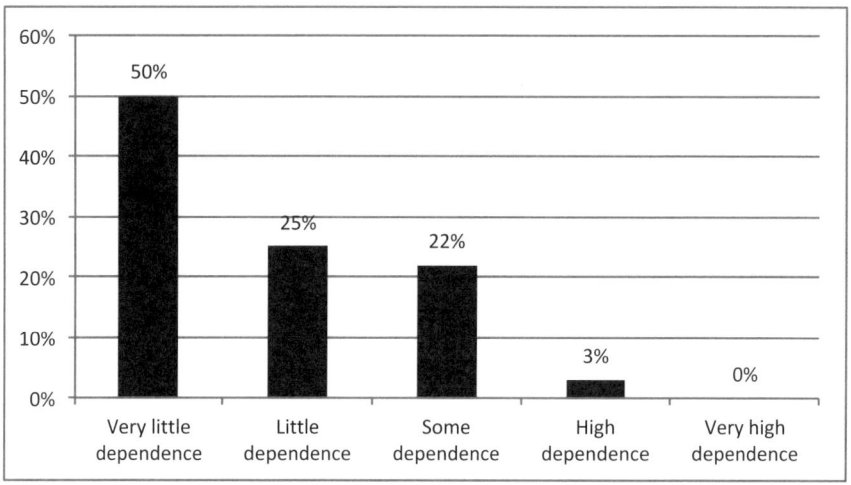

Figure 11: Main challenges working with net working capital (mark up to 5)

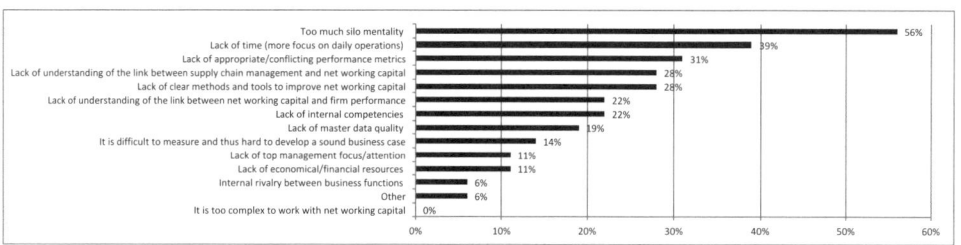

Conclusion

This mini-survey in *The Danish Supply Chain Panel* has focused on net working capital. The results reveal that the respondents are aware of the importance of net working capital but that they at the same time also acknowledge that there might be an untapped potential for improvement. The mini-survey indicates a need for competence development among supply chain executives within this area in order to establish a common language in top management. We hope this mini-survey can stimulate to put net working capital on the agenda in order to evaluate whether projects, that can improve the skills and practice within this area, should be initiated.

References

Atkinson,W. (2008), "Supply chain finance: The next big opportunity", *Supply Chain Management Review*, Vol. 12 No. 4, pp. 57-60.

Camerinelli, E. (2009), "Supply chain finance", *Journal of Payments Strategy and Systems*, Vol. 3 No. 2, pp. 114-128.

Gomm, M.L. (2010), "Supply chain finance: Applying finance theory to supply chain management to enhance finance in supply chains", *International Journal of Logistics: Research and Applications*, Vol. 13 No. 2, pp. 133-142.

Hoberg, K., Alicke, K. and Leopoldseder, M. (2015), "Time to get supply chain management to the board", *Supply Chain Management Review*, Vol. 19 No. 4, pp. 36-43.

Hofmann, E. and Kotzab, H. (2010), "A supply chain-oriented approach of working capital management", *Journal of Business Logistics*, Vol. 31 No. 2, pp. 305-330.

Pfohl, H.-C. and Gomm, M. (2009), "Supply chain finance -optimizing financial flows in supply chains", *Logistics Research*, Vol. 1 No. 3-4, pp. 149-161.

Business process outsourcing is driven by needs for increased flexibility and cost reductions[1]

By: Jan Stentoft and Ole Stegmann Mikkelsen

Introduction

In today's dynamic business environment we see that the discussion on what the firms should make inhouse and what to buy from suppliers are increasingly important, not least in the light of increasing globalisation (Arlbjørn et al., 2013). The focus has traditional been on production when discussing this strategic issue and typically focus on own core competencies and increased flexibility are often mentioned as drivers for outsourcing. However, it is not only the production of physical products that should be subject for this discussion, also administrative processes should be object for the discussion on what to keep inhouse and what to buy outside the firms boundaries (see Table 1 for examples of areas that may be subject for outsourcing). Therefore, the theme business process outsourcing (BPO) is the scope of this mini-survey distributed to *The Danish Supply Chain Panel*. The panel have been asked about their experience with business process outsourcing and the results are reported here in this brief article.

---

1 This article is reproduced from Stentoft, J. and Mikkelsen, O.S., (2015), "Business process outsourcing is driven by needs for increased flexibility and cost reductions", *DILF Orientering*, Vol. 52 No. 2, pp. 33-36.

Table 1: Examples of business processes areas being subject for outsourcing

Area for Business Process Outsourcing	Examples
Information technology and software	Applications and systems development, applications maintenance and re-engineering, IT strategy and planning, ERP implementation
Operations support services	Re-engineering, facilities management, telecommunications, logistics
Human resource services	Hiring and recruitment, payroll, training and staff development
Operations finance and accounting services	General accounting and audit, banking and financial services solutions
Marketing services	Marketing programs, sales and sales management, strategic planning, public relations, web development
Back office transaction processing	Administrative and management support services, document management and processing, general transaction processing, payment processing
Customer interaction services	Call centres, CRM and telesales, customer contact services, order processing, customer support, warranty administration
Knowledge and decision services	E-learning and education solutions, project management, data analytics, data mining, data warehousing

Source: Brown and Wilson (2005)

Almost half of the respondents in *The Danish Supply Chain Panel* reply in this mini-survey that they use business process outsourcing. Interestingly, 33% answered that they have also taken business processes back that have previously been outsourced within the last five years. Thus, the dynamic nature of the business environment might lead to shifting conditions for being attractive of having such process in control in-house or being sourced from outside. In the following we will take a closer look on the respondent's answers to statements concerning what kind of business processes that have been outsourced and what have been the drivers as well as barriers in such processes.

Business processes being outsourced

In the survey respondents were asked which kind of business processes or areas were outsourced. The results appear from Figure 1.

As shown in Figure 1, the two most common areas for BPO are within information technology and software and operations support services (both obtaining 65% of the respondents that practice BPO. 52% of the respondents have outsources HR services such as hiring and recruitment, payroll, training and staff development. Hereafter comes operating finance and accounting services with 39%. Company core areas such as the important interaction with customers and knowledge and decision services are only to a minor degree subject to outsourcing.

Drivers for Business Process Outsourcing

However, to identify the motivation for BPO, the respondents in panel have been asked about various drivers for their business process outsourcing decisions. In the following we take a closer look on the answers from those respondents that have carried out BPO. The drivers are organized into four groups:
1. organizational drivers,
2. improvement drivers,
3. financial and cost drivers and
4. revenue drivers.

Figure 1: Outsourced business areas

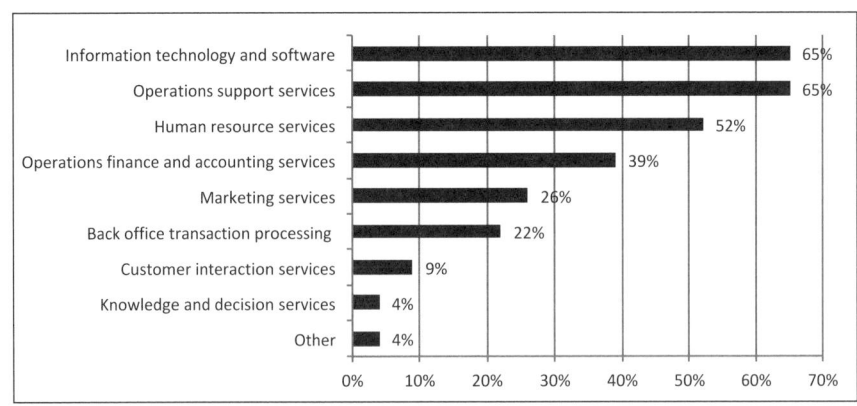

Organizational drivers are concerned with achieving a higher quantum of focus on core business, improving responsiveness to ever changing business conditions, demand for products and services, leveraging emerging technologies and achieving higher stakeholder value. Figure 2 contain the respondent's answers to statements concerning organizational drivers. The respondents were asked to answer to which degree they agreed to six statements on a 5 point Likert Scale ranging from 1 (to a very low degree) to 5 (to a very high degree). In Figure 2, the averages of answers are listed. The results show that the two drivers with the highest average scores are "to increase flexibility to deal with ever changing business conditions" and "to achieve a greater focus on core business". These two drivers is much in line with the drivers for outsourcing physical production as mentioned above. Next in line of drivers the respondents points at "assign operational issues to an outside expert" and "to redirect resources from non-core activities to the customer" with 3,0 and 2,9 in average. This may indicate a greater understanding that, also for business operations, others may be better in conducting the activity and that the companies address more focus to customers. The last two organizational drivers "to gain access products, services or emergent technologies" and "to have greater trust on market positioning and new product development" are to a lesser extend indicated as organizational drivers" for BPO.

The respondents were also asked to rate seven statements concerning *improvement drivers*. The main objectives of this group of drivers are to improve operating performance; obtain expertise, skills and technologies; improve management and control; improve risk management; acquire innovative ideas; improve credibility and image by associating with superior providers (Ghodeswar and Vaidyanathan, 2008). As shown in Figure 3 the two drivers that have obtained highest average scores are "to become more flexible and dynamic to meet the changing opportunities" with an average

Figure 2: Organizational drivers

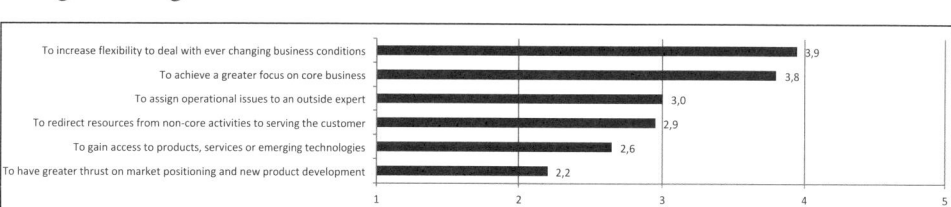

on 4.1 and "to eliminate the fixed cost of internal staff by moving the function to a supplier" with an average on 3.9. This is in line with the answers above on organizational drivers stating that companies needs to become more flexible in order to be able to cease the potential opportunities arising from the dynamic an ever changing company conditions. Also the focus on changing from fixed to variable cost helps in supports the flexibility intended. The two following performance drivers are of a more traditional operational performance nature focussing at operational performance and control of quality, productivity, processed and risk. Hereafter follows the driver "to obtain expert skills and innovative ideas" and "to obtain technologies which otherwise would not be available" with 3.2 and 2.6 in average. Compared to the four drivers mentioned above these two latter drivers are more externally focussed, suggesting that the main improvement drivers for core BPO in companies are internally focussed. The last improvement driver, with only 2.0 in average, is "to improve credibility and image by associating with superior providers". Some respondents have marked the "other" rubric and listed improvements drivers as "to reach a high level of development", "cost reduction", "cost efficiency" and "cost and flexibility", of which the three latter supports the drivers with the highest average scores.

Financial and cost drivers are focusing on reducing investment in assets, freeing-up resources for other purposes, and generating cash by transferring assets to the service provider (from fixed to variable costing). Figure 4 display the results of the respondent's answers to seven statements concerning financial and cost drivers. The most agreed driver for BPO is to reduce or control operating costs. Outsourcing processes to an external partner that have these areas as their core can save companies for costs. It is costly to maintain expertise in every step in the overall workflow. Thus, being conscious about where ones core processes are and where not provides valuable knowledge to develop plans for further business developments

Figure 3: Improvement drivers

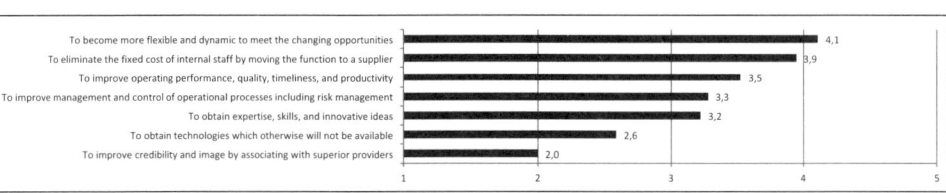

and thus competitiveness. Further outsourcing may enable increased control of the remaining cost within the company. The following five financial and cost drivers, from are all very much on an equal level of importance as stated by *The Danish Supply Chain Panel* and it is not possible to drag a conclusion based on a significant difference of importance. On the other hand they all are above the average of 3.0, indicating the five drivers from "to achieve cost reduction with enhanced performance" to "to reduce investment in assets" are of some importance for the decision to outsource business processes. The last driver "to expanding operations into a new geographical region" only have little importance (2.0 in average) when deciding for BPO.

The last group of drivers the respondents have valued is about *revenue drivers* as shown in Figure 5. The objectives of revenue drivers are to achieve growth by gaining increased market access and leveraging the service provider's best-in-class processes, capacity and systems (Ghodeswar and Vaidyanathan, 2008). The revenue drivers seem not to be as significant as the other sets of drivers as appears from Figure 5. However, the two drivers that have obtain the highest average scores are "to leverage on the service provider's best processes, capacity and systems" and "to manage demand efficiently through outsider's automation, process maturity and the latest technology" with average scores on 3.1.

The next three drivers are "to stretch the limits in handling the increased volume of business, "to focus on enablers of business growth and strategies to fulfil them" and "to expand capacity /in order) to design, test and build new products and services", all with the average of 2.6. While the two first drivers mentioned revolves around getting access to and leverage on external expertise, these three latter drivers all addresses the issue of creating internally "space" to better handle increase business. The final driver, with

Figure 4: Financial and cost drivers

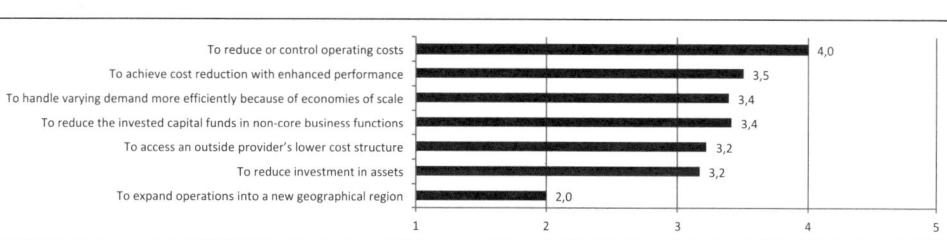

Figure 5: Revenue drivers

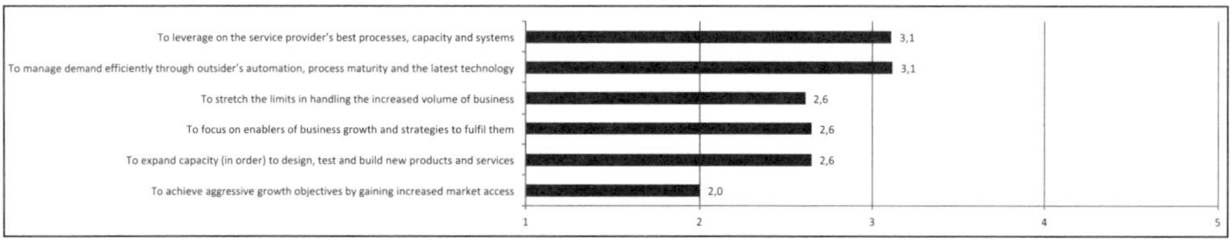

[Bar chart showing revenue drivers:
- To leverage on the service provider's best processes, capacity and systems: 3,1
- To manage demand efficiently through outsider's automation, process maturity and the latest technology: 3,1
- To stretch the limits in handling the increased volume of business: 2,6
- To focus on enablers of business growth and strategies to fulfil them: 2,6
- To expand capacity (in order) to design, test and build new products and services: 2,6
- To achieve aggressive growth objectives by gaining increased market access: 2,0]

only an average of 2.0" is "to achieve aggressive growth objectives by gaining increased market shares".

Barriers influencing the business process outsourcing decision

Finally the respondents were asked about the main perceived barriers for BPO in the firms. As it appears from Figure 6 it is especially the lack of resources and competences that are addresses as barriers. But in general, the results in this mini-survey reveal not a great amount of perceived barriers. However, we do not know whether the respondents have been responsible for the BPO's in mind, why another answers might be reported if answers have been reported by the project managers behind the BPO's.

Conclusion

This mini-survey from *The Danish Supply Chain Panel* has focused on BPO with a special emphasis on what drives such decisions and what barriers

Figure 6: Perceived barriers in BPO decision processes

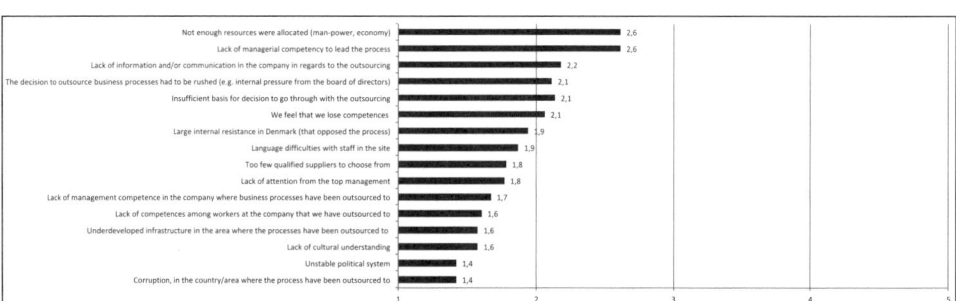

that have been experienced. Main organizational drivers for BPO is identified as being a need for increased flexibility to deal with changing business conditions and a need to focus on core processes. The data indicate that the main areas for BPO are information technology and software and operations support surveys. Main improvements drivers are to become more flexible and to shift from fixed staffing cost to variable staff costing. The main financial and cost driver for BPO is to reduce or control operating costs. The two main revenue drivers is to exploit the suppliers capabilities and being able to manage own demand more efficiently. Finally, the mini-survey the main perceived barriers in BPO, though they generally not are obtaining high scores, are lack of resources (man-power and economy) and lack of managerial competences to lead the process.

With this knowledge in mind some interesting questions arise, which has not been in focus for this mini-survey. One interesting issue to investigate is what effect the BPO have had on the performance of the companies. One might ask if the use of BPO has improved or perhaps deteriorated the performance? Other interesting questions to focus on are how the BPO process was carried out and how BPO is organised in the companies. Who has the responsibility and is it organised centrally or de-central? These questions are important but not in the scope of this mini-survey, but should be questions to address in future research projects and questionnaires. We hope this article can stimulate to discussions about your current practice, if any, about BPO.

References

Arlbjørn, J.S., Lüthje, T., Mikkelsen, O.S., Schlichter, J. and Thoms, L. (2013), *Danske producenters udflytning og hjemtagning af produktion*, Kraks Fond Byforskning, København K.

Brown, D. and Wilson, S. (2005), *The Black Book of Outsourcing – How to Manage the Changes, Challenges, and Opportunities*, Wiley, Hoboken, New Yok.

Ghodeswar, B. and Vaidyanathan, J. (2008), "Business process outsourcing: An approach to gain access to world-class capabilities", *Business Process Management Journal*, Vol. 14 No. 1, pp. 23-38.

Strategic awareness of supply chain complexity and firm performance: The missing link[2]

By: Jan Stentoft, Antony Paulraj and Ole Stegmann Mikkelsen

Introduction

Following the globalization of trade, the supply chain of companies has become increasingly more complex. Products are nowadays sourced in one continent, produced or assembled in another, and sold at the market on a third continent. This demand proximity from suppliers, thereby forcing them to follow their customers around the globe in the quest for better cost as well as access to specific technologies, knowledge, competences, and markets. All this adds complexity and risks to the supply chain, making it not only harder to manage, but also far more costly to operate than in "the good old days", thereby impacting cost of goods sold (COGS) negatively. Supply chain complexity can be related to either detail complexity or dynamic complexity (Bozarth et al., 2009). Detail complexity is the distinct number of components or parts, products, processes, suppliers, customers, locations/sites etc. Dynamic complexity refers to the unpredictability of a systems response to a given set of inputs, driven in part by the interconnectedness of many parts that make up the system (Bozarth et al., 2009). In the following sections, we present the results of a mini-survey that focused on supply chain complexity phenomenon: current practice, its relationship to financial performance, as well as challenges and needs to cope with these complexities.

---

2   This article is reproduced from Stentoft, J., Paulraj, A. and Mikkelsen, O.S., (2015), "Strategic awareness of supply chain complexity and firm performance: The missing link", included in DILF's newsletter in week 17.

Figure 1: Addressing supply chain complexity

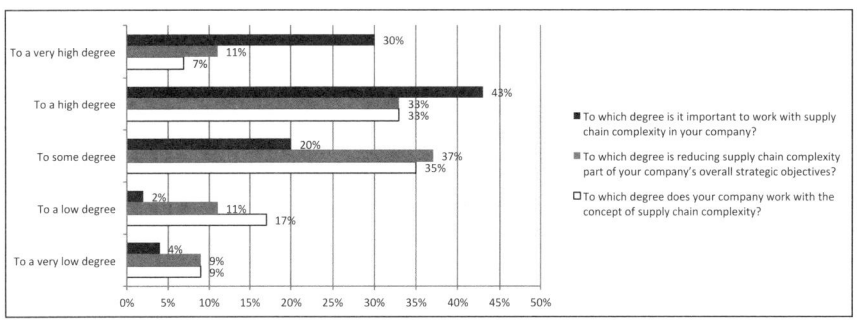

As shown in Figure 1, 73% of the respondents find that working with supply chain complexity is of very high or high importance in their companies. This clearly indicates an acknowledgement of the fact that supply chains comprise of complexities that need to be managed appropriately. Therefore, apart from evaluating the importance of complexities, it is also interesting to see how the respondents perceive they work towards coping with these complexities. As indicated in Figure 1, while 44% of the respondents indicate that reducing supply chain complexity is a significant part of their organizations overall strategic objectives (i.e., either to a very high or a high degree), 37% indicate that it is integrated only to some degree. In general, this reflects that top management understands the need to address supply chain complexity from a strategic perspective. However, the data also shows a gap between perceived importance of complexities and the actual actions taken to reduce such complexities. 40% of the companies answer that they work either to a very high or high degree towards reducing complexity. Surprisingly, majority of the respondents (60%) seem to work only to some degree, low or very low degree towards reducing complexity. This result clearly indicates that these companies might need to work more towards their reducing supply chain complexity.

Supply chain complexity and financial performance

Figure 2 shows the respondents perception of the untapped financial potential of reducing supply complexity in their organizations. While 62% perceive that there is a very high to high financial potential in working with supply chain complexity, 33% perceive that there is only limited (some) potential. Additionally, only 4% answer that there is a low to very low financial potential. Taken together, this result suggests that there seems to be a general perception that working on reducing complexity will make the companies more financially competitive. However, the survey did not focus on identifying the magnitude of this financial potential; it just wanted to explore whether a potential exists.

The perception of relatively high financial potential of reducing supply chain complexity could be very well attributed to the fact that the importance of supply chain complexity is well understood by the organizations top management teams. Accordingly, Figure 3 presents the degree to which the concept of supply chain complexity is understood by the top management. As evident from Figure 3, 38% respondents find that their top management teams understand the concept of supply chain complexity to a very high or a high degree. Additionally, 40% of the respondents perceive that their top management understands this concept only to some degree. Comparing results from Figures 2 and 3, it is surprising to see that there is a stronger perception about the financial potential of reducing supply chain complexity when compared to that of how well the phenomenon is understood in the top management team. These results clearly indicate that

Figure 2: What is the financial potential to reduce supply chain complexity in your company?

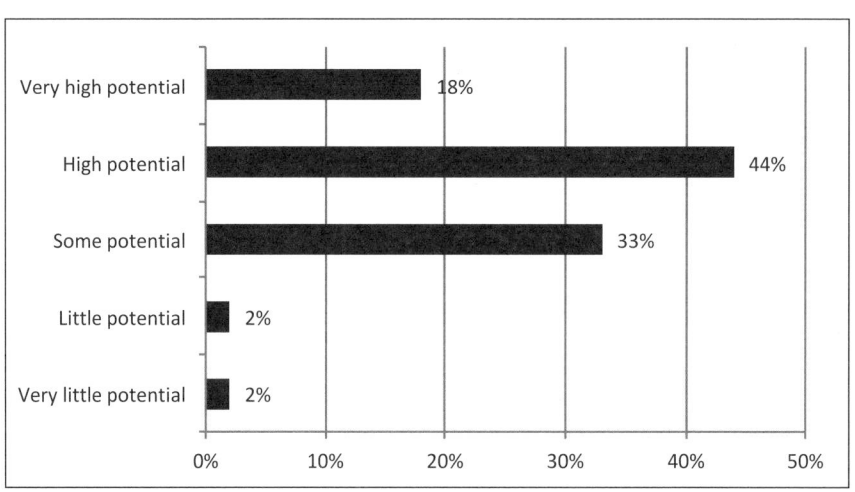

Figure 3: Degree to which the concept of supply chain complexity well understood in the company's top management group

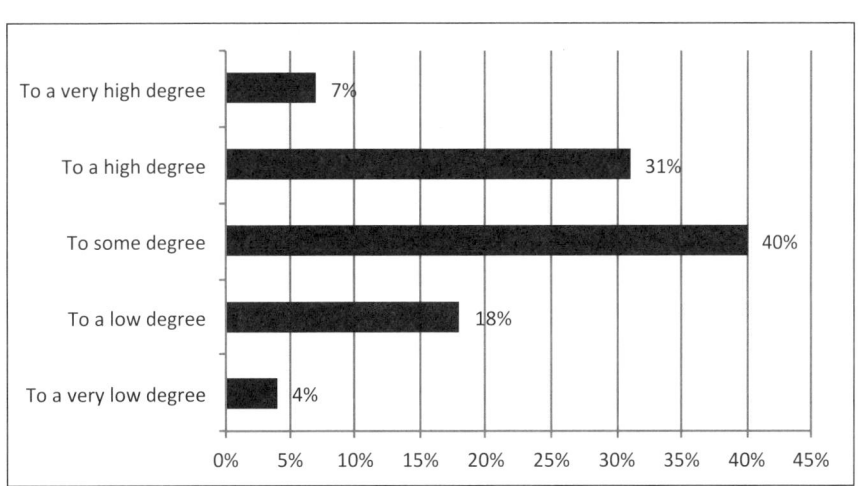

efforts must be undertaken to include the phenomenon of supply chain complexity in top management agenda of some companies.

Current practices for reducing supply chain complexity

The respondents were also asked to evaluate the extent to which they are working with different forms of supply chain complexity in their organizations. As shown in Figure 4, the highest average on a scale from 1 (to a very low degree) to 5 (to a very high degree) is 3.16 and is related to practices with reducing supply chain complexity in terms of internal inventory levels. This is followed by complexity reduction at "uncertainty level" with an average at 3.04. This type of uncertainty can be reduced through developing and implementing appropriate sales & operations planning processes. Focus on the speed level is perceived to be the third most dominant area with an average of 2.98.

Another interesting observation is that companies focus less on reducing complexity in terms of customer rationalization when compared to other areas. This result suggests that customer rationalization is a challenging task with various political views and reasons to move along with the exist-

Figure 4: Degree to which the company works with reducing complexity

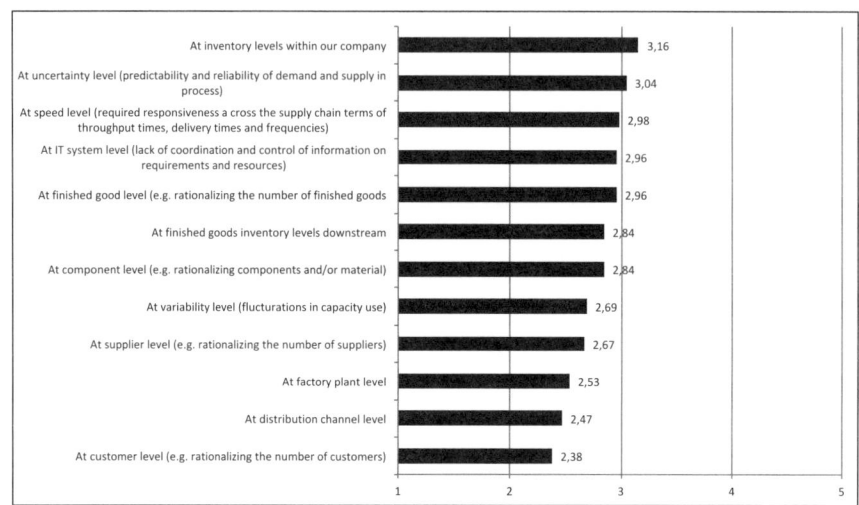

ing portfolio of customers even though some of those relationships are not as profitable.

Challenges with supply chain complexity

The strategic work focusing on reducing supply chain complexity does not come without challenges. Figure 5 illustrates how the respondents have marked on a number of prelisted challenges. A little more than half of the respondents indicate that the lack of understanding of the link between supply chain complexity and firm performance is the main challenge. Intuitively, one can recognize that the different complexity areas listed in Figure 4 do affect performance metrics of cost, lead-time, quality and flexibility. But linking the present level of supply chain complexity to firm performance seems to be quite challenging. This lack of clarity may prevent the initiation of more complex complexity reduction projects since the outcome of such efforts are not quite apparent. At the same time, this result indicates that some efforts are needed to develop and implement appropriate performance metrics. Other key challenges with percentages of respondents over 40% are: "too much silo mentality", "lack of time (more focus on daily operation)" and "lack of clear methods and tools to reduce complexi-

Figure 5: Main challenges in working with complexity

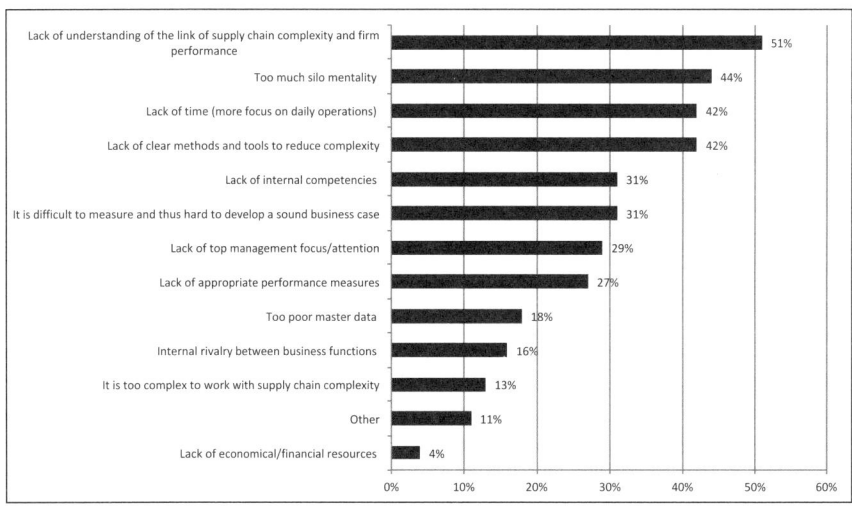

ty". The silo mentality is a challenge albeit this behavior has been a point of debate for more than 30 years now! Lack of time due to increased focus on operation is a well-known challenge that has been addressed many times during the various mini-surveys completed and reported in *The Danish Supply Chan Panels* since its establishment in 2012. Thus, it is not surprising that the respondents mark "lack of time" as a challenge. However, these results suggest that some work needs to be allocated to develop a business case for supply chain complexity reductions. Perhaps, such a process can showcase the necessity to release resources for this purpose. Furthermore, it is important for firms to develop capabilities in handling both daily operations as well as development of the supply chain – to be an ambidextrous supply chain. It is also quite interesting that 42% of the respondents mark "lack of clear methods and tools" as being a challenge for reducing supply chain complexity. This goes hand in hand with the lack of understanding of the link between complexity and firm performance. Reducing supply chain complexity is a complex task in itself. We suggest that this is an underdeveloped area that applied researchers and management consultants must focus on so as to help firms in devising tools and methods that can objectively reduce supply chain complexity.

Need for supply chain complexity reduction and resources to do so

The results of this mini-survey clearly indicate that there is a relatively strong recognition of the importance of reducing supply chain complexity. However, just recognizing the need is not enough; firms need to initiate projects to do something about it. Figure 6 shows that the respondents expect to initiate projects in the near future to reduce supply chain complexity. While 56% of the respondents indicate that some projects will be initiated, 29% of the respondents answer that "a comprehensive amount of projects" will be initiated. This result signals the awareness as well as willingness to work with supply chain complexity reductions. However, it is important to point out that the challenges of working with supply chain complexity reductions, the lack of understanding of the link towards performance, as well as the lack of tools might metaphorically suggest that these projects are initiated in the context of dimmed light.

As indicated earlier, the respondents have marked "the lack of time (more focus on operation)" as a challenge in working with supply chain complexity reductions. Figure 7 shows how the respondents have answered when it comes to the availability of right resources to achieve targets of

Figure 6: Expectations to initiate projects in the near future to reduce supply chain complexity

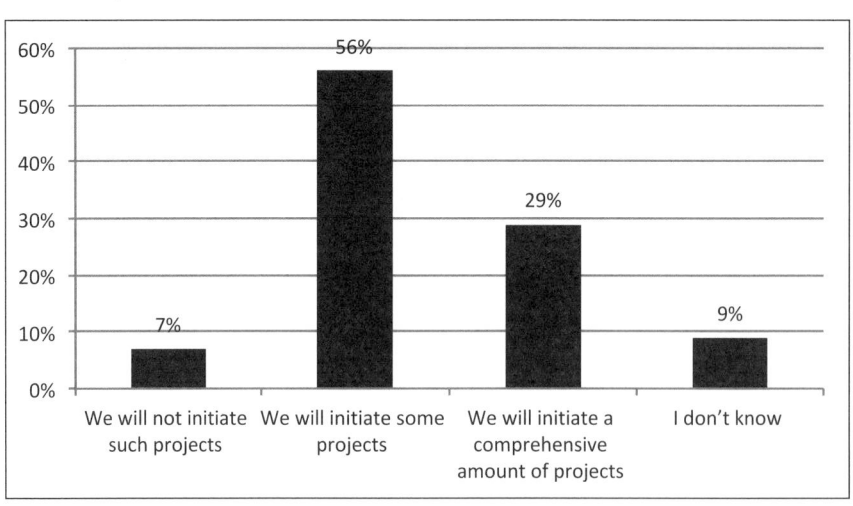

Figure 7: Do you have the right organizational resources to reduce supply chain complexity that last?

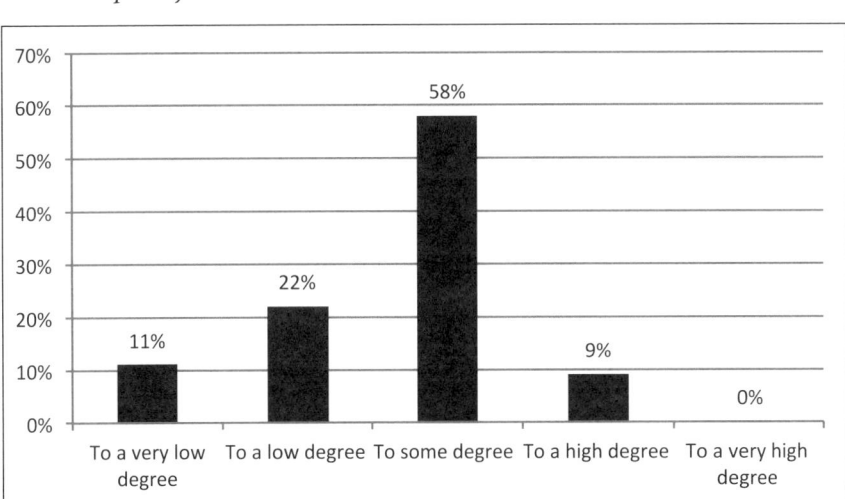

supply chain complexity reductions. It should be remarked that "right resources" can be understood in at least two different ways – a volume perspective and a competence perspective. Only 9% of the respondents answer that the right resources are in place. While 58% answer that the resources are available to only some degree, one-third answer that resources are available at a low and very low degree. This result clearly reflects the lack of resources to address supply chain complexity. Especially while 75% of the respondents indicate that they will initiate projects to curb supply chain complexity, only 2/3 of the companies respond that they have the right resources (i.e., to some degree or better) for executing such projects. Such a gap can be closed only through competence development of the existing employees; hiring more similar resources or hiring new competences either temporarily or permanently.

Figure 8 shows the respondents perception of the need for external consultancy assistance in their work towards reducing supply chain complexity. More than half of the respondents indicate that they are not as dependent (i.e., little or very little) on external assistance to achieve their targets. 22% indicate some dependence while 22% indicate a high and very high dependency on external consultancy. This result does not provide any clear

Figure 8: Perceived dependence on external consulting help in order to succeed with reducing supply chain complexity

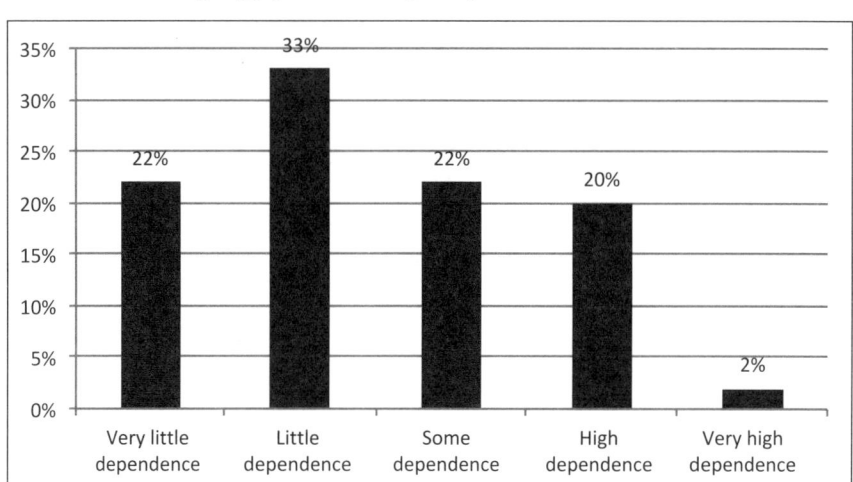

direction; on the contrary, it indicates that companies may have different resource pools, and, thus, different needs.

Conclusion

This article has provided insight into the results of a mini-survey on supply chain complexity that was distributed to *The Danish Supply Chain Panel*. The results indicate that supply chain complexity is perceived as being an important issue to be contended with; but there is still considerable room for improvements in this area. Current practices are mainly concerned with reducing complexity through inventories and minimizing uncertainty in demand and supply, and through more responsive supply chains. The panel attributes the main challenges in reducing supply complexity to a lack of understanding of how the phenomenon is linked to firm performance, silo mentality, lack of time and lack of appropriate methods and tools. Finally, the panel does also report that they want to initiate projects to reduce complexity in the supply chain. However, they do not seem to have adequate resources in-house, and does not, to the same extent, see the need for assistance.

Reference

Bozarth, C., Warsing, D.P., Flynn, B.B. and Flynn, E.J. (2009), "The impact of supply chain complexity on manufacturing plant performance", *Journal of Operations Management*, Vol. 27 No. 1, pp. 78-93.

Few CEO's have a background in SCM[1]

By: Jan Stentoft and Antony Paulraj

Introduction

Through its simultaneous emphasis on service improvements as well as cost reduction activities, the supply chain management (SCM) area has, for a long period, played a key role in enabling companies achieve sustainable competitive advantage. The supply chain area is increasingly playing a pivotal role in this globalized economy wherein raw materials and components are sourced, manufactured and even sold on a variety of continents. Historically, managers have been of the perception that products and services that are offered with the right marketing mix as being the best source of competitiveness. But more recently, this perception has changed significantly. In other words, managers believe that unless the right marketing mix is supplemented by excellence in other functional areas, it cannot be a source of competitive advantage. One such area is the supply chain! In fact, successful companies nowadays compete based on their supply chains and are realize the need to continuously as well as equally focus on supply chain innovations in the same pace as that of product, sale as well as market innovations. Supply chain innovation is rightly recognized as a dynamic capability that can often result in long-standing competitive advantage.

In spite of this growing importance of SCM, top management does not seem to acknowledge its complete potential. If this is true in your organization, why do you think this is the case? Could it be that the top management in your organization fails to see what SCM is about and what benefits it could provide. Among others, the lack of understanding could be due to (1) the lack of poor internal communication, (2) the fact that SCM is not represented in the top management, or (3) the fact that very few CEO's

---

1 This article is reproduced from Stentoft, J. and Paulraj, A. (2015), "Few CEOs have a background in SCM", *DILF Orientering*, Vol. 52 No. 2, pp. 36-42

have a background in SCM. Another major reason could be that the SCM folks are too focused on operational or tactical level and rather overlook the need to hone the skills to speak the language of the CEO/CFO. The ambition of this article is to answer some of these questions by presenting the results a mini-survey that was distributed to *The Danish Supply Chain Panel*.

Representation of SCM in top management and supply chain strategy

The first question on the survey was concerned with whether SCM is represented in top management teams. As indicated in Figure 1, close to three-fourth of the respondents considers this to be case in their company. This result clearly indicates that the importance SCM is generally acknowledged within organizations. Additionally, this result also corresponds to the recent US-based study conducted by Wagner and Kemmerling (2014). However, our analysis does not inform us about what is meant by SCM. The notion of SCM is not clearly understood both in academia and practice. While in some companies SCM is primarily concerned with the sourcing/upstream function; in others it is concerned with planning and manufacturing or with inventory/distribution/downstream part (please see an ear-

Figure 1: Is SCM represented in the top management team?

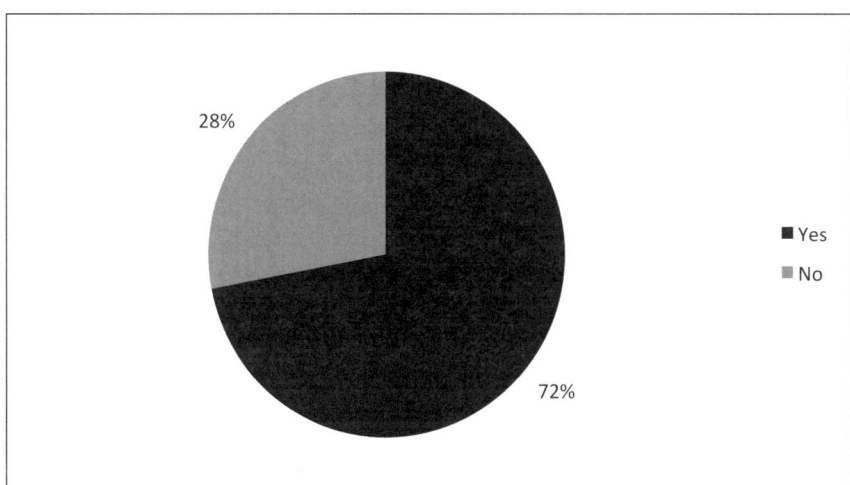

Figure 2: Does your company have a SCM strategy?

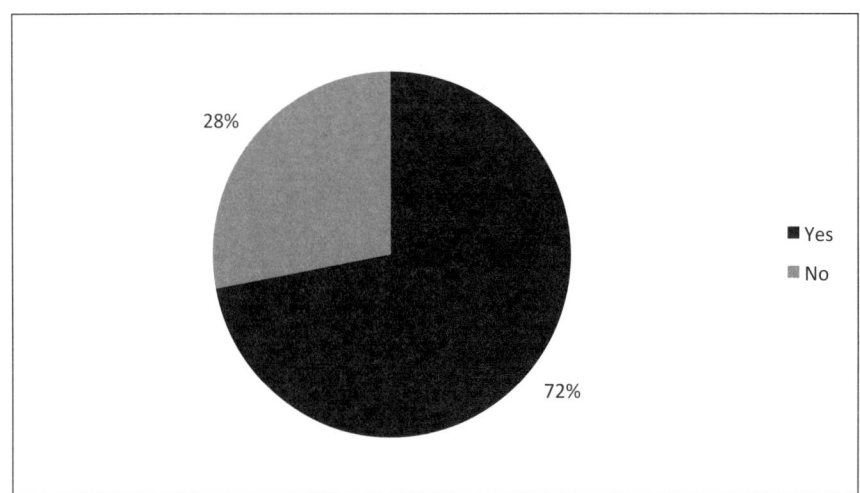

lier mini-survey conducted by Arlbjørn and Johnsen, 2013 on this topic). Other practices might even be combinations of the above-mentioned interpretations.

The respondents were also asked whether their companies have a SCM strategy. As shown in Figure 2, 72% of the respondents answered yes to this question. When combining the results presented in Figures 1 and 2, we can conclude that the strategic relevance as well as the importance of SCM is well recognized among most of the companies that are part of *The Danish Supply Chain Panel*. However, still more than one-fourth of the companies have some work to do here. While these results provide some indications about the state of SCM matureness in the Danish industry, it cannot be generalizable to all Danish companies, since *The Danish Supply Chain Panel* is made up of companies that perhaps have above average prowess in SCM. Accordingly, given that the results could be upward biased, we could conjecture that the true picture of the Danish industry is actually much lower in comparison.

Top Management and Supply Chain Management

When asked about the technical background of their CEO, 30% of the respondent answered that their CEO is from sale, 24% is from finance and

Figure 3: The technical background of your CEO

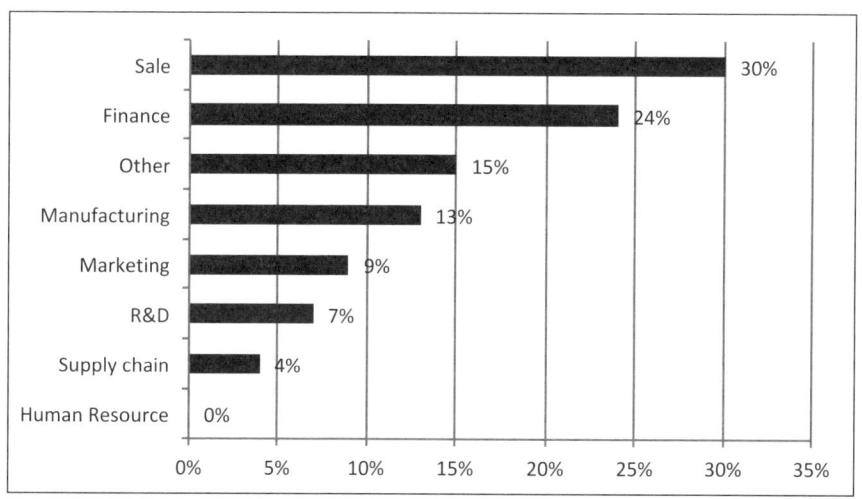

15% answered "other" indicating backgrounds within business law, agricultural and chemistry (please refer to Figure 3). Most importantly, as indicated in Figure 3, only 4% of the respondents CEO's had a background in supply chain.

Figure 4: Top management's understanding of the supply chain's role in creating competitive advantages

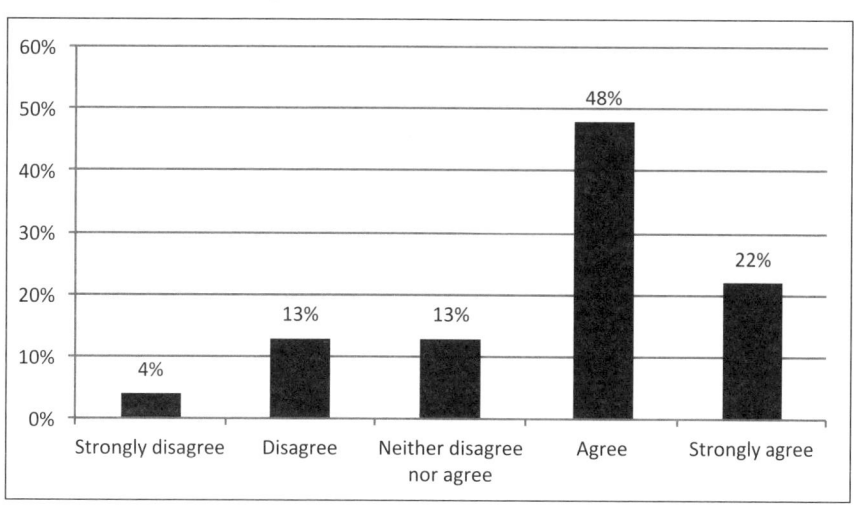

Even though a significant number of CEO's did not have a background in SCM, as evident from Figure 4, 70% of the respondents indicated that their top management has an understanding of the role of SCM in creating competitive advantages. Based on this result, we could conclude that about 30% of the companies requires a pedagogical exercise so as to articulate how the performance benefits of SCM is strongly related to the overall company performance. As a first step in this direction, supply chain executives need to make simple visualizations of the supply chains and provide facts on the costs and performance yields of their current supply chains. When contrasted with cost figures, the yield will clearly bring to light the supply chain performance outputs that could be derived from the supply chain cost inputs.

Supply Chain Strategy

The respondents in panel were also asked about "the main focus is in their supply chain strategy". In general, the area of SCM aims to fulfil the twin objectives of improving service as well as reducing costs. The service elements cover performance areas such as delivery time, delivery accuracy and delivery information. Performing well on such parameters is important for sustaining the turnover or even increasing it. Thus, the service elements constitute important factors that improve the top line of the company' annual account. In contrast, the cost part of SCM contains vital sources for improving the bottom line of the companies' annual account. The cost part could relate to a focus on net working capital, asset utilization, or cash to cash. As evident from Figure 5, the supply chain strategies among the panel members are being dominated by a cost focus with: 62% of the respondents answering 1 or 2 on a scale of 1 to 5 (with 1 displaying a cost focus and 5 displaying a service focus). Thus, cost figures still seem to dominate the strategies of most the companies that are part of the Panel. However, 31% of the companies focus on balancing both cost and service elements. We believe that these companies might have been through strategy processes that have helped them to realize the importance of sticking to concrete strategic objectives that balance cost and service targets. At the same time, this mini-survey does not tell anything about what the companies' corporate strategies are; thus, we do not have any indications of the alignment of the supply chain strategy with the corporate strategy. But as

Figure 5: Main focus of the SC strategy

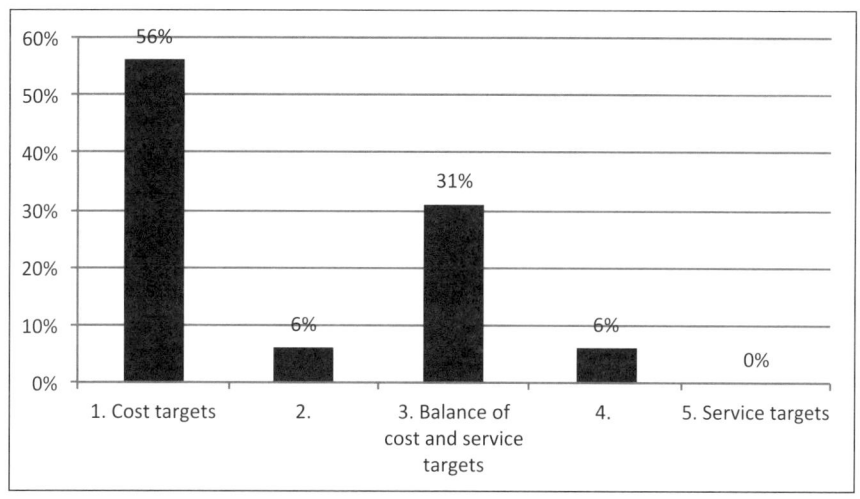

evident in practice, if the corporate strategy is dominated by cost perspective, an alignment process might cascade the cost focus down to the supply chain strategy as well.

Figure 6 illustrates that the respondents perceive that their supply chain strategy is well anchored in top management. 78% of the respondents either agree or strongly agree to this statement. This is a positive indication to the fact that top management within these companies is concerned with SCM and do give it strategic considerations. Again, we should be cautious not to overemphasize this result to all Danish companies. The respondents to our mini-survey are made up of members that have a strong interest to gain feedback on SCM issues. While we are very happy for their sincere efforts, their answers and practices may be above the general practice in the Danish industry.

The respondents were also asked about what they perceive as being the main challenge in implementing their supply chain strategy. The main challenge for 25% of the respondents is the high level of complexity in their supply chain (see Figure 7). Complexity can destroy profitability in any industry if not managed properly. But the concept of complexity is complex in itself. It might mean different things in different companies. Therefore, a first step is to start analyzing the number of stock keeping units / the number of parts/spare parts an organization holds. The higher the number of

PRACTITIONERS PERSPECTIVES

Figure 6: The supply chain strategy is well anchored in top management

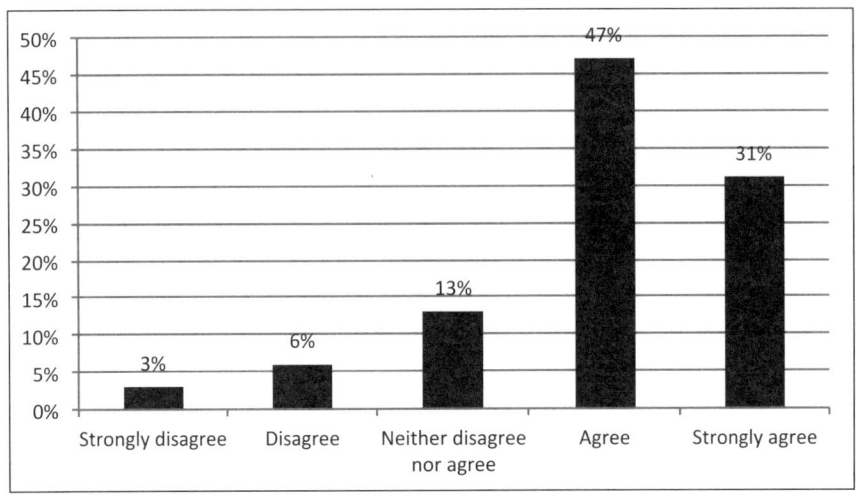

these units/parts, the higher the complexity level could be. Other areas that increase complexity can be the number of customers, suppliers, markets, inventories as well as markets. Thus, a supply chain strategy development process could benefit from fact finding of the supply chain and then develop an execution plan that takes into consideration the complexity inherent in the supply chain.

The respondents also mention "too much silo mentality", "too poor master data" and "lack of internal competencies" as being other main challenges in implementing their supply chain strategy. Silo mentality indicates not only a lack of process focus, but also misaligned performance measures.

Figure 7: Main challenge for implementing the supply chain strategy?

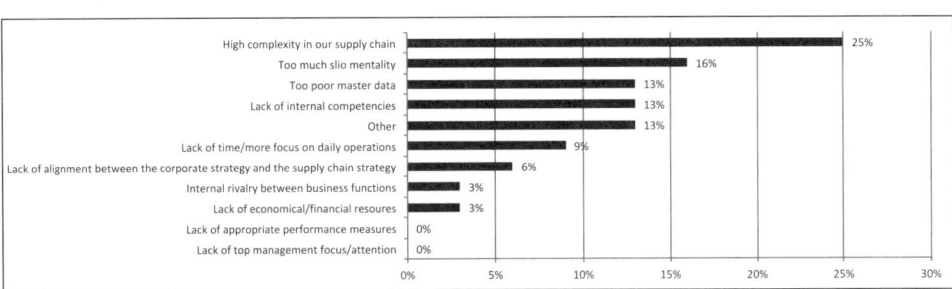

Poor master data is a challenge in many companies. Everybody knows it; but only a few are doing anything about it. It can be difficult to comprehend how costly poor data can be to companies. Additionally, poor master data will also significantly blur the visibility along the supply chain. Lack of internal competences is basically a HR issue. Are organizations in shortage of internal change agents at the expense of operational staff? In many companies, we see supply chain strategies to be unrealized mainly due to the lack of implementation resources. Finally, under the "other" category, respondents have provided answers like "lack of time (more focus on business development & projects)" and lack of "IT resources".

The current and future supply chain setup

Finally, the respondents were asked to rate different statements concerning their current and future supply chain setups. Figure 8 provide the averages for the six different statements where the respondents should their level of agreement on a five point Likert Scale (ranging from 1 = strongly disagree to 5 = strongly agreeing). Figure 8 shows an interesting finding about how well SCM as well as non-SCM staff members understand the company's supply chain structure and performance. An average score of 3.67 was ob-

Figure 8: Average scores of statements concerning the current and future supply chain setups

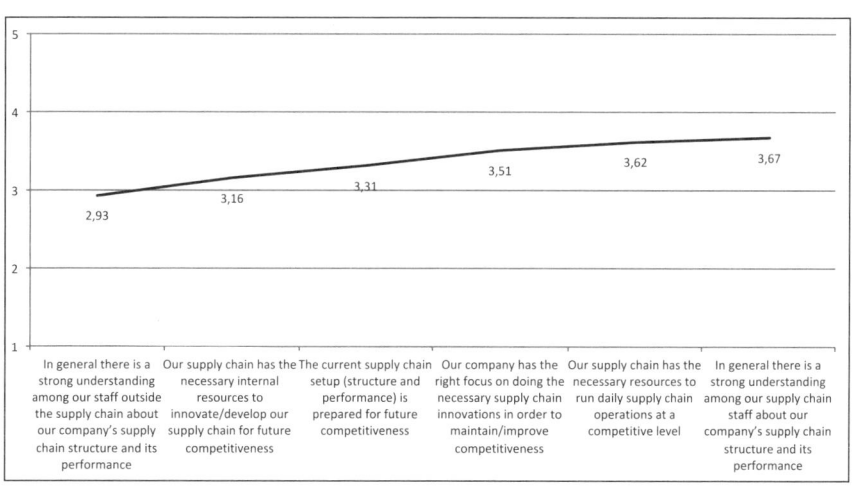

tained in the case of SCM staff members. Additionally, this average is much higher than the average score of 2.93 that was given for the understanding of non-SCM staff. While this difference in itself is not surprising, it clearly suggests a need for a marketing task that better propagates the importance of the structure as well as the function of the supply chain in companies that were part of this mini-survey.

Figure 8 also shows an average of 3.16 for the statement on "whether the organization has the necessary internal resources to develop a future competitive supply chain". First of all, this average seems to be much lower for such an important issue. Second, the average score of 3.62 for the statement "whether the right resources are on board in order to run the supply chain operations". Taken together, these average values suggest that companies are focusing more on operational issues rather than developing competitive supply chains of the future.

The respondents were also asked whether they find their current supply chains to be prepared for future competitiveness. This statement has obtained an average on 3.31, which is not that persuasive. However, the average is a little higher (3.52) for the statement on whether the company has the right focus on doing supply chain innovations. But while the statement on innovation relates to a focus, the statement regarding preparedness relates to actual execution. Unfortunately, our mini-survey was not designed to shed more light on this.

Conclusion

This mini-survey was set out to focus on the top management's understanding of SCM. The results show that SCM is highly represented in top management teams and that the responding companies not only have, but also pursue a SCM strategy. Surprisingly, only a few CEO's have a background in SCM. However, one can question whether this is really a problem as long as (1) SCM expertise is represented in the top management team, (2) the top management is aware of SCM's role in creating competitive advantages, and (3) the top management takes ownership of the SCM strategy.

Main challenges in implementing SCM strategies are increased complexities in supply chains, too much organizational silo mentality, poor master data and lack of internal competencies. However, all these issues could be managed if they are brought into the top management room along with real-life facts and figures of the state of SCM.

References

Arlbjørn, J.S. and Johnsen, T. (2013), "Organisatorisk er supply chain en pose blandet bolsjer", *DILF-Orientering,* Vol. 50 No. 3, pp. 38-41.

Wagner, S.M. and Kemmerling, R. (2014), "Supply chain management executives in corporate upper echelons", *Journal of Purchasing & Supply Management*, Vol. 20 No. 3, pp. 156-166.

Effective inventory management is permanent job in a changeable world[1]

By: Jan Stentoft

Introduction

This article aims to describe the results of a mini-survey that deals with one of the classic areas of supply chain management namely inventory management. There are many exciting issues associated with inventory management. What goods should be stored and how much? Where and how are we going to store the goods? Who is in charge of inventory management? What principles do we need for inventory management? This is just few examples of such important decisions. Of course, the inventory management function plays a different role depending on what type of business we are dealing with. Some have many item numbers; others have few. Some goods are subject to a rapid rate of change; others a slower pace of change. Some companies only have stocks of raw materials – others also have semi-manufactured and finished goods inventories. Some have outsourced the warehouse to third parties; others take care of themselves. In a dynamic business environment, there is a need for continuous evaluation of the way in which business processes take place. This also applies to business processes related to warehousing. Do we have the right items in stock and do they have the desired turnover rates? How do we ensure an effective phasing-in and phasing-out of goods?

The respondents in this mini-survey were asked a number of questions regarding some of the above issues. The first question has to do with the method by which the finished goods inventories are managed. As shown

---

1 This article is edited and translated to English from the Danish version Stentoft J. (2015), "Effektiv lagerstyring er fast arbejde i en foranderlig verden", *DILF Orientering*, Vol. 52 No 1, pp. 10-13.

Figure 1: Method for management finished goods inventories

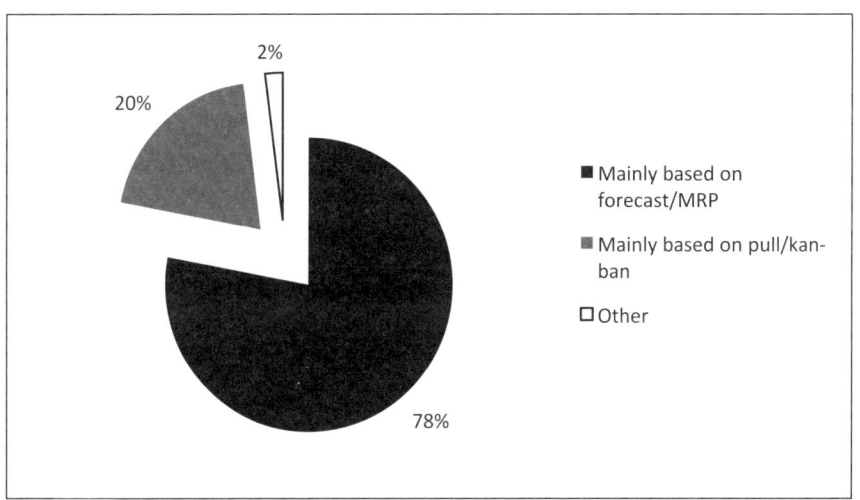

in Figure 1, the management of finished goods inventories is mainly conducted through Materials Requirements Planning (MRP) among respondents in *The Danish Supply Chain Panel*. Almost, 78% of the respondents indicate that their finished goods inventories are controlled through MRP. And, 20% of the respondents indicate that their finished goods inventory is controlled by kan-ban; i.e. a pull-based system based on reorder points.

The strategic role of warehouse management

The Danish Supply Chain Panel was asked to reflect upon the degree to which their companies' warehouses have strategic attention. As shown in Figure 2, 66% of the respondents answer that their warehouse to a high or very degree has a strategic focus. And, 23% of the respondents answer that their warehouse to some degree has a strategic focus and 11% of the respondents answer that their warehouse only to a low or a very low degree has a strategic focus. Companies' constantly increasing focus on net working capital might be an explanation that 66% of the respondents prioritize inventory levels from a strategic point of view. Effective warehouse management can reduce net working capital through lower level of capital tied up in stocks, lower level of interest costs, lower level of depreciations of inventories and lesser obsolescence. What are the reasons behind 11%

Figure 2: The strategic focus of the warehouse

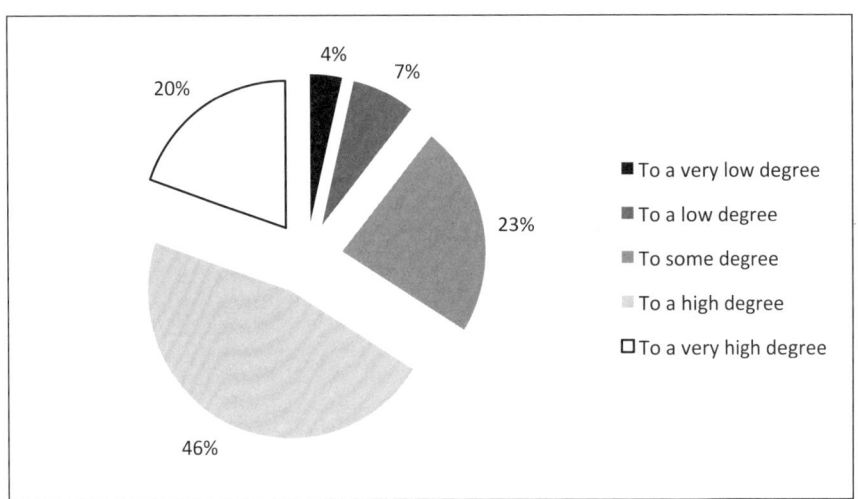

responding that they have a low strategic focus on inventory management, unfortunately this mini-survey could not provide specific answers. Possible reasons could be the fact that these companies does not have much inventories (in terms of volume and/or value) or that it reveal a signal that inventory optimizations is a true need with a focus on warehousing from a much more strategic perspective.

The respondents were also asked about their practice of outsourcing finished goods inventories. As shown in Figure 3, 11% of the respondents reply that all of their finished stocks are outsourced. 25% of the respondents answer that some are outsourced, while 57% of the respondents answer that this practice has not taken place in their companies. Thus, there are different practices in this area. Some companies outsource the warehouse successfully, while others with a lower level of success. Important success criteria during outsourcing are, among others, documentation of current processes; availability of the required master data and one or more trusted partners with the right skills.

The respondents were then asked for an evaluation of their practice with vendor managed inventory (VMI). Almost 69% of the respondents answer that this practice takes place only to a low degree or not at all (see Figure 4). Then 18% of the respondents answer that this practice takes place to a high or very high degree. It is surprising that this practice is not much

Figure 3: Outsourcing of finished goods inventory

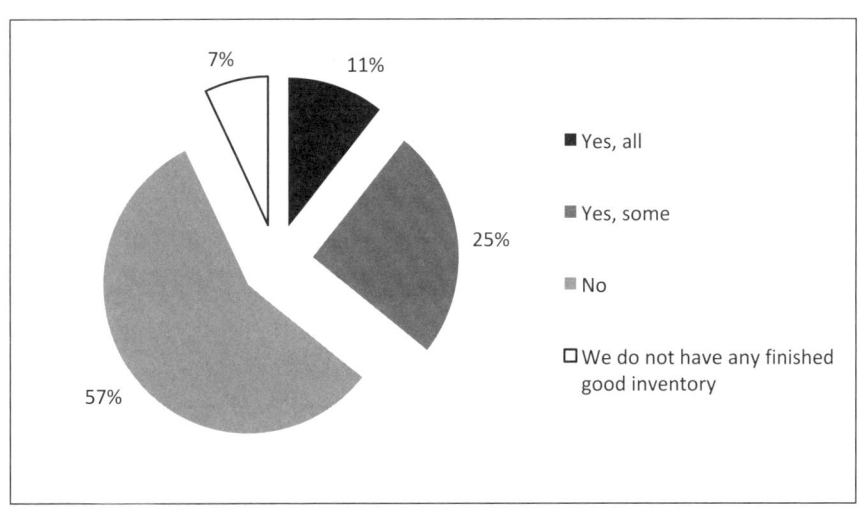

applied. Practice with VMI has been known for many years, but it does not seem like this is diffused into the Danish industry (as represented by this panel). Challenges with VMI can include: 1) too high startup costs, 2) lack of visibility of the benefits, and 3) lack of IT readiness to integrate systems and call for data quality.

Figure 4: Practice with vendor-managed inventories

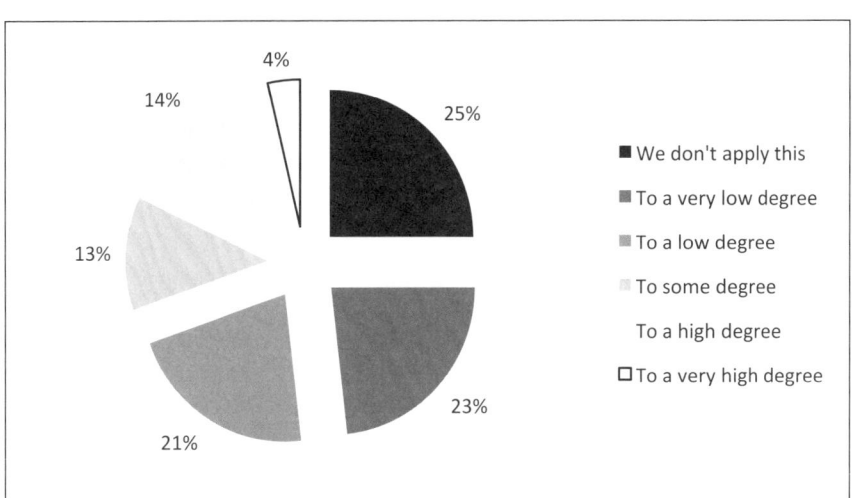

Practice with inventory optimizations

As shown in Figure 5, a large share of the respondents has implemented inventory optimizations over the last 2 years. A total of 93% of the respondents answer that they have completed optimizations of their stocks. As described earlier, a reason for this might be the management's increasing focus on reducing net working capital. The result also indicates that focus on inventory optimization does not necessarily require a strategic approach towards inventory management, but that all inventories, regardless of their type, continuously needs optimizations.

Figure 6 show that 86% of the respondents answer that they to a high or very high degree are continuously working to trim their companies' inventories (right quantities, right composition, optimal processes, etc.). It is pleasant to see that such practice is taking place. Additionally, 5% of the respondents indicate that they to some degree are working to trim their companies' inventories and 7% of the respondents indicate that they are only to a lesser degree working to trim their companies' inventories. This indicates an opportunity for some improvement in these companies.

The Danish Supply Chain Panel was asked whether their overall inventory management task has become more complex. As shown in Figure 7, 64% of the respondents find to a high or very high degree that their inven-

Figure 5: Inventory optimization practice

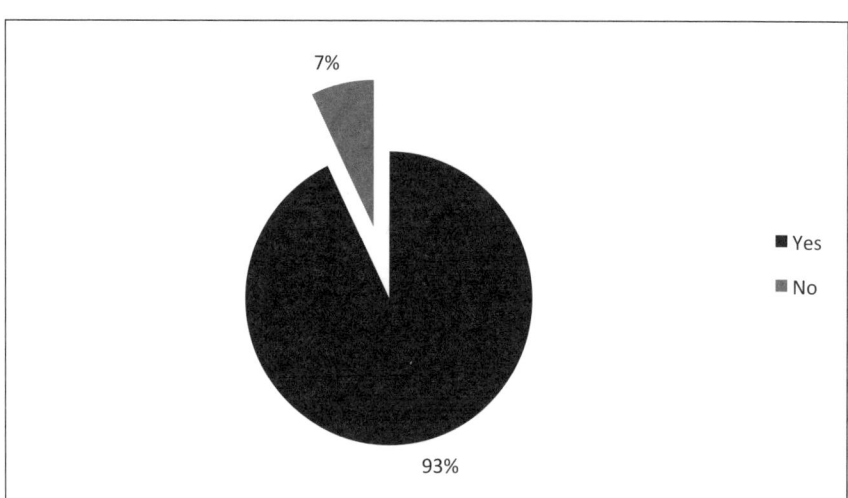

Figure 6: Practice with continuously inventory trimming

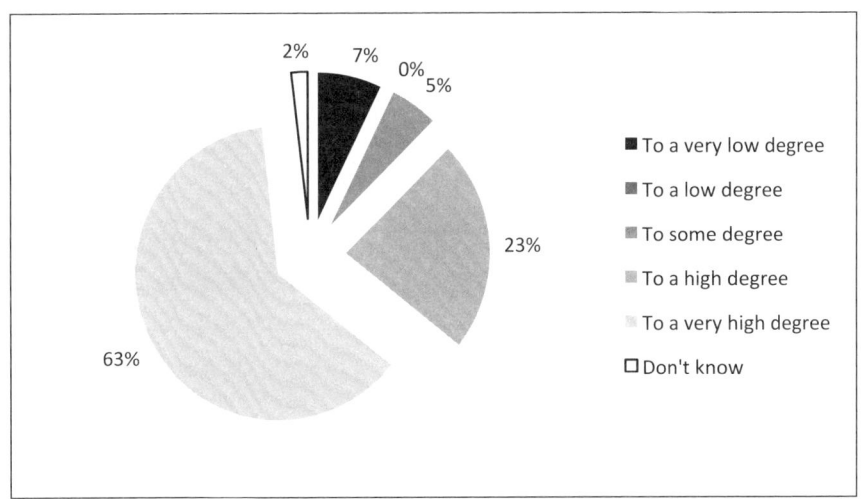

tory management task has become more complex. Such a complexity can emerge due to an increased level of stock units and/or operating with an increased number of inventory locations.

As shown in Figure 8, 50% of the respondents answer that they to a low or very low degree experience problems with obsolescence of their inven-

Figure 7: Has the inventory management task become more complex?

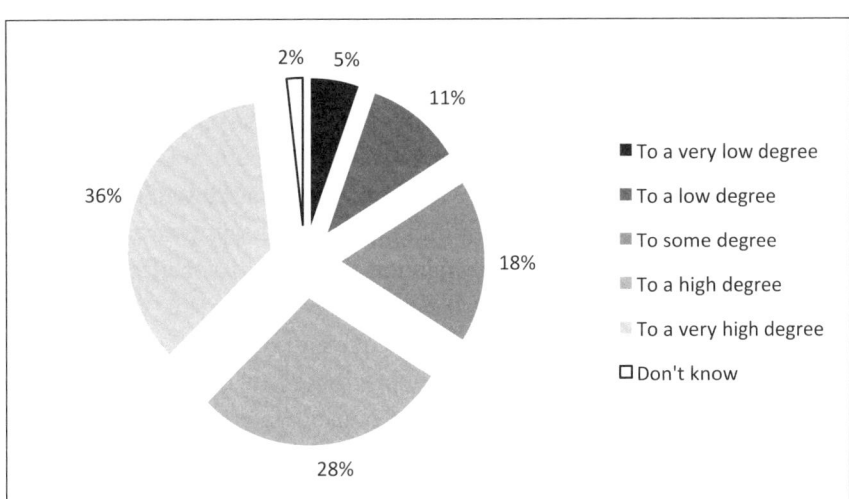

Figure 8: Problems with obsolete inventories

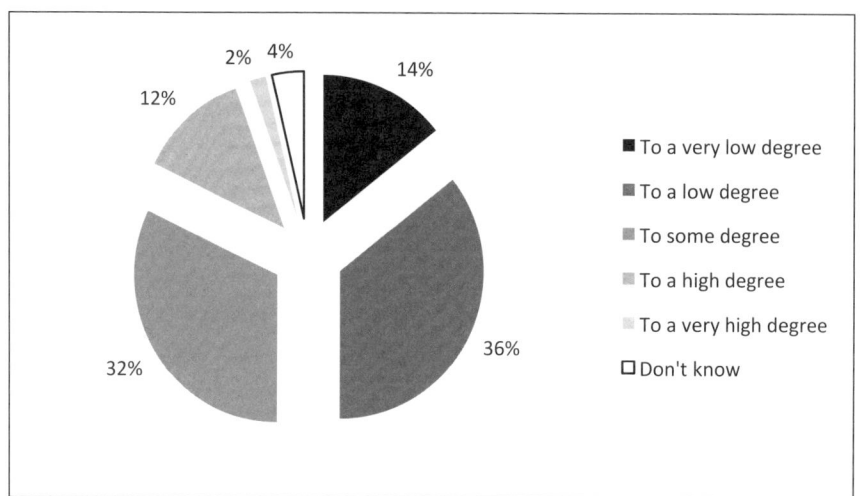

tories. This result can be seen in conjunction with the previous mentioned result, which reveals that almost 93% of the companies are working with optimizing their inventories. In other words, it has an effect. A continuous focus on inventories can thus reduce the risk of obsolescence. However, 14% of the respondents answer that they to a high or very high degree experience obsolescence, which indicate a need for improvements projects in these companies.

Challenges

The respondents were also asked to reflect upon what they consider to be the biggest challenges with their inventory management. As shown in Figure 9, 59% of the respondents answer to the fact that they have too many goods with low turnover rates. Secondly, inventory levels are perceived being too large, which 45% of the respondents indicate as a challenge. Finally, 38% of the respondents answer that their inventories are too small.

In the light of the before-mentioned challenges, it is interesting to see that one fourth of the respondents indicate that they will make significant investments in the warehouse over the next 2-3 years (see Figure 10). Then 53% of the respondents indicate that they will make minor investments. Overall, 80% of the respondents answer that they will carry out invest-

Figure 9: Challenges with inventory management

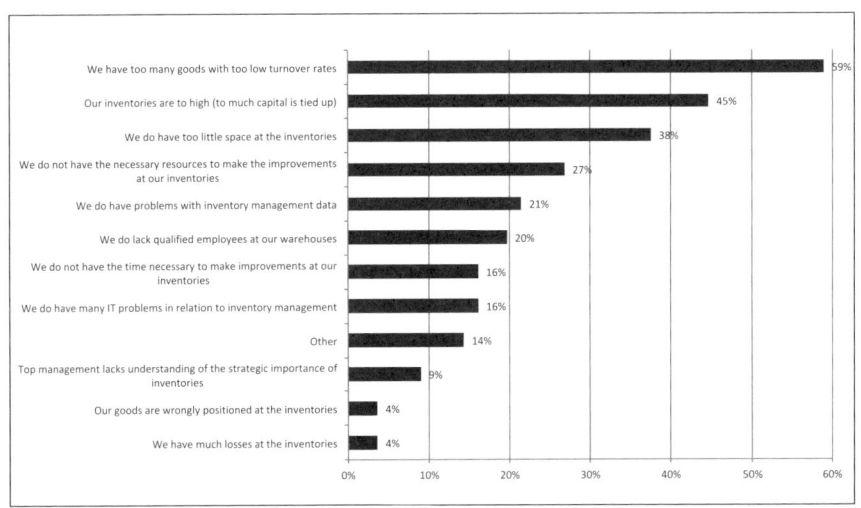

ments and thus work on improving their warehouses. Such investments may be in automation, locations, storage systems, etc.

This article has focused on one of the classic topics in the supply chain management. Effective inventory management is an important source for competitiveness as it assist in ensuring the ability to deliver the right quan-

Figure 10: Expectations for investments in warehousing

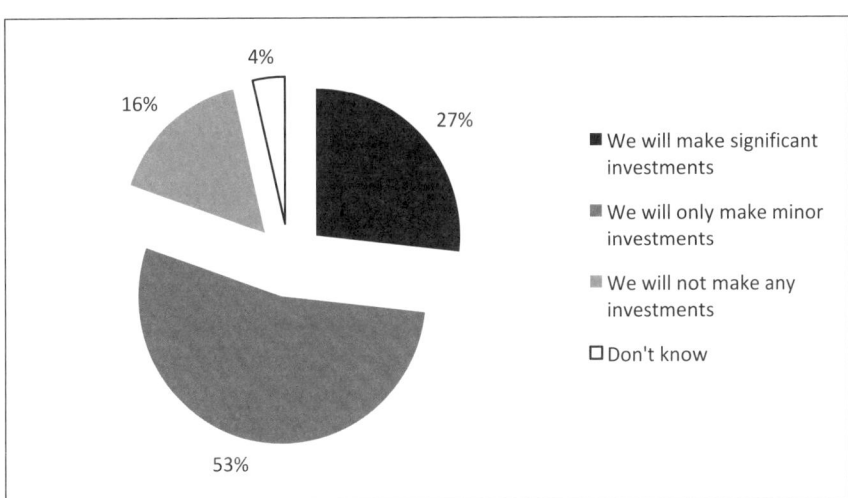

tities, right quality at the right times. The role and function of the warehouse should be analyzed on a regular basis. The business environment is dynamic, for instance, continuous changes in customer demands, assortments, demand patterns, suppliers, and business processes. Such changes can increase the pressure continuously in optimizing inventories. There is often a lot to gain and the investment in improvements in warehousing could prove to be a strong business case. It is expected that the results in this mini-survey foster discussions about the role and function of warehousing in the companies in order to clarify where and to what degree there is a need for improvements.

ns 3 – Panel articles in 2014

Risk management in supply chains is considered important but resource allocation is difficult[1]

By: Jan Stentoft

Introduction

This article aims to describe the results of a mini-survey, which deals with risk management in the supply chains. This theme has become increasingly relevant as global trade continues to grow. To source, produce and sell globally can mean that the companies' supply chains become more vulnerable. Factors that contribute to increased risk in the supply chains include:

- Globalization of supply chains (longer lead times, risk of obsolescence)
- Trend against outsourcing and offshoring (longer lead times, less flexibility, quality issues)
- Reduction of supplier base
- Lack of transparency in supply chains
- Demand vulnerability

There are several examples of companies that have been hit hard as a result of natural disasters, accidents such as Incineration of factories and terrorist acts. Such conditions can cause severe disturbances in the supply chains that can affect performance even very much negatively. Risk management in the supply chains is an important issue and should be a part of the Danish companies' sourcing and / or supply chain strategies. It is expected that the article might provide an inspiration to relate to this topic in their re-

---

1 This article is edited and translated to English from the Danish version Stentoft J. (2014), "Risikostyring i forsyningskæderne anses som vigtigt, men det kniber med ressourcerne", *DILF Orientering*, Vol. 51 No 4, pp. 35-39.

spective organization in order to assess whether current practice is satisfactory. Discussion of such issues occurs in several names, for example, Risk management, vulnerability, disruptions, and natural disasters. Managing such issues is referred to in this article for risk management. With this little introduction, we will look into how *The Danish Supply Chain Panel* perceives the importance of risk management in the supply chains and how they do practice risk management.

As shown in Figure 1, 72% of the respondents in this mini survey answer that they either to a high or very high degree consider risk management as important in the supply chains. In addition, 25% of the respondents consider risk management to some degree as important in the supply chains. Compared with the respondents' responses to the degree of risk management work in their supply chains (see Figure 2), it is seen that the perceived importance of the subject is stronger than the specific practice in the field. Almost 32% of the respondents answer that they to a high or very high degree work with risk management in the supply chains. We will return to the possible explanations of this gap between perceived importance and concrete practice later in the article in connection with a presentation of respondents' responses on their perceived barriers for working with this topic.

Figure 1: Perceived importance of risk management in supply chains for the company's long-term competitiveness

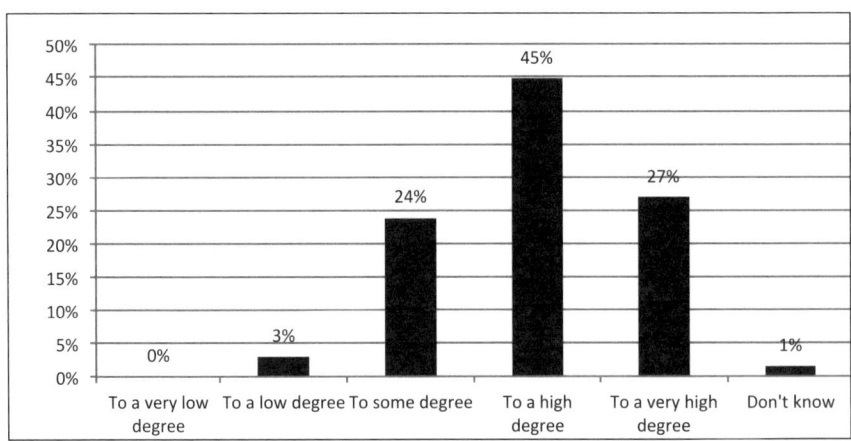

Figure 2: Actual work with risk management in supply chains

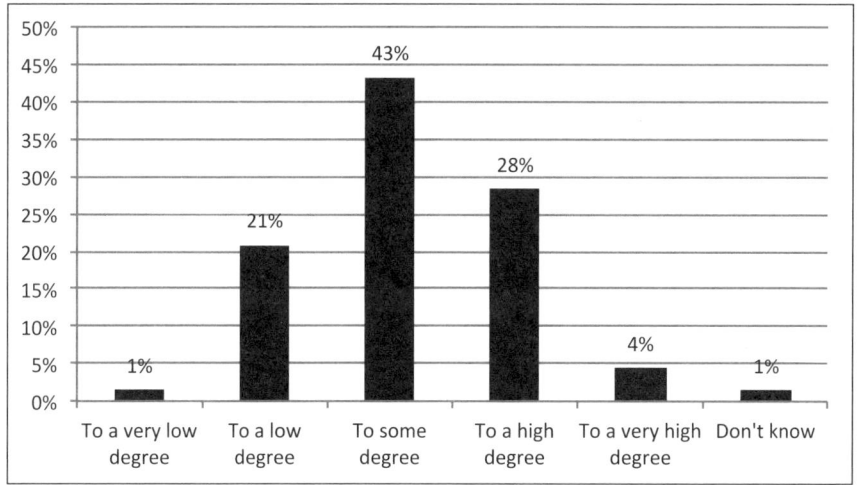

Performance and risk factors

The panel members were also asked about their assessment of the degree to which performance in their supply chains has been affected by disruptions. As shown in Figure 3, 17% of the respondents reply that this has happened to a high or very high degree – i.e. almost one fifth of the respondents. A total of 44% of the respondents reply that this has happened to some degree. The answers do not inform how many times this has happened, but the results indicate that the issue of "right" risk management is an issue that the Danish companies should take seriously.

The respondents were asked about what they consider as risk factors in their respective supply chains. There can of course be differences across industries and companies – some are more vulnerable to changes in commodity prices, exchange rates and wage increases than the others are. As shown in Figure 4, 50% of the respondents answer that fluctuations in commodity prices represent a risk factor. In addition, 44% of the respondents indicate market changes as a risk factor. Furthermore, 33% of the respondents indicate shortage of raw materials as a risk factor. Under "other", some respondents mention "natural disasters", "logistics/transport", "wrong products/delivers from suppliers" and "too many single sourcing setups" as a risk factor.

Figure 3: Degree of impact on supply chain performance caused by supply chain disruptions

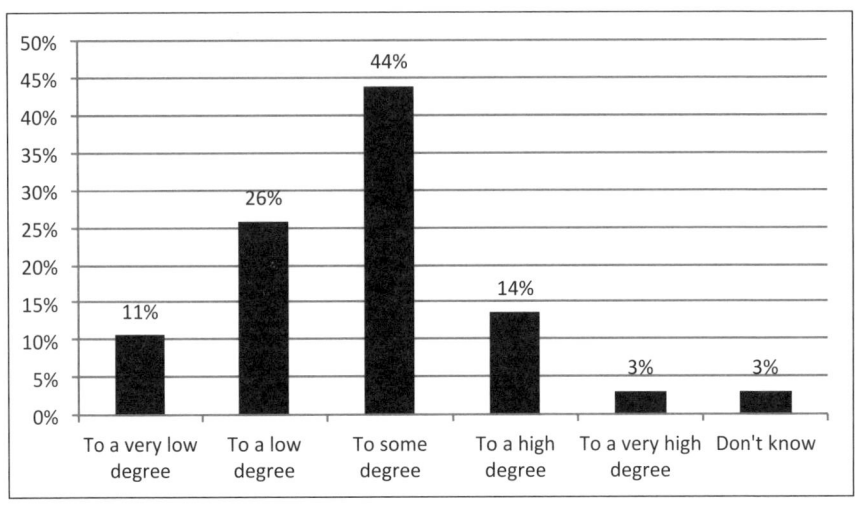

Figure 4: Risk factors in supply chains

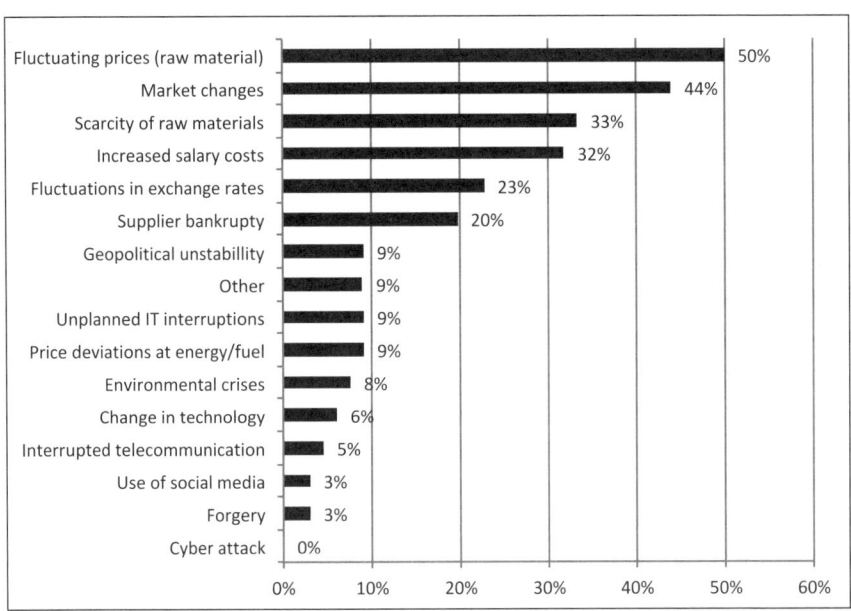

Sensitivity

The Danish Supply Chain Panel was asked to assess what they consider as the most sensitive risk factors to which their supply chains are exposed. Respondents have been able to specify upto three factors. As shown in Figure 5, "dependency on specific skills" is the factor that has achieved the most markings (42% of the respondents). For example, it might be specialized subcontracts for own production. Here it is important to have alternative plans ready if such deliveries should fail. "Dependence on a small supplier base" is indicated by 39% of the respondents as a sensitivity factor. This point may also play a central role in corporate strategies. Around 33% of the respondents report that price control of raw materials is a sensitivity factor. Under "other factors" respondents indicate "fluctuations in demand" and "suppliers" ability to deliver within a short period of time", which excludes sourcing from e.g. Asia.

One thing is to become conscious about how the supply chains are exposed for risk. Another thing is to be capable to minimize such risks. *The Danish Supply Chain Panel's* perceptions on this aspect are shown in Figure 6. It is clear from Figure 6 that 56% of the respondents work with dual sourcing strategies. Safe guarding is a practice for critical goods and suppliers. The price for such a solution may be more expensive material prices as well as additional management costs. However, this practice varies from business to business. In some companies it is a requirement that there are

Figure 5: Most sensitive risk factors in supply chains

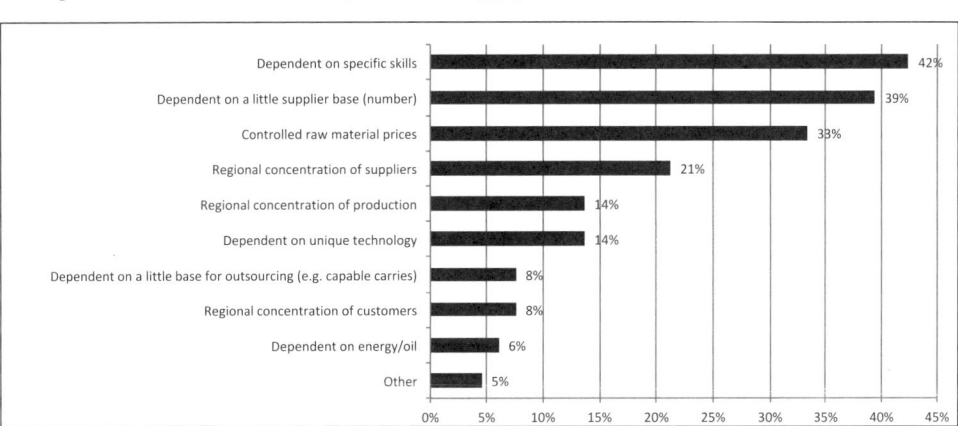

Figure 6: Risk mitigation factors

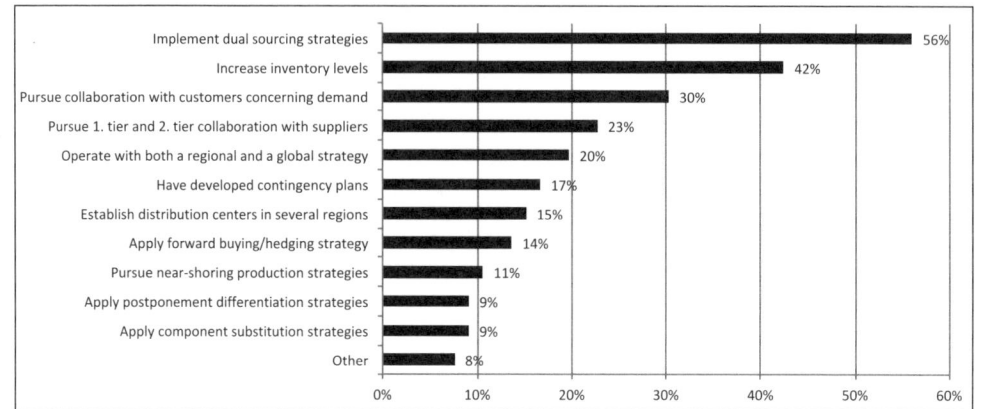

two suppliers on e.g. commodity goods while in other companies allowing single sourcing setup. And, 42% of the respondents answer that they operate with higher stock level for goods being exposed for risks. The price here is extra tied-up capital in stocks. Around 30% of the respondents answer that they try to minimize risk through collaboration with their customers. Moreover, 23% apply this practice towards their suppliers. Again, there is a difference between companies' reported practices. Some are more risky averse in the supply-side, while others are more risk averse towards customers. Under "other actions" some of the respondents mention "multiple vendors are used", "we make sure that we are not becoming too dependent on one customer", "we are continuously monitoring the developments and make corrective actions if needed" and "we have established a closer collaboration between sales and supply chain about forecasts (Sales & Operations Planning)".

Barriers for risk management

The respondents were asked about their judgement as to whether there are barriers to working with risk management in supply chains. Figure 7 shows that almost half (47%) respond that this is experienced to a low degree a very low degree. While 39% respond that this is experienced to some degree, and 9% respond that this is experienced to a high degree. In the

Figure 7: Degree of perceived barriers for risk management in supply chains

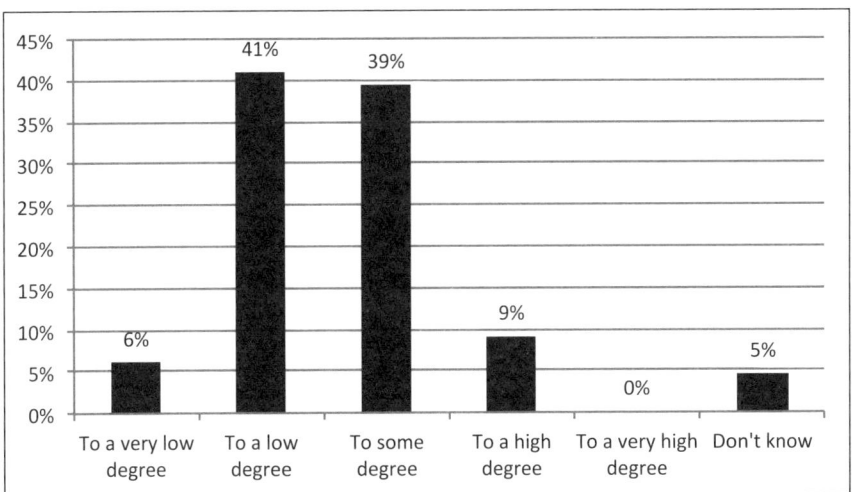

following we take a closer look at what the panel indicates as main barriers for risk management.

About half (52%) of the respondents in this mini survey indicate that a barrier is a predominant operating focus at the expense of development (see Figure 8). This challenge has been ongoing in almost all mini surveys conducted in *The Danish Supply Chain Panel* since its establishment in 2012. It shows that there seems to be constant challenges in balancing operations and development activities in the Danish supply chains. Therefore, we take the opportunity to send an invitation to the Danish companies' senior executives to raise awareness towards this dilemma and specifically to act on it, so the development activities in the supply chains are also prioritized and secured for survival in a busy working day. Half of the respondents report that lack of resources is a barrier to work with risk management in the supply chains. If one conduct even small-level analyses about the likelihood of different risks and their consequences can perhaps help the company in allocating more resources to this important activity. Nearly one third of the respondents answer that they lack knowledge in the field. Approximately one quarter lacks concrete tools. Firm specific or more general courses can be a solution for closing this competency gap. Under "other", respondents mention "missing volume on purchases"; "lack of financial instruments", "priority of work that gives something now vs.

Figure 8: Main barriers for risk management in supply chains

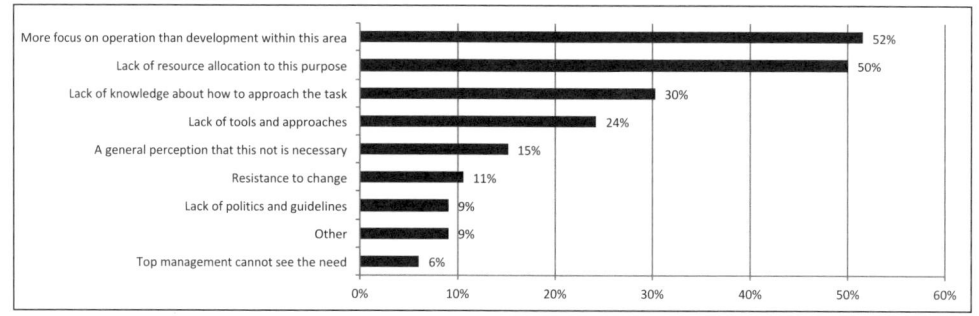

work that might give something in the future if the accident occurs" and "coordination (3.000 items divided at 100 suppliers)".

Risk management in practice

The respondents were asked to evaluate a number of solutions of risk management in the supply chain (see Figure 9) from a scale of 1 (to a very low degree) to 5 (to a very high degree). In general, there are no flashy average values achieved. A potential source of error, however, could be that they were asked wrong questions. Alternatively it gives some indications about that there is a need for developing new knowledge in this area for the benefit of practice. "Alignment and integration between internal business functions" has achieved an average of 2.8, which is the highest average score of their actual practice. This in turn could be interpreted that the companies are working with this only to some degree. The establishment of risk management (structure, processes and culture) also achieves an average of 2.8. Integration upstream and downstream achieves an average of 2.5. It is the same for "create flexibility and redundancy in product network and process architecture" (an average of 2.5).

Almost 51% of the respondents have answered that they actively work with strategic risk management of purchased products (see Figure 10). However, it is noteworthy to remember, that 38% of the respondents answer "no" to this question and 11% of the respondents answer "I do not know". This result indicates that there is an opportunity for development

Figure 9: Specific risk management practices

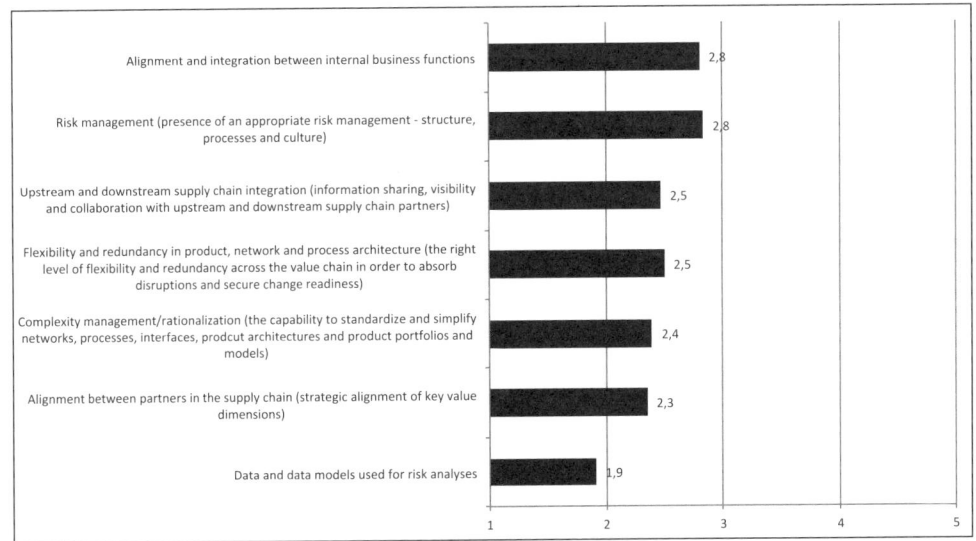

in these companies, but can be vulnerable as a result of an uneven distribution between operation and development oriented activities from a resource allocation perspective.

Figure 10: Working actively with strategic risk management of purchased products (finished goods, semi-finished products, raw materials, etc.)

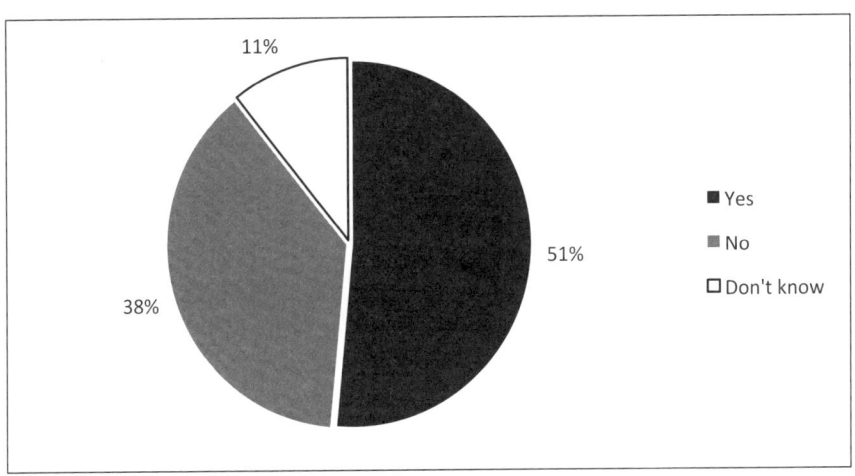

Figure 11: Criteria for segmentation of the purchased products in different strategic risk groups

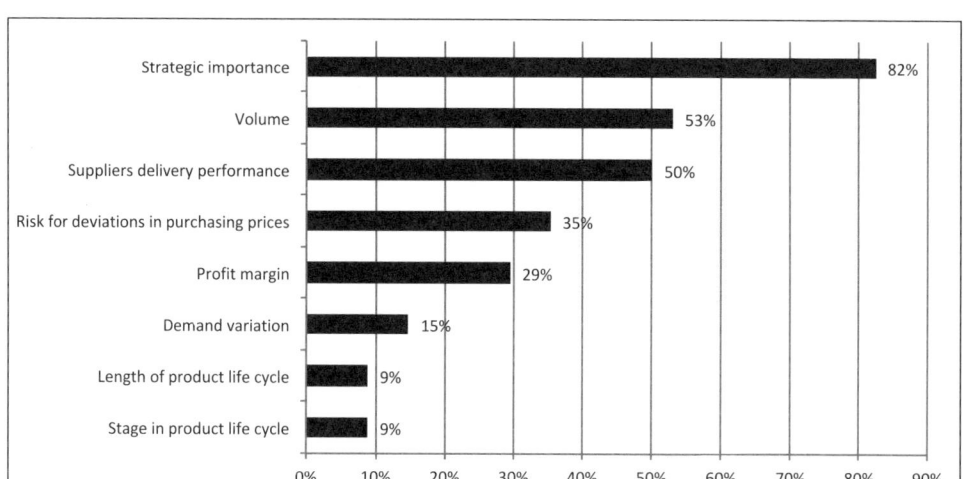

The Danish Supply Chain Panel was also asked to determine the criteria for segmentation of the purchased products in different strategic risk groups. As shown in Figure 11, 82% of the respondents agree that this is based on a "strategic importance" criterion. Next, 53% of the respondents indicate volume criterion, and 50% of the respondents report that their segmentation is based on suppliers' delivery performance.

This article has addressed the answers to a mini-survey from *The Danish Supply Chain Panel*, where the lens is focused on the phenomenon of risk management in the supply chain. The results from this study show that the respondents in general are aware of the importance of this topic, but their actual practice is lagging behind. A too much focus on operation at the expense of development and lack of resources are the main explanations of this gap. The data also point to a need for development and supply of courses focusing on risk management in the supply chains and concrete tools as well as more sharing of experience in this subject area.

Supply chain planning: An area with room for improvements[1]

By: Jan Stentoft

Introduction

"Plans are nothing; planning is everything", Eisenhower should have said this according to reliable sources. There is doubt whether this also applies to Danish supply chains in their efforts to create and further develop competitiveness. This mini-survey focuses on one of the classic themes in supply chain management, namely supply chain planning. The article's results can serve the purpose of initiating discussions about what are their own capabilities within this area and what are the plans for the future. Supply chain planning as concept has not achieved the great academic space. The area spans widely, though there might be several perceptions of what is included in the supply chain planning and this article in turn seeks to unfold.

Content elements in supply chain planning

Figure 1 shows that 60% of the respondents in this mini survey consider that they have implemented supply chain planning to a high or very high degree. While 25% of the respondents indicate that they have implemented supply chain planning only to some degree. In the following, we will dig deeper into the content behind supply chain planning.

Supply chain planning covers various types of planning. The literature seems not to be precise with definitions and specifications of content elements. Therefore it has been of interest to investigate practitioners' percep-

---

[1] This article is edited and translated to English from the Danish version Stentoft J. (2014), "Supply chain planning: Et område med muligheder for forbedring", *DILF Orientering*, Vol. 51 No 3, pp. 10-14.

Figure 1: To which degree supply chain planning been implemented?

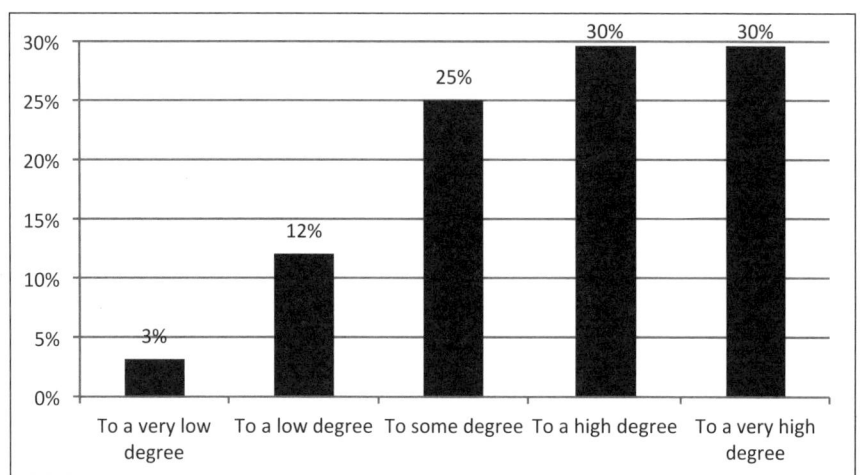

tions of the elements in supply chain planning. As shown in Figure 2, "Sales & Operations Planning" achieves an average of 4.2 on a scale of 1 (very much disagrees) to 5 (very much agrees). This might indicate that Sales & Operations Planning is a synonym for supply chain planning. "Supply planning" has achieved an average of 4.1 while both distribution planning

Figure 2: Perceptions of content elements in supply chain planning in theory

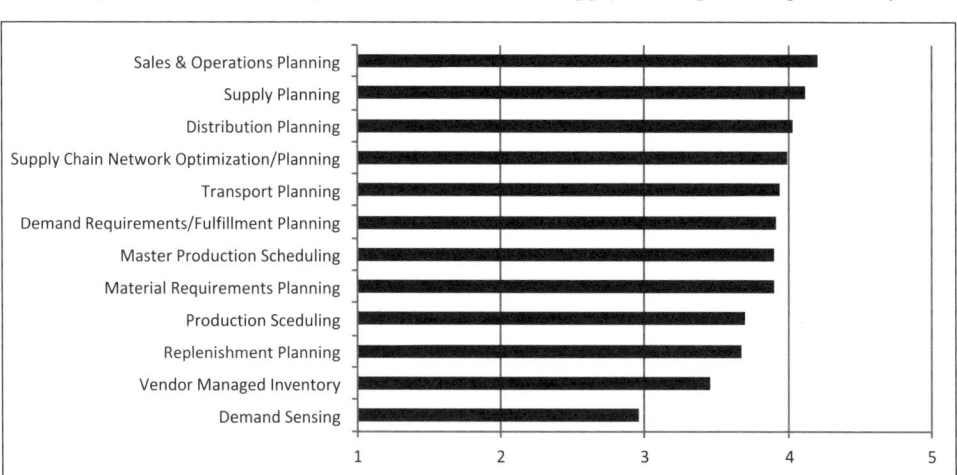

Figure 3: Panel members' perception of contents elements in supply chain planning in their practice

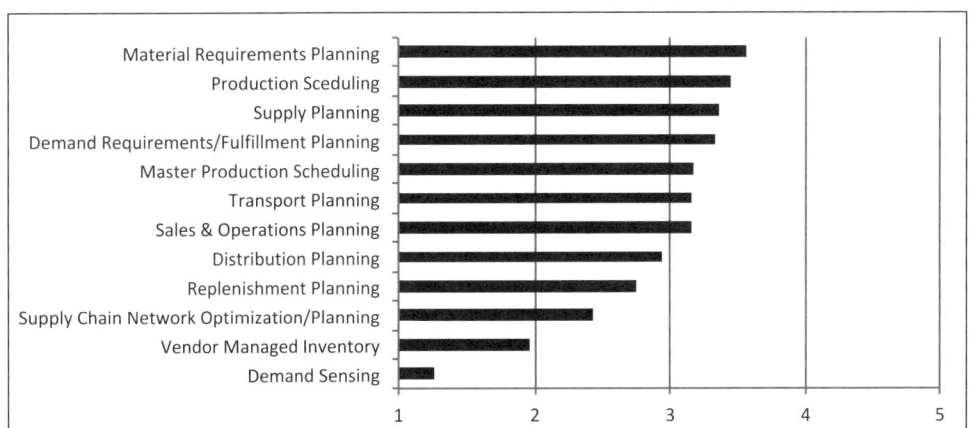

and supply chain network optimization has achieved an average of 4.0. These elements indicate a different content in supply chain planning than in Sales & Operations Planning.

Figure 3 shows the perception of the elements of supply chain planning. It is interesting to see that the highest average score is obtained by internally oriented areas as "planning requirements" and "production scheduling" with average scores of 3.6 and 3.5, respectively. When the results in Figure 3 is compared with the results in Figure 2, there seems to be a discrepancy between the content elements that are perceived being part of supply chain planning and the concrete practice of the content elements of supply chain planning. Figure 2 shows that internally oriented planning elements achieve lower average scores than externally oriented planning elements, whereas the actual practice, as shown in Figure 3, shows the opposite! Figure 2 also shows that there is still room for improvements for Danish companies to implement planning that moves into the network level. It is surprising that practice with supply chain network optimization /planning only achieves an average score of 2.4.

Overall, the results in Figures 2 and 3 points towards a need for a stronger conceptual clarification of supply chain planning. It is recommended that the individual companies spend resources on what they really understand about the term to ensure a common understanding.

Experience with supply chain planning

The respondents were asked about how concrete they work with supply chain planning. As shown in Figure 4, the respondents have been able to choose from different options such as "mainly ERP-based", "mainly self-developed applications", "best-of-breed", "mix of ERP and Best-of-Breed", "other and "I don't know". Best-of-Breed is a term that covers the best application in the field. Companies can thus decide to buy software from different suppliers to get the best solution on a particular site. The actual work on supply chain planning is mainly based on the company's main ERP system (see Figure 4). Almost 44% of the respondents answer that supply chain planning is based on their ERP system. About 29% of the respondents answer that they work with a combination of ERP and Best-of Breed solutions, where Best-of Breed is directed into the ERP system. This can, on the one hand, point out that corporate ERP systems provide adequate solutions to meet the need for supply chain planning. On the other hand, the result may also point to a lack of understanding of which solutions are available with Best-of-Breed software. As previously shown in Figure 2, the current practice of supply chain planning is primarily focused on internal planning elements that most ERP systems can handle.

Figure 4: Current supply chain planning solutions

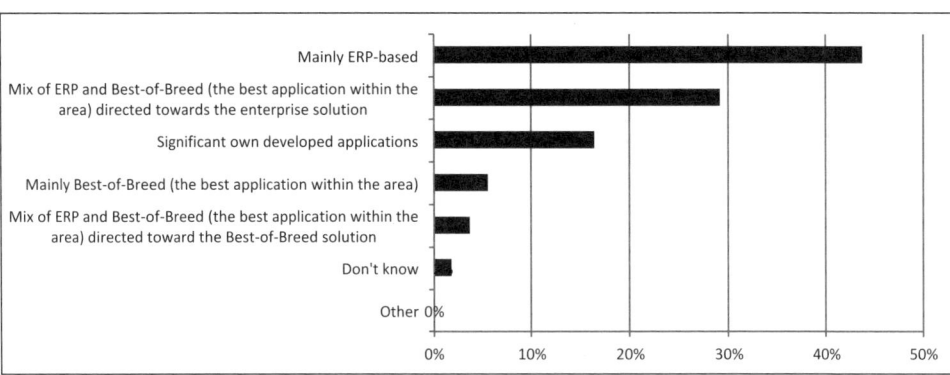

Possibilities for improvements and expected investments

The respondents were also asked to answer about the improvement areas they notice in their supply chain planning. According to Figure 5, 87% of the respondents answered a need for higher forecast accuracy. Thus, the result indicates that there is a development area to improve the forecasts. This work can, for example, begin with mapping current practice as well as analyzes of what is needed for forecasts. In addition, 71% of the respondents indicate that they also can see possibilities for improvement within Sales & Operations Planning. A previous mini-survey on this issue concluded that there still is a great potential in Danish companies for implementing Sales & Operations Planning. Under "other", some of the respondents indicate that there are possibilities for improvement within price lists and better product knowledge.

In general, there seems to be expectations of creating improvements in supply chain planning within the next 2-3 years. Almost 43% of the respondents indicate that they expect significant investments (see Figure 6) and 39% of the respondents indicate that they expect investment only to a smaller degree; however some investments are expected after all.

Figure 5: Areas for improvements in supply chain planning

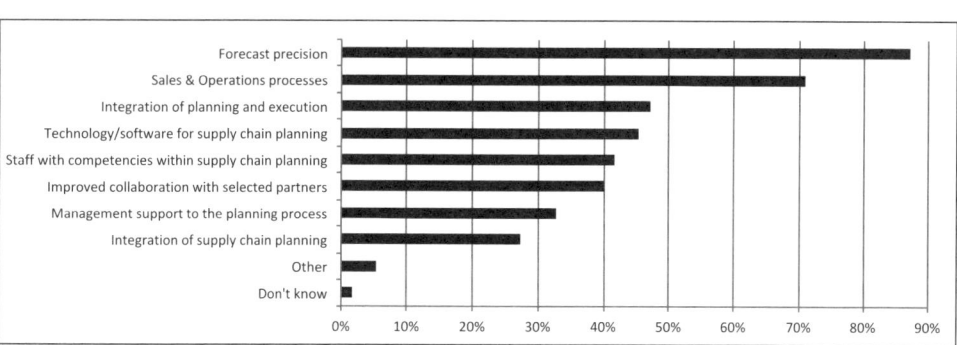

Figure 6: Expectations about investments in planning over the next 2-3 years

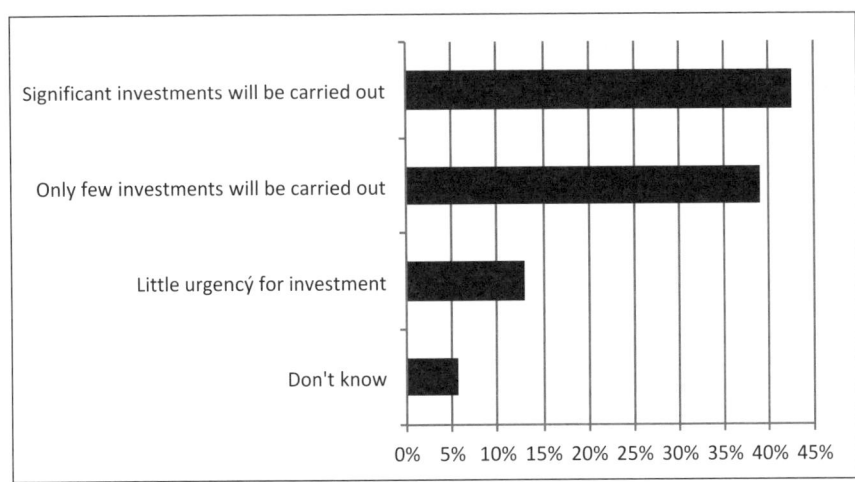

Is the technological platform up-to-date?

As shown in Figure 7, 35% of the respondents indicate that their technological platform for planning has been updated within the last 1.5 years, while 19% of the respondents indicate that this has taken place during the period of 2011-2012. A total of 41% indicate that their technology platform was last updated in 2010 or earlier. This may indicate there is an investment backlog in this area.

Figure 7: When is your current planning technology platform updated?

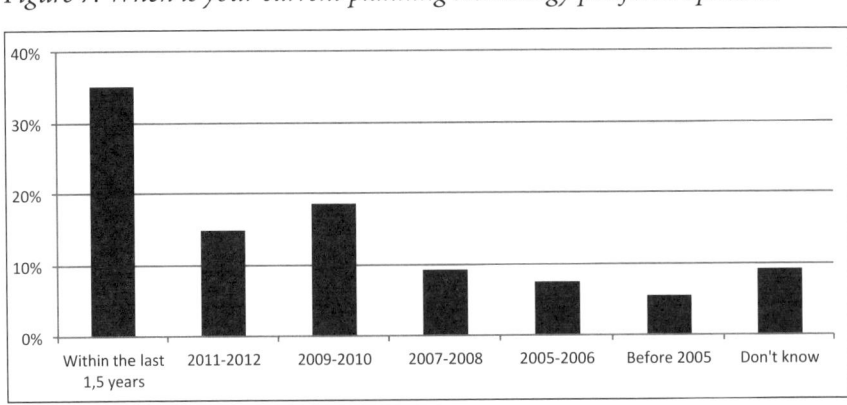

Figure 8: To what degree do your current supply chain planning applications meet your needs?

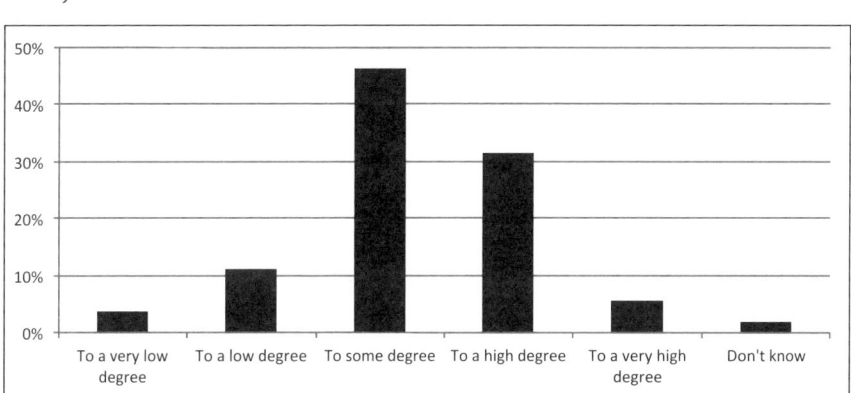

The respondents were asked to assess the degree to which their current supply chain management applications cover the company's real needs. As shown in Figure 7, 37% of the respondents indicate that their applications to a high or very high degree cover actual needs. Figure 7 also indicates that there is a need for better applications, with 46% of the respondents indicating "to some degree" and 15% of the respondents indicating "to a low or very low degree". Next, we will look into the possible reasons for the need for improvements within this area.

Challenges with supply chain planning

Figure 9 reveals that 46% of the respondents consider the main challenge of their current supply chain planning applications to be inappropriateness to model and process data. And, 37% of the respondents indicate that they do not have the relevant/required applications/functionalities. At the same time, 35% of the respondents indicate that they actually have the desired applications; however they simply do not use the options in applications available. Finally, 33% of the respondents indicate that they lack training in using the applications. Figure 9 thus points to a number of key areas of action – either in the form of investment in new applications or in the form of investments in improvements in business processes around supply chain planning. Under "other", the respondents identify challenges like collecting data from several units for the purpose of economic follow-up and joint ca-

Figure 9: Main challenges of current supply chain planning applications

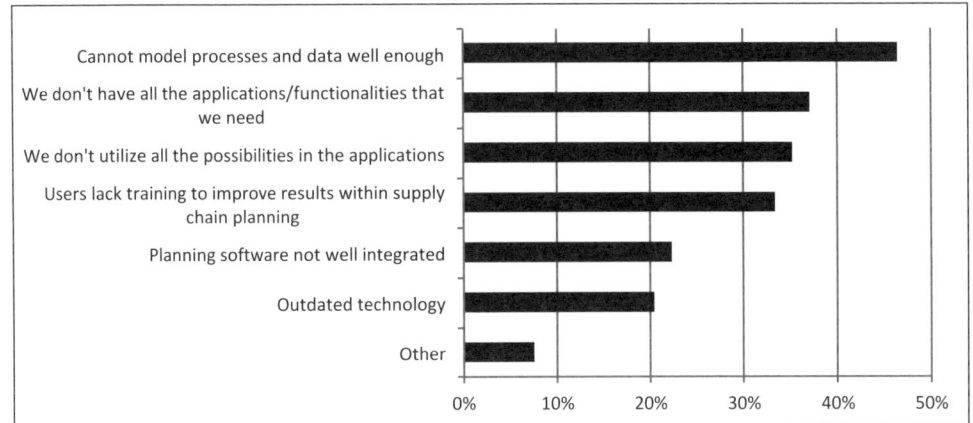

pacity planning; strong unpredictable markets and too many local changes in the plan after it is aligned across the supply chain.

Development of supply chain planning technology and its barriers

The respondents have been asked about their expectations for developing supply chain planning technology in their respective companies over the next two to three years. As shown in Figure 10, 35% of the respondents in this mini-survey expect that there will be a major upgrade of the current supply chain planning technology. While, 30% of the respondents expect that there will be acquisitions of sub-applications /functionalities, and 20% of the respondents expect that they will be at the current level also in coming two to three years. In addition 15% of the respondents report that they expect to initiate a process with regard to reviewing their current supply chain planning setup to identify new applications that can improve their work.

The concrete work of developing supply chain planning is not without challenges. Figure 11 includes the respondents' answers to questions about perceived barriers towards the development of supply chain planning in

Figure 10: Expectations for development of supply chain planning technology in the coming 2-3 years

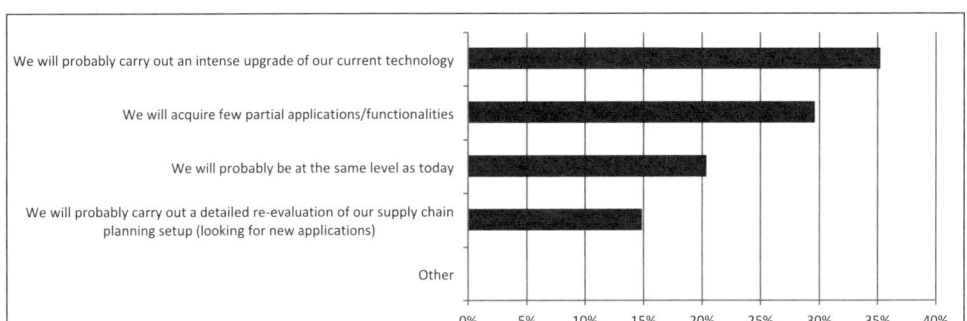

their companies. Almost 44% of the respondents indicate that they lack competencies internally in the company to improve the task. And, 41% of the respondents indicate that the operations are prioritized higher than the development of this area. The problem with prioritization of operational task at the expense of development has also been significant in previous mini-surveys. Almost 26% of the respondents indicate that it is a challenge to get the top management focused on the need for developing supply chain planning. Under "other" of the respondents indicate that the current systems have just been upgraded, why some change tasks now are queuing up; other activities have higher priority; and human resources are the biggest bottleneck to achieve the most beneficial solution.

Figure 11: Barriers for developing of supply chain planning

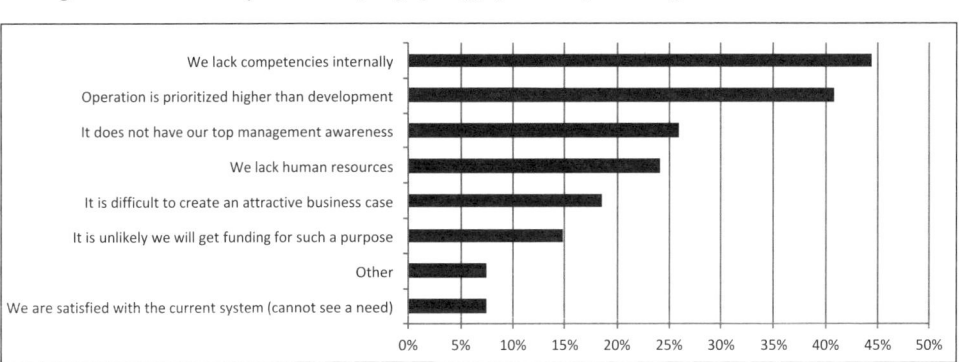

Conclusion

This article has focused on a mini-survey about supply chain planning. The results indicate that there is still some way in practice in implementing planning solutions that moves beyond the individual company. The study also shows that there are several different concepts in play under the "supply chain planning" label, for which conceptual clarification would be appropriate. The respondents expect an increase focus on supply chain planning in the coming years. The main challenges are lack of internal competencies and prioritization of operations over development activities in the area. It is expected that this article might assist in addressing supply chain planning among Danish companies for assessing whether there should be developments, appropriately where, how and to what extent within the field.

Sustainable sourcing: Supplier control or development[1]

By: Ole Stegmann Mikkelsen, Thomas Johnsen and Jesper Kronborg Jensen

Introduction

Although many companies still believe that their suppliers' environmental and social problems are not their responsibility, the companies are increasingly realizing that they can no longer ignore such issues. Let us just think of some of the examples that created headlines in the media over a longer period such as the Rana Plaza textile plant in Bangladesh that collapsed in April 2013 and killed more than 1.100 employees, BP's oil spill in Mexico in 2010 or Apple's difficulties with, among other things, suicide due to the hard working conditions of an Asian supplier (Foxconn).

The challenges have emerged in particular because supply chains often span several countries, including developing countries (i.e. low cost countries), and supply chains are often very long and complex and therefore non-transparent (Johnsen et al., 2014; Jensen et al., 2013). The companies themselves have chosen to operate in such countries and so various stakeholders, including customers, have the viewpoint that such companies also must take the responsibility. A study by Save the Children shows that 45% of the Danish consumers deselect goods because of the fear of child labor. We share the Save the Children's point of view that there is an urgent need for more nuances in the debate. However, this does not change the fact that companies have to work to reduce the risks associated with social and environmental problems with suppliers and sub-suppliers.

First and foremost, sustainable supply chain management implies an in-

---

[1] This article is edited and translated to English from the Danish version Mikkelsen, O.S., Johnsen, T. and Jensen, J.K. (2014), "Sustainable sourcing: Leverandørkontrol eller udvikling, included in DILF's newsletter in week 19.

creased need for monitoring and control of the company's suppliers. However, as problems often arise further upstream in the supply chain, one of the challenges is to control the indirect suppliers (the suppliers' suppliers). In addition, experience shows that it is often insufficient only to control, but that resources must be allocated to help the suppliers. This is the issue that we are focusing in this mini-survey. A previous survey of *The Danish Supply Chain Panel* focused on sustainability as part of the company's supply chain strategy (Arlbjørn and Mikkelsen, 2012) and it was concluded that work on sustainability is primarily driven by economic motives, and that responsibility for sustainability is anchored widely in the organization. In this study we focus on how companies work to integrate sustainability with their suppliers and their suppliers.

Sustainability and strategy

As mentioned, companies' approach to sustainability was investigated by Arlbjørn and Mikkelsen (2012) based on the companies supply chain strategy. The respondents were asked whether there is a reasonable focus on sustainability in their supply chain strategy. We have chosen to repeat this question to see if there has been development over time, despite the relative short period. The answer is shown in Figure 1, which also contains the answers from the previous survey which was conducted in 2012.

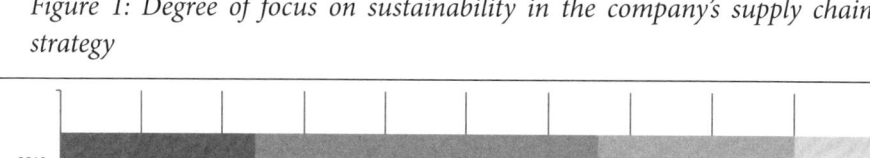

Figure 1: Degree of focus on sustainability in the company's supply chain strategy

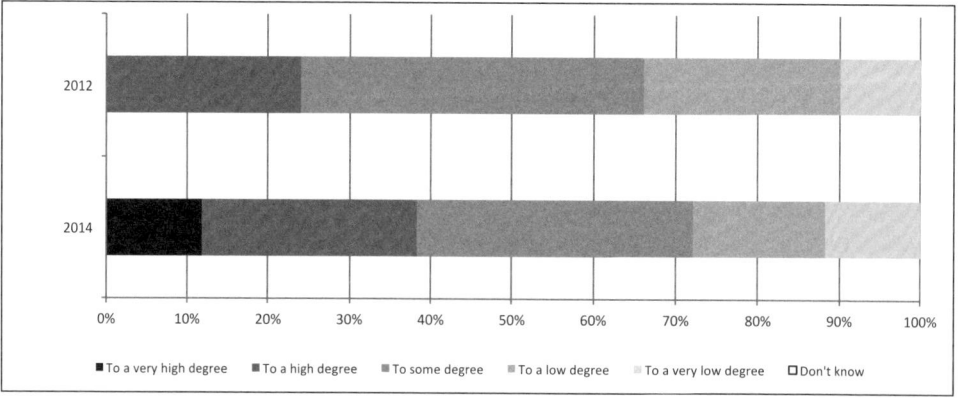

Figure 1 shows that well over 38% of the respondents indicate that there is a high or very high focus on sustainability in the company's supply chain strategy. 34% of the respondents indicate that there is a focus on sustainability in the company's supply chain strategy to some extent, while about 28% of the respondents indicate that there is only a low or very low degree of focus on sustainability in the company's supply chain strategy. Comparing these results with the results from the 2012 survey, a positive development can be seen as only 24% of the respondents at that time indicated that there was a high degree of focus on sustainability in the company's supply chain strategy. No respondents in the 2012 survey reported that there was a very high focus on sustainability in the supply chain strategy. However, there are 2% more here in 2014 that indicate that there is a very low degree of focus on sustainability in their supply chain strategy. Thus, the gap between the companies' focus on sustainability in the supply chains and the general perception of the society on the development potential as well as the responsibility of the companies seems to be reduced.

Monitoring and controlling the suppliers

Since sustainability, as highlighted in the introduction, involves defining requirements for environmental and social performance in companies' supply chains, we then asked whether the companies measure the performance of their direct (first-tier) suppliers in terms of sustainability.

As shown in Figure 2, only 20% of the respondents do measure to a high or very high degree the direct (first-tier) suppliers' performance in terms

Figure 2: To what extent is the sustainability performance of the suppliers directly measured?

of sustainability. Nearly 32% of the respondents indicate that this only take place to a very low degree, while almost 17% of the respondents indicate that this take place to a low degree. However, in spite of sustainability has attained more focus in the supply chain strategy, still 50% of the respondents answer that they do not spend much resources to monitor their first-tier suppliers' performance of sustainability. The fact that such a large proportion of the respondents indicate such a low degree of performance measurement on their first-tier suppliers is suggestive since the company, as stated in the introduction, will be measured assessed and hold accountable for environmental and social problems caused by their supplier chain. Thus, it represents definitely an important challenge. Similarly, it is a problem if no systematic measures take place then any improvement efforts taken will not be visible. The fact that it is difficult to visualize the gains of effort was identified as a major barrier for implementing sustainability in the 2012 survey (Arlbjørn and Mikkelsen, 2012).

Collaboration with suppliers

In the 2012 survey, respondents stated that external cooperation on sustainability is mainly focused upstream against suppliers. In this 2014 survey, we asked the respondents who they involve and cooperate with in monitoring and developing sustainability by the company's suppliers.

Although Figure 3 shows that the majority of the respondents do not involve some of the stakeholders to a high or very high degree, but apparently handle it themselves, there are still some interesting observations. As shown in Figure 3, it is especially the company's own customers that are involved in the development of the suppliers' sustainability. About 24% of the respondents indicate that own customers are involved to a high or very high degree in the development of suppliers' sustainability, while just over 18% of the respondents indicate that this take place only to some degree. Following, 15% of the respondents indicate that the public authorities are involved to a high or very high degree and 27% of the respondents indicate that the public authorities are involved only to some degree. NGOs are not only important stakeholders who help to set the agenda for public sustainability, but also potential collaborators that can help to provide credibility and legitimacy. We had expected that companies, to a certain degree, would have established collaboration with them. The panel responses indicate that

Figure 3: The degree of involvement/collaboration in monitoring and developing suppliers' sustainability

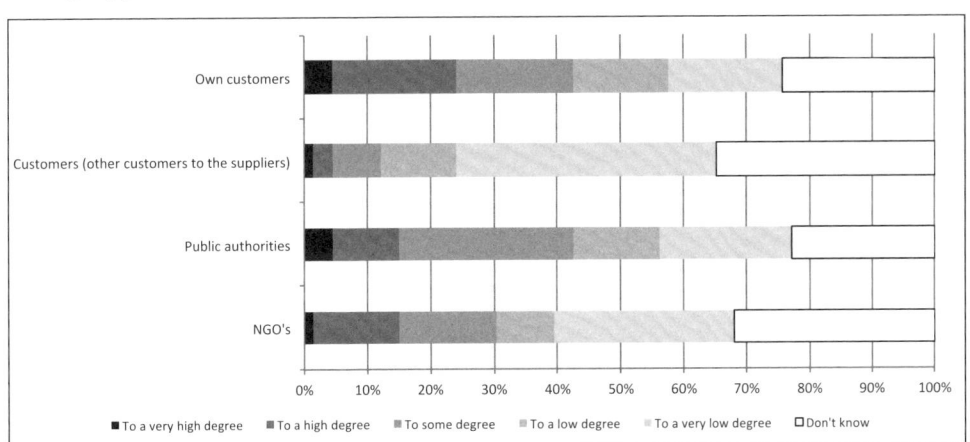

about 30% of the companies, from some degree to a very high degree involve NGOs in the development of sustainability of the suppliers. This can be perceived as being a low number, but not when this is compared with 2012 survey, where only 13% of the companies had established some form of collaboration with NGOs in sustainability. Thus, there been a positive development, but there is still a potential for great development. Compared with Figure 2, about measuring performance, collaboration could focus on how sustainability is measured and implemented in the supply chain. Collaboration with other supplier's customers does not seem to appeal to the panel's participants in spite of the number of benefits that can be achieved through such cooperation (pooling of resources etc.).

Supplier audits

A specific method of controlling suppliers' sustainability performance is to audit them. Here we are particularly interested in highlighting the companies' degree of approach in auditing the suppliers in the supply chain. In other words, the respondents were asked how far back they are in auditing their suppliers.

As shown in Figure 4, companies are to a higher degree auditing their direct suppliers (first-tier). About 17% of the respondents answer that they

Figure 4: How far back in the supply chain are suppliers audited?

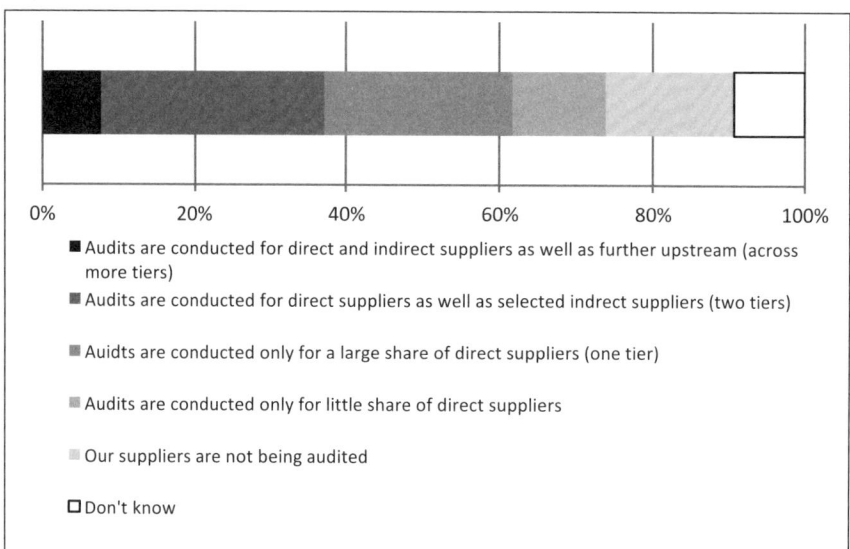

do not audit their direct suppliers, while about 9% of the respondents indicate that do not know whether they are auditing or not. In addition, it appears that approximately 37% of the companies, to a greater or lesser degree, carry out auditing of the supply base beyond the first-tier level suppliers. The same share of the companies audits only a greater or lesser part of its direct suppliers. The remaining part of the respondents indicate that does not audit their vendors or do not know if they do. We have not investigated these relationships with regard to the size and/or industries of the companies, but will emphasize that auditing of suppliers is not for free and we notice that it is especially the larger companies that have access to the resources of auditing demands.

As resources often are a scarce factor in companies, the companies have a strategy for auditing their suppliers based on, for example, geography, volume of trade, supplier size, etc. Thus, a small local supplier with small trade volume will not be exposed to the same degree of auditing as a major trading partner located in a high risk country. In other words, a company can differentiate its approach to sustainability in the supply chain in relation to suppliers, for example, by allowing some companies to sign a Code

Figure 5: Responsibility for auditing

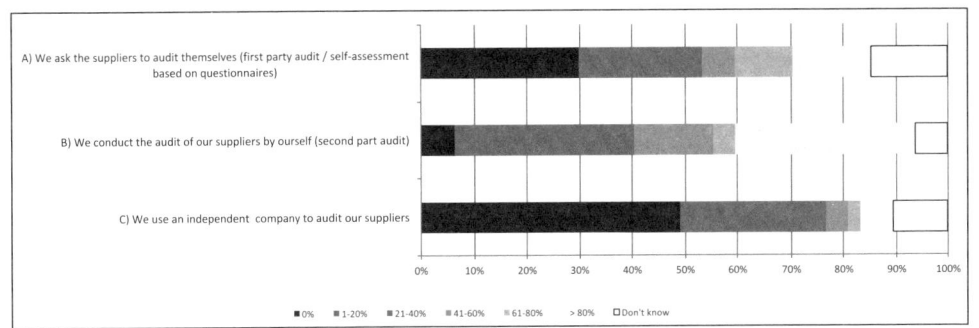

of Conduct, whereas other suppliers are audited several times during the year. Therefore, we asked who audits the suppliers, how often and to what degree this takes place. The answers are shown in Figures 5 and 6.

As shown in Figure 5, companies prefer to audit their suppliers themselves (second party auditing). 34% of the companies indicate that they themselves audit more than 80% of their direct suppliers. This partly confirms the results we noticed in Figure 3. An explanation may be that companies in this way feel that they have more control over the audit process and do not bear the costs that might be associated with third party auditing. The figure shows that auditing of an impartial third party is the option that is used to the lowest degree. Almost half (48.9%) of the respondents thus indicate that they do not use this type of audit of their direct suppliers. About 21% of the respondents use a third party to audit up to 20% of their suppliers, while 19% of the respondents use third parties to audit more than 20% of the supplier base. This indicates a clear differentiation. According to the respondents, first-party auditing is also used to a certain degree (suppliers are auditing themselves). Nearly 32% of the respondents indicate that they use first-party auditing for at least 41% of their suppliers. First-party auditing can be popular, as it is the audit form that results in the lowest costs. However, first-party auditing, compared to the other two practices, must be considered to be associated with the highest risks in terms of ensuring an objective assessment of the suppliers and even second-party auditing is associated with limitations as they can reduce the credibility of the results.

Another interesting aspect of auditing being worthwhile to investigate is the frequency of auditing, i.e. how often the respondents indicate that they audit their suppliers. The answers are shown in Figure 6.

Figure 6 shows that it is very different how suppliers are audited and with what frequency that takes place. Relatively few companies use a particular practice or frequency for the majority of their suppliers. It is interesting to note that just over 23% of the respondents state that none of their suppliers simply have to comply with the company's Code of Conduct. Conversely, almost 28% of the respondents indicate that they apply this practice to more than 41% of their suppliers. Thus, there is no ongoing follow-up in these cases but the companies react relatively only if they realize that a sup-

Figure 6: Frequency of auditing

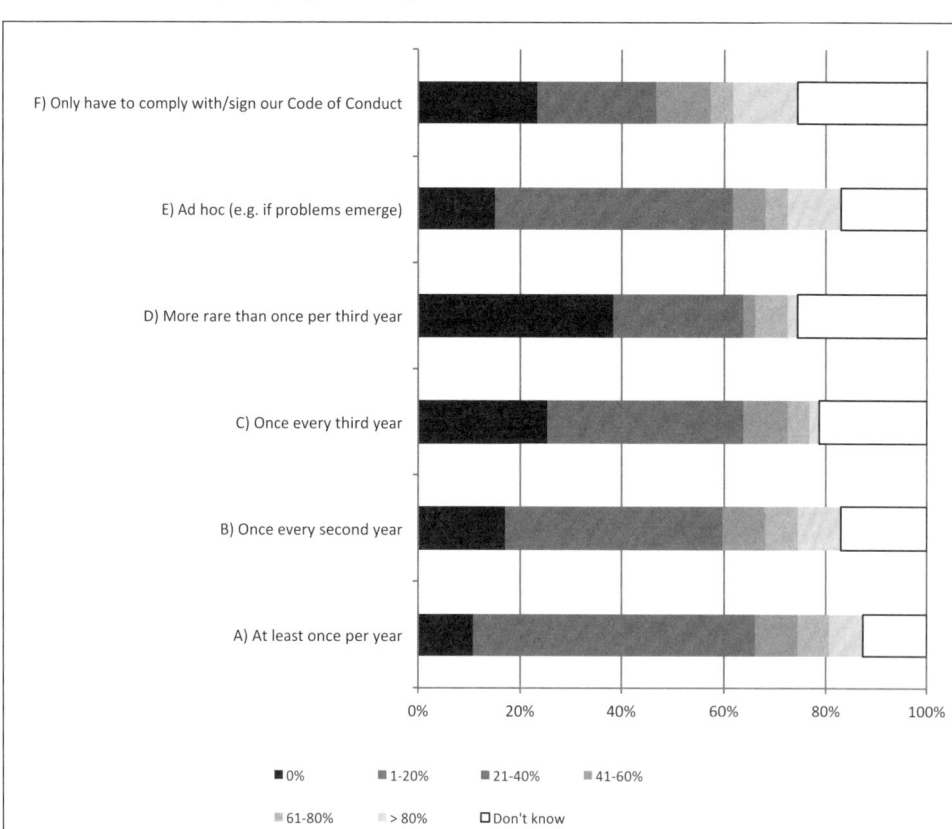

plier fails to comply with the signed Code of Conduct. This may be related to the relatively widespread practice of auditing ad hoc if there is suspicion or exposure to environmental or social issues of a supplier. It is also interesting to note that over 21% of the respondents report that over 41% of suppliers are audited at least annually, indicating that there is a relatively large group of suppliers where the frequency of auditing should be considered frequent. Therefore, it is supposed to be a relatively large group of suppliers that are positioned in high-risk countries, which can support the importance of monitoring suppliers due to global sourcing.

Requirements for suppliers

Some companies have gradually developed their own Codes of Conduct, which provide guidelines on how the companies themselves will act and how they expect the suppliers to act. In addition, several companies choose to be certified in the field of sustainability in order to demonstrate proven evidence of their systems and actions. Therefore, we asked the respondents whether this is transferred as a requirement to suppliers or not.

As shown in Figure 7, about 68% of the respondents indicate that to a high or very high degree the main focus is that the suppliers must comply with the guidelines in the corporate Code of Conduct. Including the

Figure 7: Requirements when purchasing raw materials, components, products and services

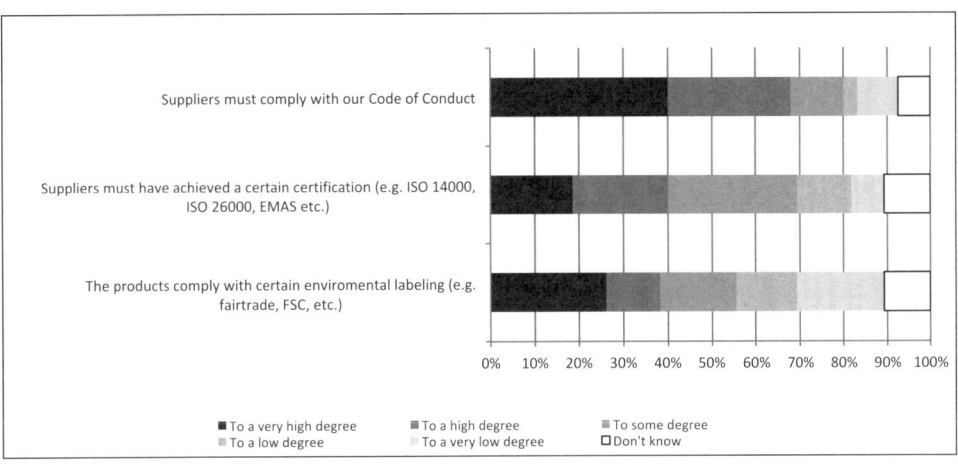

answer 'to some extent', it is clear that 80% of the companies have this as a requirement. Only just over 11% of the respondents indicate that they make low or very low demands. A large proportion of the supply chain panel participants also emphasize that suppliers have obtained certifications (e.g. ISO 14000) and Ecolabelling (for example, the FSC Forest Stewardship Council). Almost 40% of the respondents reported this practice to a high or very high degree. Figure 7 further reveal that there seems to be an overweight to certification. Almost 31% of the respondents have evaluated requirements concerning environmental labeling to a low or very low degree. It is not surprising that companies emphasize that suppliers comply with the buyer's own requirements for Codes of Conduct. The fact that certifications seem to have an overweight in relation to environmental labeling can be explained by the companies that are better known with the ISO system than different environmental labels, and that ISO certifications can be fine in line with the company's own management of environmental and social affairs.

Practices for development of suppliers

If a supplier fails to meet the requirements by its customers, there are typically three options. Another supplier can be identified; the supplier can be taken over or the buyer can engage in developing the supplier. This commitment can include everything from transferring and communicating knowledge about sustainability, investing and transferring resources to the supplier, as well as training efforts to help the supplier to address any problems. Thus, in addition to monitoring and auditing, it is interesting to illustrate the tools that companies otherwise make use of in improving the sustainability of their suppliers. The answers are shown in Figure 8.

As shown in the figure, it is especially the feedback that is made in connection with evaluation, focused on and being used against the suppliers. Approximately 24% of the respondents indicate that it happens to a high or very high degree, and about 25% of the respondents indicate that it happens only to some degree. We are not surprised that problems are being addressed in the evaluation of suppliers. What is more surprising is that about 40% of the respondents indicating that this only happens to a low or very low degree. Green advices are also a tool used to some degree. Another interesting aspect is that only about 14% of the respondents indicate that

Figure 8: Practices for supplier development

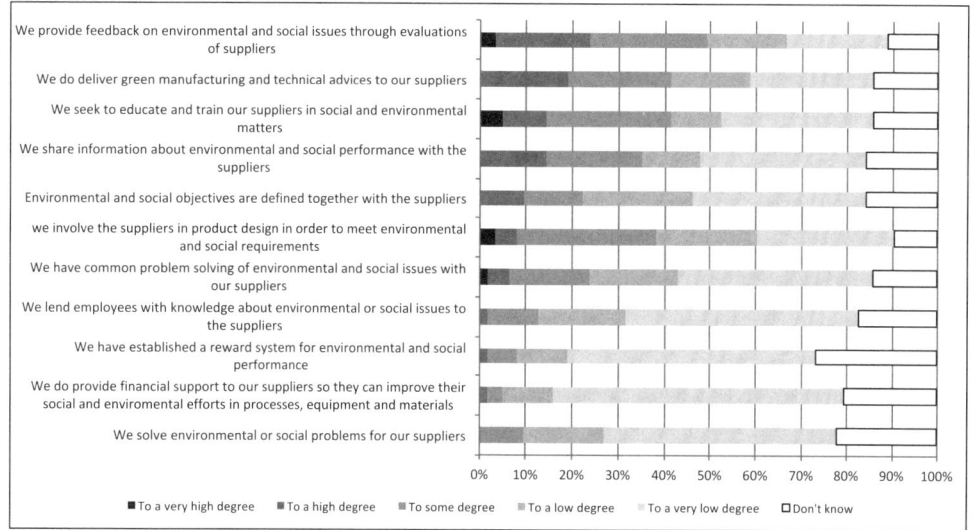

they largely share information about sustainability performance with the vendors; while almost 21% of the respondents indicate that they share this type of information to some degree. Thus, all 49% of the panel members share only this type of information at a low or very low degree with the suppliers. But how should suppliers improve if they do not receive information about their performance? Defining common goals, involvement of suppliers in product design, common problem solving, etc., are apparently not instruments that are being used.

Who has the responsibility?

Given the increased focus on sustainability, as well as the complexity of supply chains faced by companies in these years, Danish companies are beginning to analyze sustainability in the supply chain, also beyond first-tier levels. But is this a responsibility that they fully or partially believe as the responsibility of the company? The answers to this question are shown in Figure 9.

As shown in Figure 9, it does not seem like that the companies' regard it as their responsibility, since approximately 67% of the respondents believe

Figure 9: Who do you think is responsible for the indirect suppliers' sustainability?

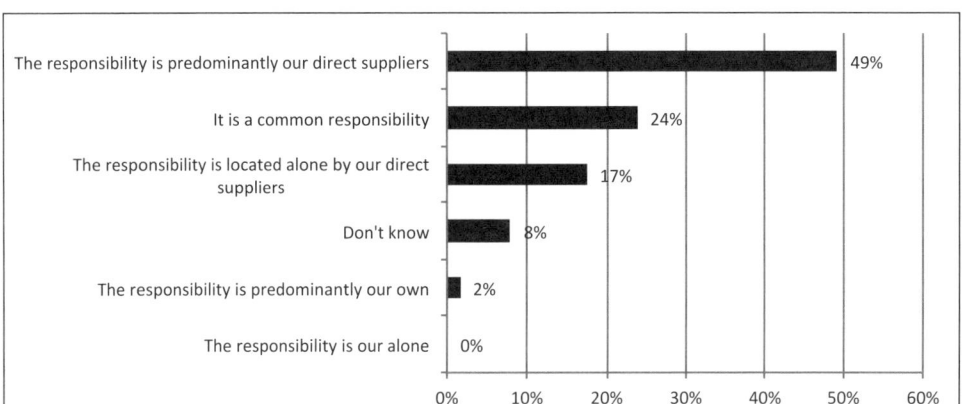

that it is, or predominantly, the direct suppliers' responsibility. However, we reported earlier in the article that a large number of companies actually audit beyond their direct suppliers. This indicates, that even if the companies think it is the supplier's responsibility, the customer does not fully believe that the direct suppliers can handle the responsibility satisfactorily – at least not if the chips are down.

Conclusion

This mini-survey has focused on sustainability in Danish companies' supply chains. It is a hot topic, both in Denmark and internationally, and it seems to be a challenge for supply chain management (especially the sourcing and purchasing function). The results reported here show an improvement from the 2012 survey (Arlbjørn and Mikkelsen, 2012); but it also reveals that there still is a long way to go for many Danish companies.

The biggest challenges are, in our opinion that Danish companies seem to be too passive and reactive in relation to the need to ensure that there are no social and environmental problems in their supply chains. We could be tempted to say that, in some companies, there might be some naivety by saying that "it is not our responsibility". It is unclear whether the responsibility for indirect suppliers can be handed over to the direct suppliers, and it is unclear who in the company will be responsible for the task. However, regardless of its responsibility, we see a great need for Danish companies to engage much more in the issue of developing sustainable supply chains.

Improvement efforts must be more systematic. There is a need to be proactive in meeting problems, and companies must realize the limitations of only using monitoring – especially methods that are not being considered credible (Meqdadi et al., 2012). Here, co-operation with third parties can be put in place, for example, many NGOs have gradually gained expertise in cooperating with companies in auditing and training of suppliers in developing countries.

Finally, we recommend that the development of a sustainable supply chain should not only be perceived as a matter of risk minimization. In fact, there are many examples that there are opportunities for creating value and competitive advantages in a business model based on a sustainable supply chain. We believe that this is an obvious opportunity for Danish companies, which in general should not compete for costs, but for quality and innovation, including supply chain innovation (Arlbjørn et al., 2013). This requires a strategic approach to the problem, as we hope an increasing number of companies will pursue.

References

Arlbjørn, J.S. and Mikkelsen, O.S. (2012), "Arbejde med sustainability er primært drevet af økonomiske besparelser", *DILF Orientering*, Vol. 49 No. 6, pp. 14-15.

Arlbjørn, J.S., Mikkelsen, O.S., Munksgaard, K.B, Schlichter, J. and Paulraj, A. (2013), *Konkurrencekraft gennem Supply Chain Innovation*, Industriens fond og Institut for Entreprenørskab og Relationsledelse, Syddansk Universitet.

Jensen, J.K., Munksgaard, K.B. and Arlbjørn, J.S. (2013), "Chasing value offerings through green supply chain innovation", *European Business Review*, Vol. 25 No. 2, pp. 124-146.

Johnsen, T.E., Howard, M. and Miemczyk, J. (2014), *Purchasing and Supply Chain Management: A Sustainability Perspective*. Routledge, London.

Meqdadi, O., Johnsen, T. and Johnsen, R. (2012), "The role of SME suppliers in implementing sustainability", In Proceedings of the 20th IPSERA Conference, 1-4 April, University of Naples Federico II, Italy.

Social media in Danish supply chains: A top or pop phenomenon?[1]

By: Jan Stentoft, Ole Stegmann Mikkelsen and Thomas Johnsen

Introduction

The word "social" has been increasingly used through the media landscape over the recent years as millions of people use online communities and social platforms like Facebook, LinkedIn and YouTube (see an overview of some forms of social media in Table 1). Although there has been a huge growth in the use of social media, this is perhaps only the beginning of new ways to do businesses. There are still great business opportunities using social media. A recent survey shows that IT-supported communities have grown to over 1.5 billion users globally and the proportion of online users using social media regularly is 80%. In addition, 70% of the companies use social technologies and 90% of them are reporting on the benefits of this use. Knowledge workers use the social media on average 28 hours per week in writing emails, information search and for internal collaboration (Chui et al., 2012). In a business context, the use of social media has taken place especially in connection with sales and marketing activities and as means to recruit new employees or market own labor skills. The use of social media in the supply chains are underexposed and have not yet been widely used; neither in professional trade journals nor in academic journals. Rozemeijer et al. (2011) has considered some of the studies conducted on the use of social media in the supply chains. This study focuses on the use of social media by buyers and reveals that over 90% use LinkedIn, 40% use Facebook and Twitter, and over 75% of the respondents expect their use of

---

[1] This article is edited and translated to English from the Danish version Arlbjørn, J.S., Mikkelsen, O.S. and Johnsen, T. (2014), "Sociale medier i danske forsyningskæder: Et top – eller et popfænomen?", *DILF Orientering*, Vol. 52 No 2, pp. 18-23.

social media to increase over the next two years. Although it is not clear how social media can be used, several answered that they believe social media, among other things, could be used to improve:
- Purchasing performance
- Collaboration with suppliers
- Quality of sourcing decisions

Social media can thus be used to collect information about suppliers. Other benefits might be access to experts in the field; promoting professional careers and exchange of best practices, news, etc. It is clear that social media play an increasing role in consumers buying behavior, but it seem like they now also play an increased important role in professional procurement.

According to Gonzales (2013), social media should play a more central role in supply chain management. Basically, social networks are not a matter of socialization, but rather a matter of facilitating communication between people. And as Gonzales (2013) expresses, is it not precisely the fact that the management and execution of supply chain processes are about to achieve the objectives? Therefore, this mini-survey focuses on the use of social media by highlighting the degree to which social media are used in Danish supply chains, what forms of social media are used and what are the driving forces as well as barriers for using social media.

Table 1: Forms of social media

Social media	Brief description
Facebook	Facebook is a social network where one, among others, can share pictures, text updates and chat with each other.
LinkedIn	LinkedIn is a business-oriented social network where you can create professional contacts and business relations. It is increasingly used as a medium for recruiting new employees and to recommend each other.
Twitter	Twitter is a micro-blogging website where you can send your own and read other users' updates. Such updates are called tweets.
YouTube	YouTube is a web portal where it is possible to share their video clips for free. Videos can be uploaded. You can see and comment on other people's videos.

Industry blogs	A blog is a website that is regularly updated with short texts (posts or comments, where the latest ones are at the top). The person who edits the blog is called a blogger. It is possible that readers can comment on individual posts, and here at industry blogs typical industry-specific knowledge.
Web sites	Traditional websites have for a long time been and are often not associated with the term social media, but websites are increasingly equipped with blogs or chat features. In this study, it is not clear whether they are with or without these "social characteristics".
Snapchat	Snapchat is a program for distributing photos, videos with text and drawings. The messages are visible for a number of seconds, after which they destroy themselves.
Instragram	Instagram is a social network in the form of an app for iPhone and Android smartphones. Users can update with a photo with a short text. You can follow other users by searching for their name and clicking 'follow'. It's possible to 'like' a photo and comment it.

Forms of social media

The respondents were asked to assess the degree to which they use social media in their daily work in the supply chains. As shown in Figure 1, the use of social media in the supply chains does not appear to be particularly common in Danish companies.

Websites are the medium that has the greatest use with an average of 3.28 on a 5-point Likert scale from 1 (to a very low degree) to 5 (to a very high degree). Such websites are typically industry or company-specific portals, allowing searching for information about markets, companies/suppliers and products. Often, e-mails can be sent from such pages and in some cases a blog or chat service is also available making interaction possible. The social media with the second highest average is LinkedIn, with an average of 2.34, which is under "to some degree". Then follows, Facebook with an average of 1.67; YouTube with an average of 1.53 and Industry blogs with an average of 1.46. Under "Other", answers like SAP-JAM and Pinterest (a social network focusing on sharing photos and interests, where the company can be promoted) were listed. Overall, these results indicate that social

Figure 1: Practice of using social media in supply chains

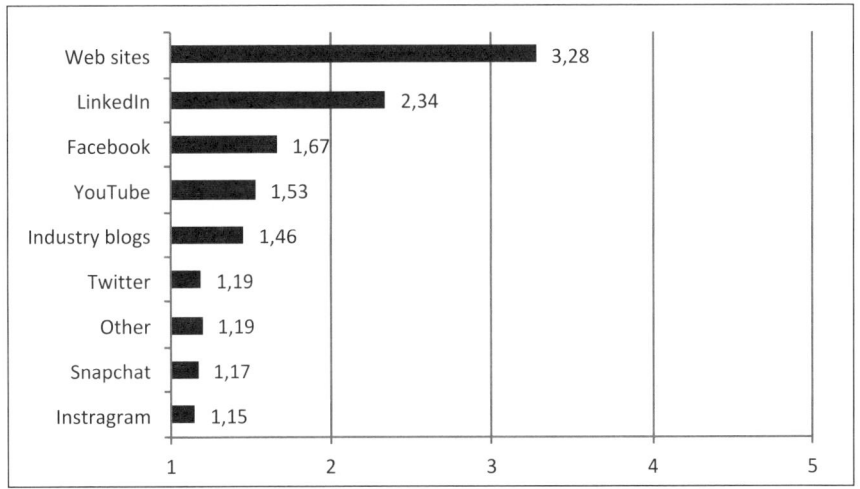

media have not yet had the big breakthrough in Danish supply chains. Possible reasons for this are discussed later in this article.

Driving forces for using social media

With the relatively limited use of social media in the supply chains, the respondents were also asked to reflect on the primary reasons for using social media. Figure 2 shows that social media is used to search for new suppliers among 38% of the respondents. This is followed by "interaction with other companies (forum for the exchange of experience)" and "interaction with customers" among 37% of the respondents respectively. In addition, 32% of the respondents state that social media is used to search for information from current suppliers; while 31% of the respondents indicate that social media is used to explore market conditions and trends. Furthermore, 22% of the respondents indicate that they do not use social media at all. Compared with the previous results, where websites dominated the use, it is not surprising that searching for new suppliers and searching for information by current suppliers being relatively much high. However, the use of social media internally in the company is surprisingly not a widespread practice (see "cross-functional interaction" with 14% and "interaction with colleagues" with 9% of the respondents). The data reveals that there seem

Figure 2: Drivers for using social media (more marks is allowed)

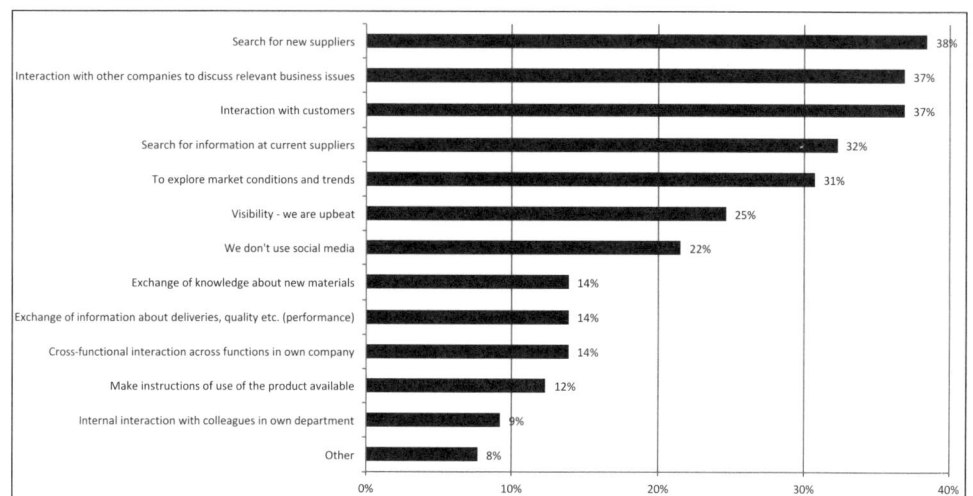

Note: More marks have been allowed

to be opportunities for using social media, both external and especially internal, as a mean to break down the functional silos. Under "other", respondents mention "searching for candidates for supply chain positions (e.g. through LinkedIn)", "outplacement of employees", "global supply chain communication (24 hour time zones)", and to stay updated on CSR and sustainability issues.

Experience and the frequency of using social media

The respondents were asked to assess whether their supply chain organization has been slower to use social media compared to other departments in their company. This question does not take into account the respondents' perception of the company's use of social media in general, but do alone compare the supply chain function with the other functions. Thus, one can answer "no" and actually indicate that one function is as slow as the other functions of the company. According to Figure 3, 28% of the respondents report that their supply chain function has been slower to use social media, while 45% of the respondents respond that they have not been slower. Additionally, 27% of the respondents respond "do not know". The respondents

Figure 3: Has the supply chain been slower to use social media than other functions in the company?

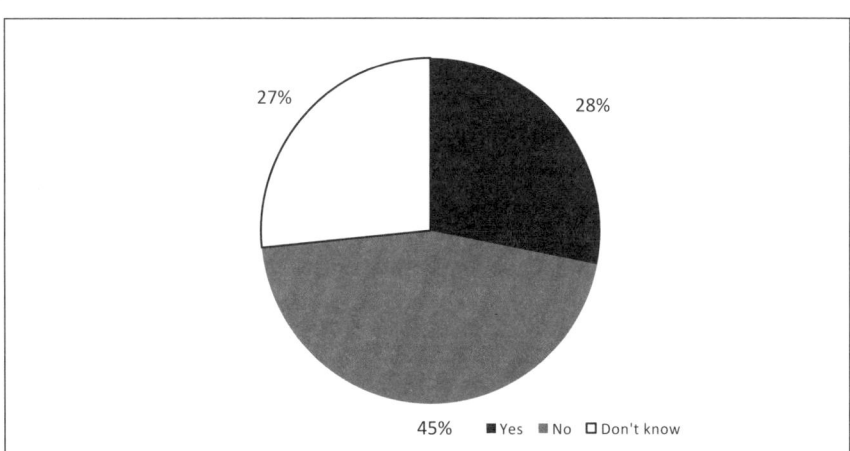

who have answered that they have been slower were asked for reasons for this slowness. In the open question about why the supply chain area is perceived as being slower to use social media than other functions, there have been many different answers. Examples of responses are that there must be

Figure 4: Frequency in the use of social media in supply chains

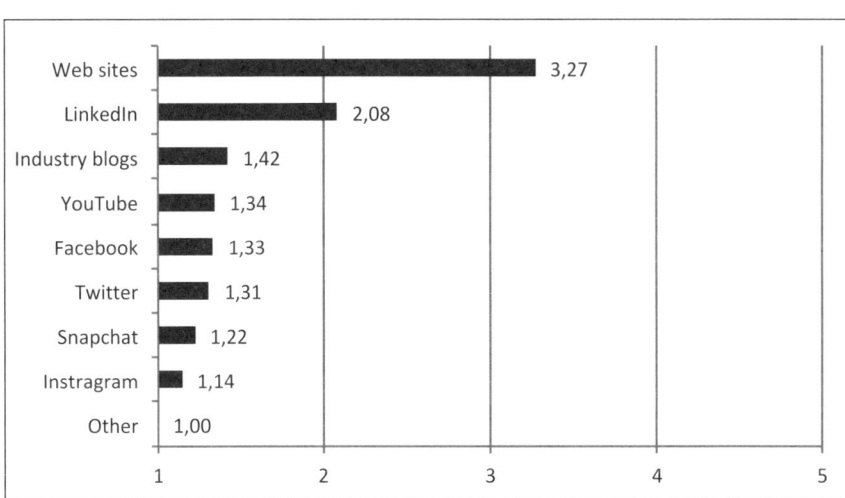

a real need before it is used; that one cannot see the benefit/value of it; that the right skills are not present; that sales and customers have first priority; that there is a lack of maturity and that "we are focusing on operation – social media seems to be a little bit arty-party".

Respondents who have answered that they use social media were also asked to indicate how often this happens. As shown in Figure 4, "websites" is the social media that is used most often with an average of 3.27 times per week. This is followed by LinkedIn with an average of 2.08, which is equivalent to "once per week". The other forms of social media are rarely used. This indicates that the other social media still lack to offer anything useful to the supply chain staffs and also indicate that information search as well as information sharing in a supply chain context so far primarily is related to search for professional skills and industry-specific websites and blogs.

Barriers for using social media in supply chains

Despite the fact that the use of social media explodes in the society, companies seems to be reserved to apply these technologies. Therefore it is interesting to investigate why companies to a lesser degree have adopted social media technologies. The respondents were therefore asked to assess what they consider to be the main barriers for using social media in their

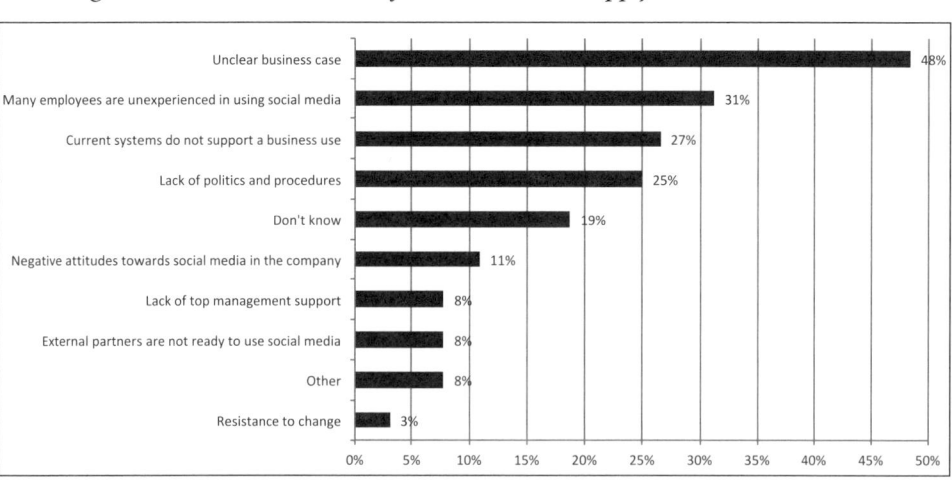

Figure 5: Barriers to the use of social media in supply chains

supply chains. As shown in Figure 5, an "unclear business case or value" is the most widely perceived barrier for applying social media in the supply chains (with 48% of the respondents indicating this barrier). "Lack of experience in the use of social media" is then followed with 31% of the respondents indicating this as barrier for applying social media in the supply chains. Almost one fourth of the respondents believe that current systems do not fit their business and lack of policies and guidelines. Under "other" the responses were "one cannot see the same advantage in the supply chain as in marketing/sales" and "security is too insufficient for customers, suppliers, and the company itself to use the media".

Knowledge from social media is not shared in the supply chain

An often critical point to social media is that it is time-consuming. Several companies also operate with policies for whether social media can be used during the normal working hours, including what types of social media and to what extent. Too much silo mentality is an often referred barrier in supply chain development initiatives in the Danish supply chains in various studies (see Arlbjørn, 2013 and Arlbjørn, 2014). Figure 6 indicates

Figure 6: Formalized processes and systematic methods for studying and sharing information from social media with other functions

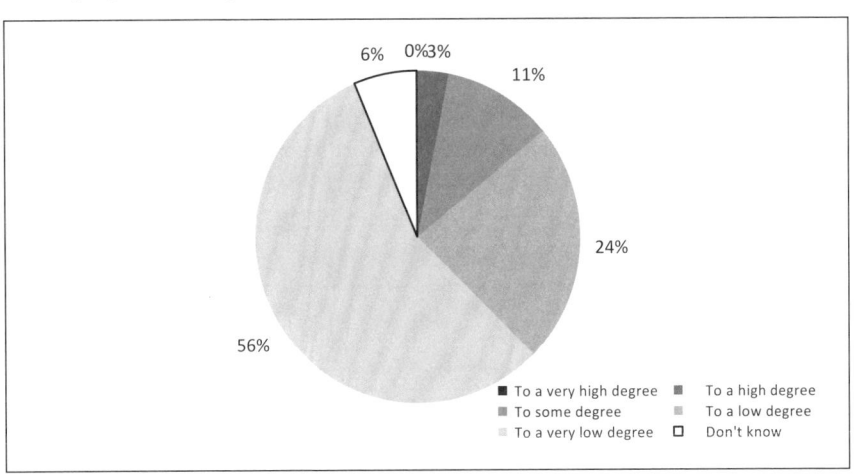

that knowledge sharing of information obtained through social media does not take place with other functions within the supply chain. Thus there is even a silo mentality within a silo! Almost 80% report that such closed loop feedback processes within their own supply chain is prevalent only to low or very low degree.

Risks of using social media

Social media technologies are open platforms, where, as a user, you have the opportunity to express your opinion in both writing and speech. Many discussions have taken place whether a lack of a filter actually can do more harm than good things when using social media. Of course, one should not generalize because the concept of social media is wide. Furthermore, one should use the media with care. Without any specific risk definition, the respondents were asked to assess whether they consider the use of social media in work contexts as a commercial risk. As shown in Figure 7, there are no clear answers to this question. A response probably depends on what is actually understood by risk. Therefore it can be recommended to investigate whether it poses any risks to work with social media in the supply chains including what constitute risks, their probabilities and mitigation plans.

Figure 7: Perceptions of social media from a risk perspective

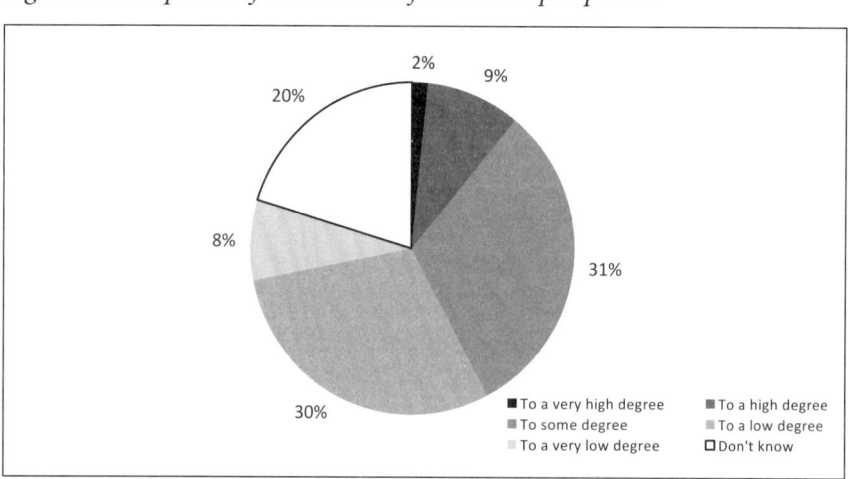

Expectations for future use of social media and its impact

The most stable thing is that change will take place. This is an often-stated statement. One thing that is certain is that the younger employees have stronger experience with using social media than older employees and are also used to a different form of communication than older colleagues. Therefore it is interesting to investigate whether companies expect an increasing use of social media in the supply chain. Figure 8 shows that 21% of the respondents agree to a high or very high degree that the use of social media within the supply chain area is expected to increase over the next 5 years. The results do not say anything about how much the usage will increase. The answers should be seen in the light of what respondents are considering at the time of writing. In addition, 45% of the respondents answer that agree "to some degree". Moreover, 18% of the respondents answer that "no, not at all" and "do not know". These answers indicate a need for further clarification of opportunities and potentials using social media in the Danish supply chains. Therefore we encourage the Danish companies to share experience in this area in order to inspire others to implement solutions that create concrete value to the company.

The respondents were also asked to assess the expected impact of their use of social media in the supply chain area over the next 5 years. As shown

Figure 8: Expectations for increased use of social media in the supply chain within the next 5 years

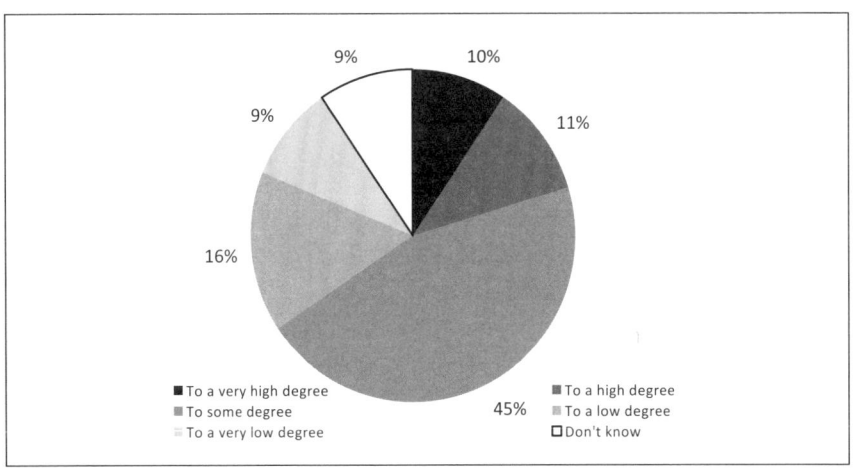

Figure 9: The expected effect of the use of social media in the supply chain within the next 5 years

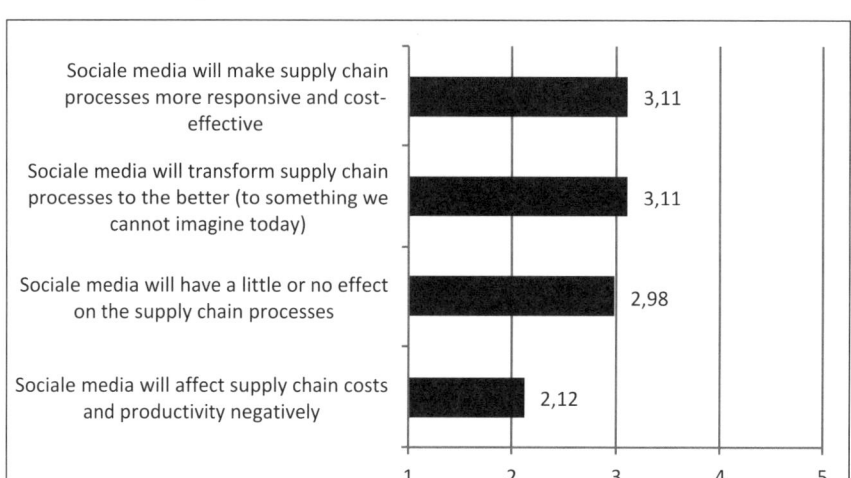

in Figure 9, there is a mixed perception that social media will make supply chain processes more responsive and cost effective with an average of 3.11 (ranging from 1 "highly disagree" to 5 "highly agree"). The same is true for the statement that "the social media will transform the supply chain processes better in a way we cannot imagine today". However, there is also a mixed perception of whether or not the social media will actually affect the supply chain processes. There seems to be some opportunities here to develop that supply chain innovations simultaneously are focusing on the use of technology, supply chain processes and supply chain network structure (see Arlbjørn et al., 2013a and Arlbjørn et al., 2013b). Finally, Figure 6 shows that there is less agreement with regard to that the use of social media in the supply chain will have a negative effect on cost and productivity.

Social media as a recruitment platform

As mentioned earlier, one of the purposes of using social media is the ability to attract new employees through such media. Almost, 47% of the respondents believe that it to a very high or high degree is important to attract new employees through social media as shown in Figure 10. On the other hand, 27% of the respondents find that this is not important. The

Figure 10: The importance of social media in attracting new employees

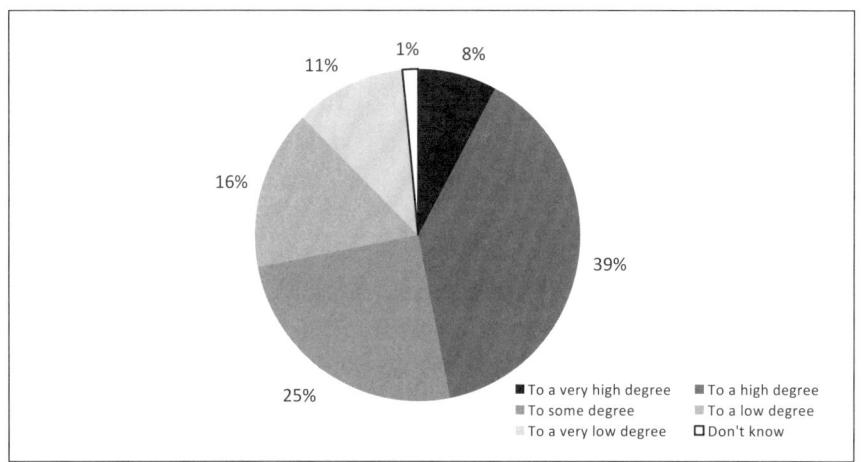

answers to these questions should perhaps be seen in the context of the specific job category for which the companies are looking for a new employee. There might be contradicting views regarding whether the social media are a suitable medium for finding the right candidate.

Conclusion

This article has focused on the use of social media within the supply chains. The results indicate that social media does not seem to be widely used in the Danish companies' supply chains. The study points to several possible reasons for this result including lack of practical relevance, lack of concrete knowledge usage and concrete skills. There are different views on the use of social media, and social media as a headline also contains many different technological directions where each technology may have different degree of usability in a supply chain context. The survey also acknowledges an immaturity in the use of social media in the Danish supply chains. We hope this study can help to exchange more experience with the use of social media, including the types used; how they are used; the degree to which they are used and what specific results are being achieved. Thus, we hope the article can foster discussions about the use of social media in the supply chains, so we can come closer to deciding whether such a phenomenon is in the top or just is pop!

References

Arlbjørn, J.S. (2014), "Det Danske Supply Chain Panel – hvad har vi lært I 2013?", *Dilf-Orientering*, Vol. 51 No. 1, pp. 24-25.

Arlbjørn, J.S. (2013), " Det danske supply chain panel 2013", *Dilf-Orientering*, Vol. 50 No. 1, pp. 48-49.

Arlbjørn, J.S., Mikkelsen, O.S., Munksgaard, K.B., Schlichter, J. and Paulraj, A. (2013a) *Konkurrencekraft gennem supply chain innovation*, Industriens Fond, København K.

Arlbjørn, J.S., Mikkelsen, O.S., Johnsen, T. and Møller, M.M. (2013b), "Supply chain innovation: Om dilemmaet mellem drift og udvikling af forsyningskæder", *Dilf-Orientering*, Vol. 50 No. 6, pp. 52-57.

Chui, M., Manyika, J., Bughin, J., Dobbs, R., Roxburgh, C., Sarrazin, H., Sands, G. and Westergren, M. (2012), *The Social Economy: Unlocking Value and Productivity through Social Technologies*, McKinsey Global Institute.

Gonzales, A. (2013), "The social side of supply chain management", *Supply Chain Management Review*, Vol. 17 No. 4, pp. 16-21.

Rozemeijer, F., Quintens, L. and Konstantin, K. (2011), *Social Media use by Purchasing Professionals*, Final Report, Maastricht University.

Sengupta, S. (2013), "10 trends for the next 10 years", *Supply Chain Management Review*, Vol. 17 No. 4, pp. 34-39.

Section 4 – Panel articles in 2013

Supply chain innovation: About the ambidextrous dilemma in the supply chains[1]

By: Jan Stentoft, Ole Stegmann Mikkelsen, Thomas Johnsen and Morten Munkgaard Møller

Introduction

Over the last decades, there have been many discussions about how Danish companies can ensure continued competitiveness at a time when globalization of trade has been said to have been fully achieved. There have been major discussions about whether the Danish wage level is too high in comparison with other Western countries and not least in relation to low-wage countries in Eastern Europe and Asia. Similarly, there has been a focus on improving productivity in both production and administrative processes. There is simply a need to get a higher output from input resources. Finally, there is also a need to ensure better framework conditions (e.g. in the form of lower taxes and duties, less administrative burdens and access to employees with the right qualifications) for Danish business to ensure competitiveness. These points are undoubtedly essential elements. However, the problem is complex and what works for one company does not necessarily work for another.

This article focuses on how companies' supply chains can function as a key player in improving competitiveness. A research report funded by The Danish Industry Foundation (www.industriensfond.dk) shows that there

---

1 This article is edited and translated to English from the Danish version Arlbjørn, J.S., Mikkelsen, O.S., Johnsen, T. and Møller, M.M. (2013), "Supply chain innovation: Om dilemmaet mellem drift og udvikling af forsyningskæder", *DILF Orientering*, Vol. 50 No. 6, pp. 52-57.

is a positive correlation between efforts to improve supply chains and concrete production in terms of improved supply chain performance (Arlbjørn et al., 2013). However, the research report reveals that there is still a great potential for Danish industry to improve competitiveness through supply chain innovation. The present article delivers data from *The Danish Supply Chain Panel* on the issues of managing both supply and development of supply chains. As shown in Figure 1, 93% of the surveyed companies have carried out improvement initiatives over the past two years and this indicates that there is much focus on such development activities. On the other hand, 7% of the surveyed companies have not carried out improvement initiatives and mention absence as lack of time, resources and top management awareness as reasons for not carrying out improvement initiatives.

The article is further structured in six sections. The following section briefly presents a framework for understanding supply chain innovation. Then a section that examines the supply chain panel's responses with regard to the concrete content elements of the implemented improvement projects in the light of the framework. This is followed by two sections, which indicate the supply chain panel's perceptions of both driving forces and barriers in connection with the implementation of improvement initi-

Figure 1: Share of respondents which has implemented improvement initiatives in their supply chain

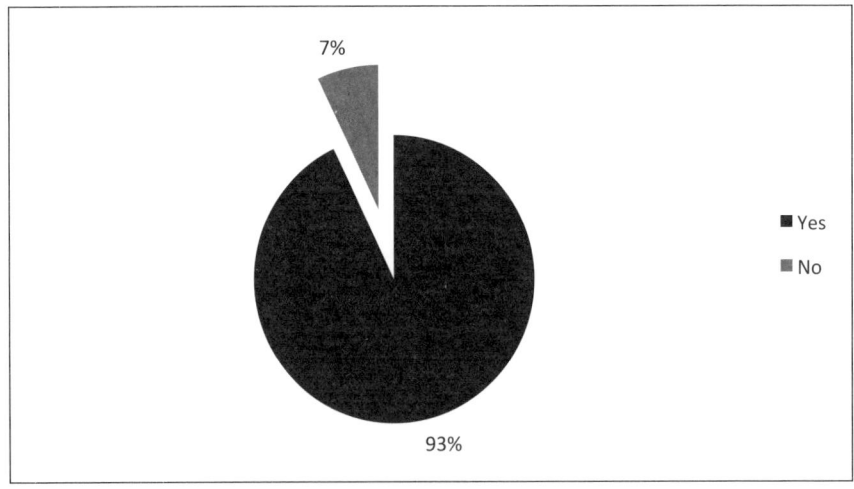

atives. Later a section that shows the goals and the effects of the improvement projects carried out. A brief conclusion ends the article.

Supply chain innovation

Supply chain innovation consists of three components, as shown in Figure 2: a) business processes, b) technology and c) network structure. A given supply chain innovation can take place within one of the components, but will typically more or less affect all three components.

Business processes are a structured set of activities that provide measurable output. Supply chain-related business processes run across the traditional functional "silos" of a company, such as sales, logistics, manufacturing and procurement. Examples of business processes relevant to the supply chain are demand management, order management and supplier management. The technology component refers to all types of IT technology that can be applied to ensure a more efficient and transparent flow of materials and information in the supply chains. Examples of such technologies are

Figure 2: A framework for supply chain innovation

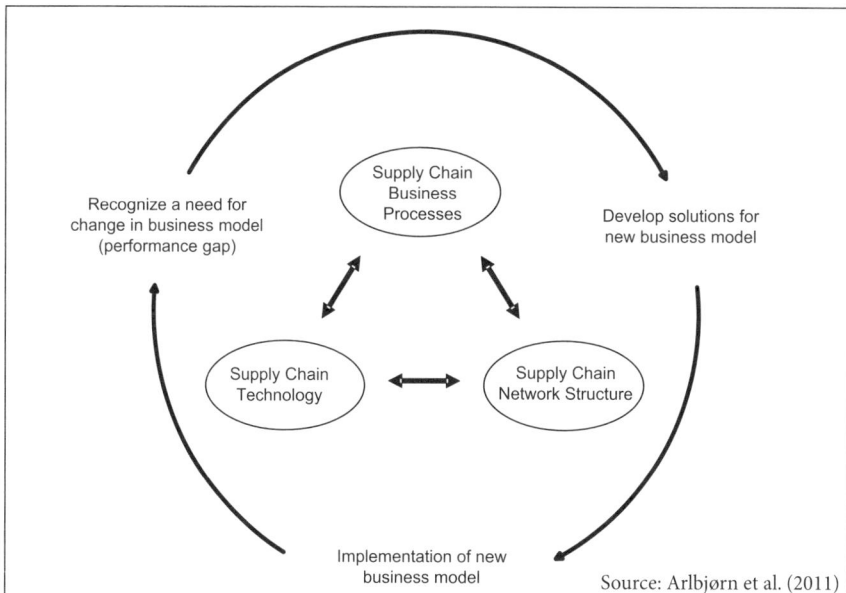

enterprise resource planning (ERP) applications, warehouse management systems (WMS) and global positioning systems (GPS). Network structure refers to the depth and breadth of upstream and downstream relationships as well as the different forms where they can be unfolded. Examples include outsourcing, vendor-managed inventory (VMI) and 3rd party logistics.

Content of the improvement initiatives

This section focuses on the respondents' answers to the elements of the supply chain improvement projects they have implemented in the past two years. The structure follows the three supply chain innovation components from previous sections.

Figure 3: Content elements in improvement projects focusing on business processes

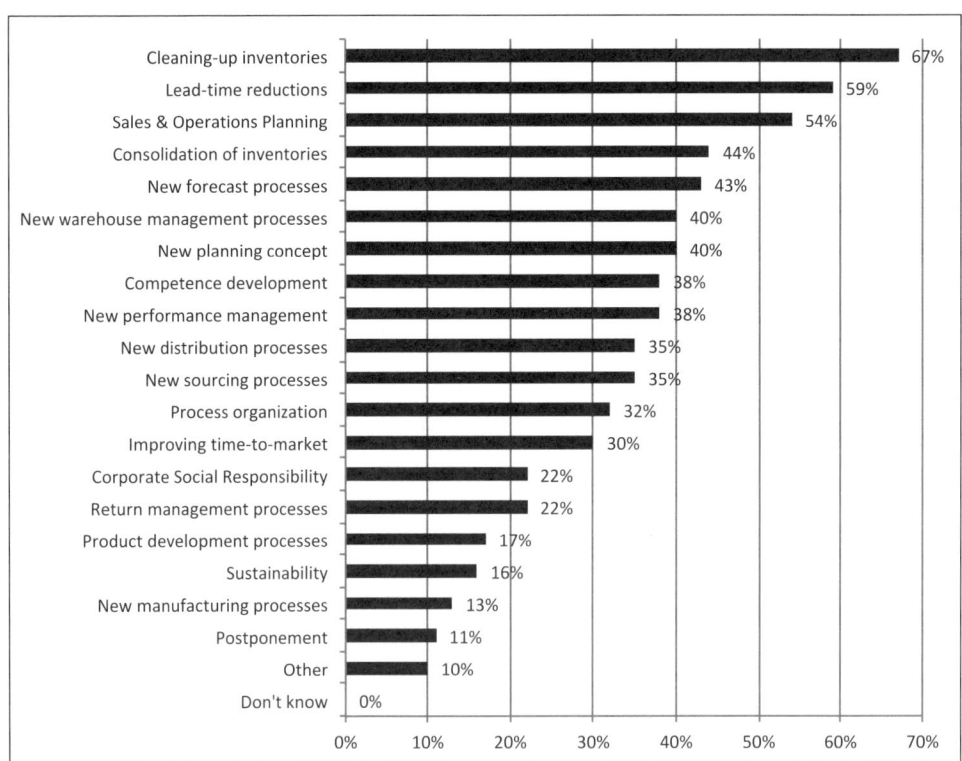

Note: Multiple selections have been possible for the respondents.

Business processes
The content of the improvement projects that focused on business processes is illustrated in Figure 3. It can be seen that "cleaning up inventories" and "lead-time reductions" are the areas that have occurred in most improvement projects. Then, follows the implementation of Sales & Operations Planning (S&OP), which is in line with a previous mini-survey in *The Danish Supply Chain Panel* is an emerging practice in Danish companies (Arlbjørn and Møller, 2013). There seems to be an overweight of the directly measurable and short-term improvement projects in the form of cost and time reductions and improved quality.

Under "other" some respondents have provided answers such as cash flow, lean, quality management, sourcing processes and transport management.

IT technology
The improvement projects reported in *The Danish Supply Chain Panel*'s supply chains have also included changes in IT. Figure 4 show that business

Figure 4: Content elements in improvement projects focusing on IT technology

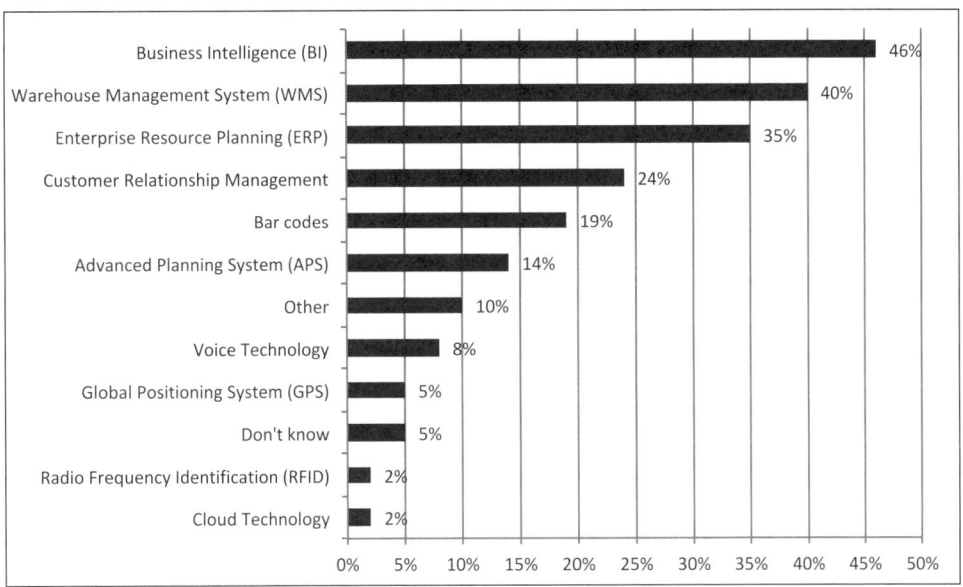

Note: Multiple selections have been possible for respondents.

intelligence (BI) technology has been the subject of improvement projects among 46% of the respondents followed by WMS and ERP. It indicates that one can see a strategic importance in delivering management information with reference to supply chain performance. Surprisingly there are few projects that have included voice technology, GPS, radio frequency identification (RFID) and cloud technology.

Under "other", the respondents indicate advanced transport optimization, project management and information sharing systems as well as extract from the ERP system to Excel. It indicates that you do not necessarily have to power up all supply chain improvement projects. There are still something to be gained using simple pens and paper!

Network structure

The respondents have also been asked whether they have implemented supply chain improvement projects which include changes in the company's network structure. From Figure 5 it is clear that four themes are mainly in focus, namely outsourcing, vendor-managed inventory, partnership formation and implementation of new distribution channels.

Figure 5: Content elements in improvement projects focusing on network structure

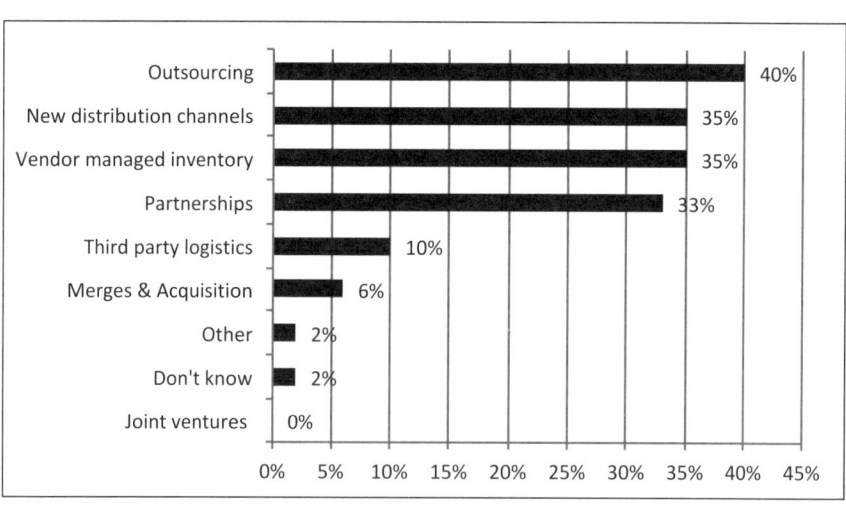

Note: Multiple selections have been possible for the respondents.

Under "Other", the respondents mention that work is provided to locate suppliers in relation to the company's geographical location to reduce the lead time and increase the flexibility.

Driving forces

Decisions to implement improvements projects in supply chains can be initiated due to different reasons. Therefore, out of special interest the panel was asked about the drivers for improvement initiatives they have implemented. Figure 6 shows that improvement initiatives primarily are driven by a desire to provide better service to customers.

Under "Other", the respondents mention additional driving forces such as a need for a constant focus on cost minimization, government requirements, input from the purchasing function and an increased growth that necessitate developments of their supply chains.

Barriers

Implementing improvement projects in supply chains is not necessarily without challenges. Often there are a number of challenges associated with carrying out such activities. The respondents were therefore asked to indicate the main barriers that they have experienced during their efforts to create supply chain improvements. As shown in Figure 7, the highest

Figure 6: Driving forces for implementing supply chain innovation projects

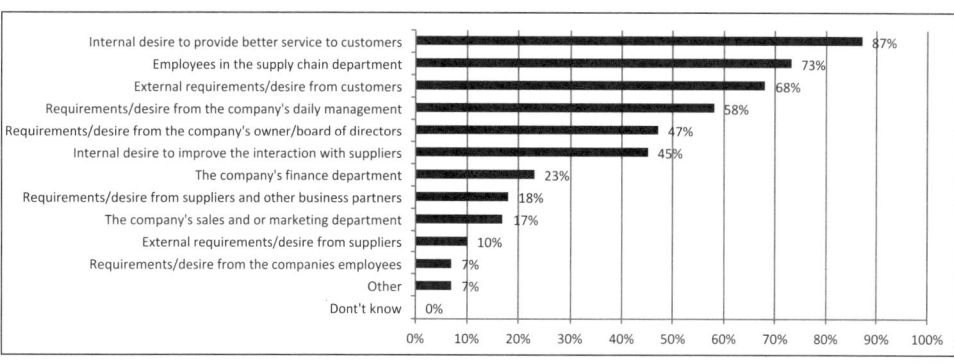

Note: Multiple selections have been possible for the respondents.

Figure 7: Barriers for implementing supply chain innovation projects

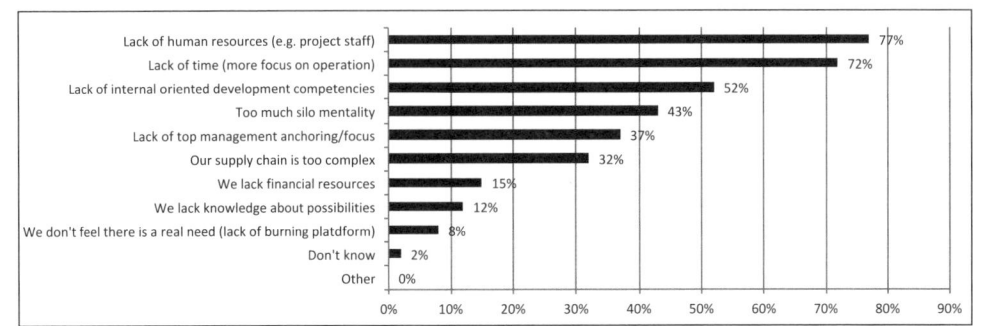

Note: Multiple selections have been possible for the respondents

ranked barrier is "lack of human resources" followed by "lack of time (more focus on operation)". Thus, the work with preparing for supply chain innovations projects can be improved in order to obtain stronger objectives and performance potentials which in turn also can lead to better resource allocation. Of course that is not always the case. However, efforts to strengthen the basis for decisions are seldom wasted. It is also noteworthy that half of the supply chain panel participants responded that there is a lack of "internal development-oriented skills". This should give substance for reflections in future recruitment activities. Finally, silo thinking is the fourth highest ranked barrier with a total of 43%. Even though we have been trying to tear down the silos for more than three decades, the silo phenomenon still seem to be active and kicking in practice.

Under "Other" a respondent mentioned that there is a lack of proper skills at the middle management level.

Operations versus development

In their research report focusing on supply chain innovation and performance, Arlbjørn et al. (2013) has also examined how managers are able to balance operations and development activities in Danish supply chains. The conclusion is very clear in this work. There is a clear emphasis on operational-oriented activities rather than development. It has therefore been of interest to investigate the same issues of balancing operations and development among the members of *The Danish Supply Chain Panel*. The answers to these questions are shown in Figures 8 and 9, respectively. We refer to Arlbjørn et al. (2013) for a deeper management of the dilemma to balance operation (exploitation) and development (exploration) activities at the same time in a supply chain context, also called ambidexterity (March, 1991; Tushman and O'Reilly, 1996).

Operation

Figure 8 shows the average scores for the respondents' responses to seven statements related to operational tasks in the supply chains. The average scores are calculated based on the respondents' answers to each statement based on a 5-point Likert scale, where 1 is the lowest possible score and 5 is the highest. The respondents have been asked to assess both the importance of the individual statements and their actual practice. As shown in Figure 8, the importance is generally considered to be higher than their perceptions of their actual practice. A focus on "improving cost effectiveness in supply chain processes" achieves the highest average score of 4.58 measured by its importance followed by "implementing small adjustments in the supply chain processes" with an average of 4.55. In general, the aver-

Figure 8: Operation-related activities in the supply chain – perceived importance and actual practice

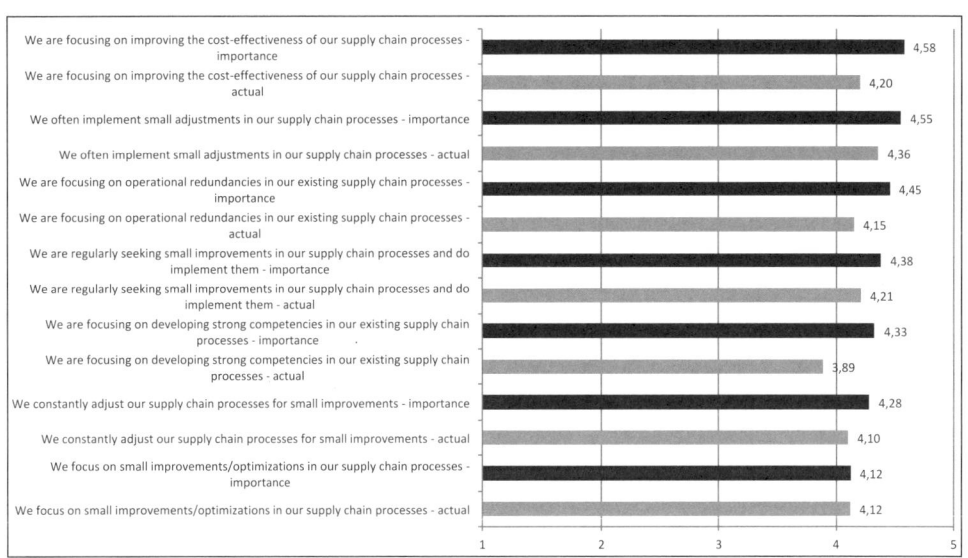

age scores of over 4.0 are based on perceived practices in developing competencies in the supply chain processes. Here, of course there is a room for improvements, which is in line with the conclusions of Arlbjørn et al. (2013).

Development
Figure 9 shows the average scores for the respondents' responses to seven statements related to development activities carried out in the supply chains. Again, he average scores are calculated based on the respondents' answers to each statement based on a 5-point Likert scale, where 1 is the lowest possible score and 5 is the highest. The respondents have been asked to assess both the importance of the individual statements and their actual practice. It is clear that the perceived importance achieves higher mean values than the perceptions of own practice. Please note that the average scores of development activities are lower than the scores for operation activities. In other words, respondents agree more in the statements about their operation of supply chains than on developing them. This is also in

Figure 9: Development-oriented activities in the supply chain – perceived importance and actual practice

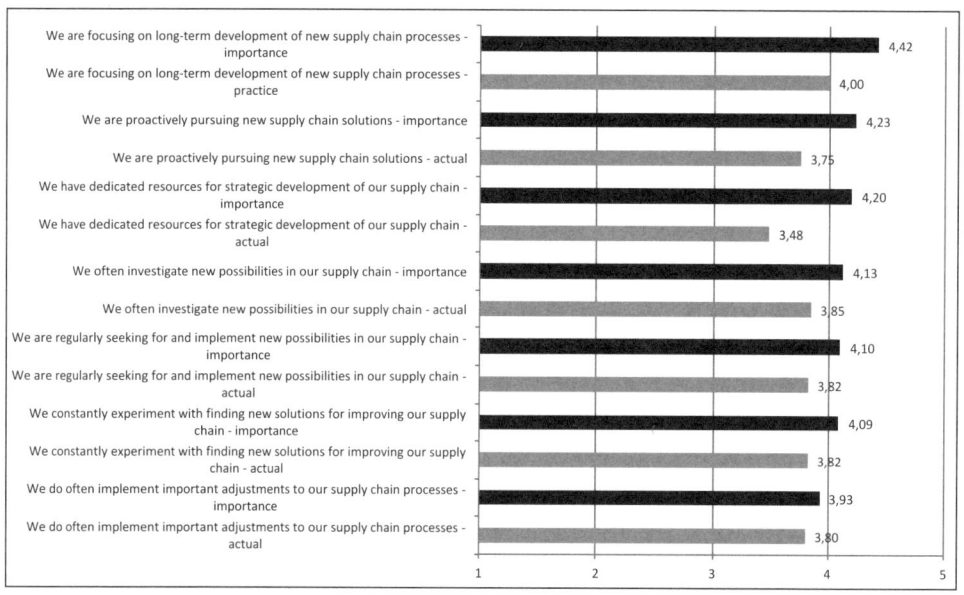

line with the results of Arlbjørn et al. (2013). The development statement that have achieved the highest average score are "focus on long-term development of supply chain processes" with an average of 4.0. This in turn indicates some efforts towards development of supply chains processes. The most significant gap in Figure 9 is the difference between the perception of importance and the actual practice of having "dedicated resources for the strategic development of supply chains". A suggestion is therefore to spend resources to develop a business case including costs and benefit calculations to establish a supply chain innovation department in the company, aiming continuously to initiate, implement, and monitor improvement efforts in supply chains. Such a function might be often self-financing and share similar characteristics as we know for technical departments in manufacturing companies.

Performance measurement and effect

The panel members were asked to reflect on the achieved performance improvements within the following five areas: 1) reduced cost, 2) improved flexibility, 3) improved lead time, 4) improved service level and 5) im-

Figure 10: Performance management and the impact of supply chain innovation initiatives

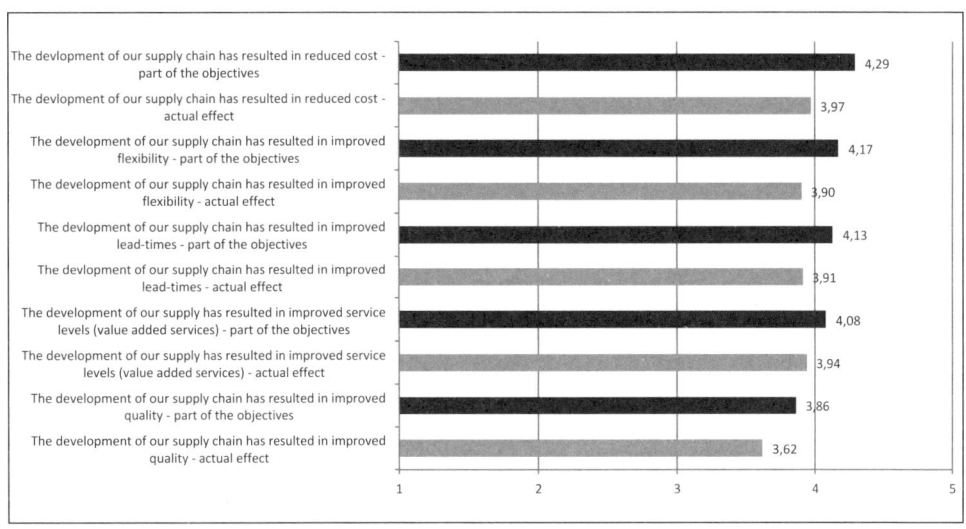

proved quality. The respondents should evaluate both the specific objectives for these areas as well as the actual achievement. As shown in Figure 10, the objectives for the five performance areas have achieved higher average scores than the respondents' perceptions of the actual effect of the objectives. The average scores for cost reductions, flexibility, lead time and service are approximately the same (average score of above 4), while the average score for improved quality is only 3.62. Conflicting goals is not uncommon in supply chains and here it looks like quality has paid the price.

Conclusion

This mini-survey has focused on operation and development activities in supply chains. Data reveals that development activities of supply chains in Denmark take place albeit it seems difficult to get it prioritized in relation to daily operations. Process-related improvements are primarily focused on cleaning-up inventories and reducing inventory levels. Implementation of BI and WMS systems is the most common initiatives in projects that have the involvement of IT. Changes in the company's network structure as a result of the supply chain innovation projects are primarily done through outsourcing. Main drivers for initiating innovation projects are internal desire to serve customers better and concrete input from employees in the supply chain departments. The main barriers are reported to be lack of human resources and lack of time (more focus on operation), which indicates that there is more focus on operation than on development.

It is our hope that the present article may stimulate discussions in Danish companies about the supply chain's contribution in companies overall efforts to create competitive advantages. However, discussions alone seldom move many stakes. Action is needed. Therefore, we refer to the research report from The Danish Industry Foundation that focuses on improved competition through supply chain innovation (Arlbjørn et al., 2013). This may include a sharper top management awareness of dilemmas between operation and development, and between strategic thinking and execution as well as a greater focus on competence development of supply chain staff that enables them to pursue readiness for the challenges of the future.

References

Arlbjørn, J.S., Mikkelsen, O.S., Munksgaard, K.B., Schlichter, J. and Paulraj, A. (2013), *Konkurrencekraft gennem Supply Chain Innovation*, Industriens Fond, København K.

Arlbjørn, J.S., de Haas, H. and Munksgaard, K.B. (2011), "Exploring supply chain innovation", *Logistics Research*, Vol. 3 No. 1, pp. 3-18.

March, J.G. (1991), "Exploration and exploitation in organizational learning", *Organization Science*, Vol. 2 No. 1, pp. 71-87.

Tushman, M.L. and O'Reilly, C.A. (1996), "Ambidextrous organizations: Managing evolutionary and revolutionary change", *California Management Review*, Vol. 38 No. 4, pp. 8-30.

Danish companies practice with Sales & Operations Planning[1]

By: Jan Stentoft and Morten Munkgaard Møller

Introduction

How many have not experienced getting to meetings where staff from, for example, sales, manufacturing, product development, finance and shopping are sitting with their own set of data about stock levels and expectations for the future? Not everyone could discover this now, but might have previously experienced it. One way to create a clear and shared vision of the company's situation and future demand can be made through implementing Sales & Operations Planning (S&OP). S&OP are also software applications, but the software only constitutes a small part of the task. The major task is about people and the way they work together in structured processes. Implementing S&OP and a loyal commitment to new processes can provide companies with a use of scare resources on value-adding activities. S&OP has become even more important in an era of business climate termed VUCA (Volatility, Uncertainty, Complexity and Ambiguity) (Goodfellow, 2012). S&OP is a tool which helps in conducting "what-if" analyses and thereby contributes to scenario planning.

S&OP is a critical cross-functional planning process that helps companies to balance supply and demand of goods and services. It is a process to develop tactical plans that enables management to gain competitive advantage. As a concept, S&OP emerged in the 1980s, there was a need to think beyond just production planning. The process brings the company's plans of sales, marketing, product development, production, procurement and

---

[1] This article is edited and translated to English from the Danish version Arlbjørn, J.S. and Møller, M.M. (2013), "Danske virksomheders S&OP-praksis", *DILF Orientering*, Vol. 50 No. 4, pp. 16-20.

finance together as an integrated design. The process runs at fixed time intervals – typically once per month and the result of the planning process are then handled by the top management. Thus, S&OP contributes to ensure readiness to deliver business results in line with the overall strategic plans.

Based on a review of research articles Thome et al. (2012) have summarized the objectives of S&OP according to the following five categories:
1. Alignment and integration (vertical alignment, balancing supply and demand, cross-organizational alignment, redefinition /adaptation /improvement of functional plans, horizontal alignment within the supply chain).
2. Operational improvements (improving the forecast, improving operational performance, reduction of inventories, management /balancing /alignment of volume and mix, management /balancing /alignment of capacity, management of uncertainty and risk, allocation of critical resources, assisting new product launches, measuring value creation, measuring and reviewing business performance).
3. Profit focus from a holistic perspective (improving business/supply chain performance, improving earnings, improving customer service, minimizing business/supply chain costs, minimizing sources of noise in demand).
4. The creation of results based on trade-offs (increase /optimize profits, improving customer service vs. inventories, responding to demand of lesser inventory, meeting customer requirements with minimized cost).
5. The end results (return on investment, inventory turnover rates, customer/product profitability analysis, and contribution margin).

This article aims to present the results of the mini-survey of *The Danish Supply Chain Panel* concerning their experience with S&OP. To meet this purpose, the article further organized into six main sections. The following section highlights the respondents' perception of S&OP as a competitive factor. The next section, illustrates different maturity stages of S&OP. The following two sections include drivers as well as barriers for implementing S&OP. This is followed by a section about the concrete practice of S&OP of the surveyed companies. The article ends with a brief summary.

Table 1: Key characteristics of Sales & Operations Planning

1. Use the KISS principle – Keep It Simple, Stupid
2. Avoid reinventing the wheel
3. S&OP is about planning in the medium term for the whole organization
4. Bridge-building to close the gap between strategy and operations
5. S&OP creates value and is closely linked to business performance
6. It is a cross-functional and integrated tactical planning process within the company
7. The planning horizon typically varies between 3 to 18 months
8. An S&OP goal is to balance supply and demand and to maintain this balance
9. There is an integration of all levels of an overall plan
10. S&OP has focused on ensuring that financial plans will be fulfilled
11. It is a decision-making process
12. S&OP is owned by a senior management team – it is their window to the future
13. It is a process that no organization can survive without completing
14. It plans and manages the outcome in terms of storage and / or specific customer order
15. S&OP is more than just a process; it is a new way of working

Source: Goodfellow (2012), Thomé et al. (2012), Feng and Sophie D'Amours (2008), Grimson and Pyke (2007).

Sales & Operations Planning as a competitive parameter

The supply chain panel was asked to what extent they believe that S&OP is an important competitive parameter. The results are shown in Figure 1. S&OP is largely agreed as an important competitive parameter. In total, over 80% of the respondents did agree to a very high or to a high degree S&OP as an important competitive parameter.

The respondents were also asked whether their respective companies have implemented S&OP. As shown in Figure 2, 56% of the respondents indicate that they have implemented S&OP, while 44% specify that they have not implemented S&OP. This result indicates that there seem to be con-

Figure 1: Perception of Sales & Operations Planning being an important competitive factor

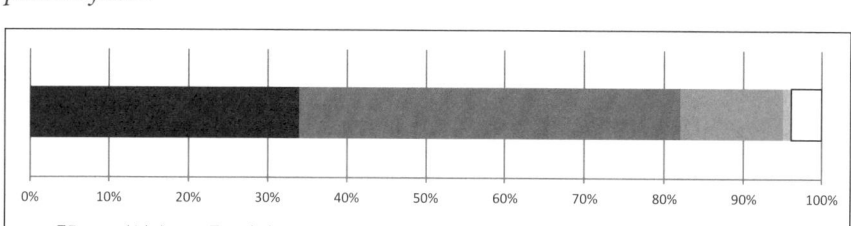

Figure 2: Implementation of Sales & Operations Planning

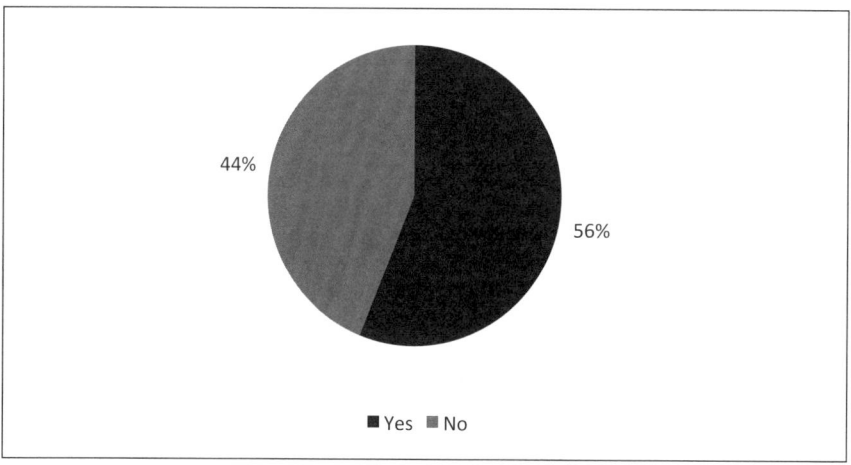

sensus on the usefulness of this cross-functional planning process. Later in this article, we will deal with the barriers reported by the companies for implementing S&OP. These answers might be the various reasons for those respondents (44%) who mentioned that they do not implement S&OP.

Maturity stages of Sales & Operations Planning

Gartner, Inc. has developed a four-step model for S&OP maturity (see Barret, 2010). The four stages are briefly summarized below.

Stage 1: Marginal processes
- Informal meetings and sporadic planning
- Separate processes (plans for demand and supply are separated)
- Large amount of Excel spreadsheets

Stage 2: Elementary processes
- Routine-based planning; uneven participation
- United demand, supply plans are juxtaposed with demand
- Stand-alone demand planning system

Stage 3: Classical processes
- 100% participation from relevant parties
- Demand and supply plans are aligned; external cooperation with a variety of suppliers and customers
- Demand planning and supply planning applications are integrated

Stage 4: Ideal processes
- Event-driven meetings; is held when an imbalance between supply and demand is spotted
- Demand and Supply processes are aligned; external cooperation with most suppliers and customers
- Advanced use of S&OP; integration of external software

Figure 3 shows that 4% of the respondents state that they are in stage 1; 37% of the respondents state that they are in stage 2; 46% of the respondents state that they are in stage 3 and 7% of the respondents state that they are in stage 4. This is a surprising result compared with the practice discussed by Barret (2010), who indicate that relatively few companies have moved to stages 3 or 4. Therefore, the result of this panel survey indicates that there has been some development since 2010. However, there might be some uncertainty with regard to the outcome concerning a clear distribution in the four stages. On the other hand, the results and stages can be a contribution in the running task of evaluating S&OP.

Figure 3: The respondents' perception of their S&OP maturity levels

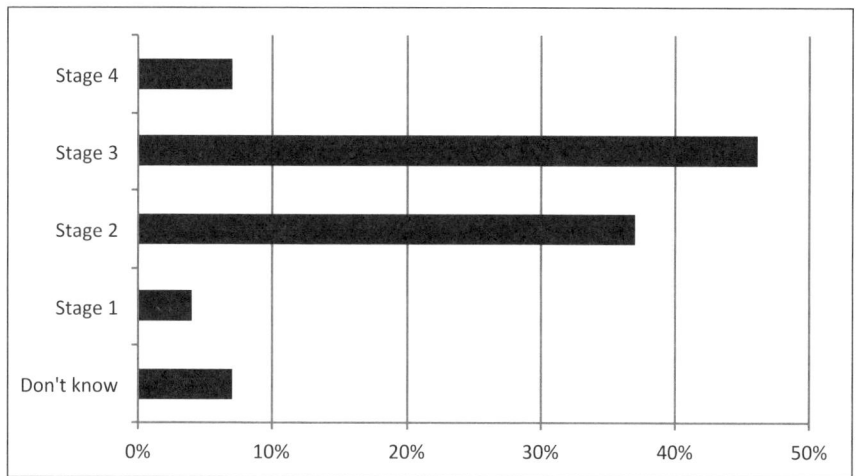

Barriers for implementing Sales & Operations Planning

The companies that have not implemented S&OP were asked to list the top three (major) barriers that stop them from implementing S&OP. This mini-survey shows that 40% of the respondents consider lack of internal development-oriented skills as the topmost barrier. We interpret this in such a way that operation is the primary focus, and that there is a lack of energy and resources to drive the developmental task of implementing S&OP. One can say that you put jugs up to pick up the water from the upper floors instead of isolating the cause and then solve it. Or to put it another way, it is expensive to be poor, as there is no development resources available for the implementation of S&OP. This is followed closely by the other two barriers such as lack of Human Resources and lack of top management anchoring, respectively. It is interesting that one fifth of the respondents indicate silo working as a barrier, as this answer implies the recognition of the existence of the silo, the possibility of the introduction of S&OP practice actually can minimize (see Figure 4).

Figure 4: Barriers for implementing S&OP

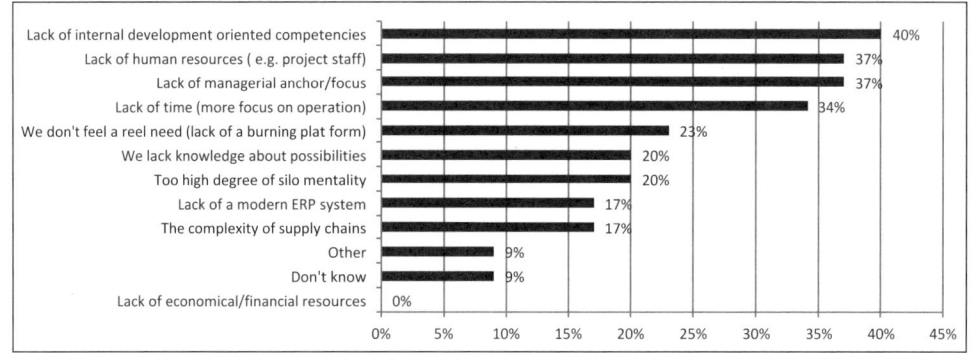

Driving forces for implementing Sales & Operations Planning

The Danish Supply Chain Panel was asked to list the topmost drivers for the implementation of S&OP. The respondents indicate that it is primarily internal forces that drive towards the decision (see Figure 5). The highest-ranking external driving force, i.e., external requirements/demands from suppliers ranks eighth out of the thirteen answers. This is consistent with the goal of implementing S&OP to strengthen internal cross-functional collaboration in order to achieve consistency between the sales organization and operations.

Figure 5: Drivers for implementing S&OP

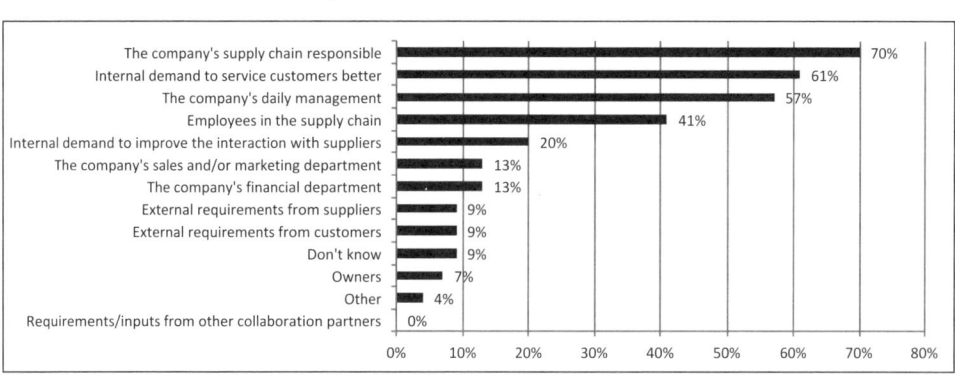

Practice with Sales & Operations Planning

So far we have considered the factors that seem to influence the implementation of S&OP. Now we take the opportunity to clarify the current practice of S&OP among the respondents in this mini-survey, which has already implemented S&OP.

Figure 6 shows there is an even distribution of experiences with S&OP over and below three years, respectively. This indicates that S&OP can be perceived as a relatively new practice among the respondents albeit it was introduced for more than twenty years ago. Thus, there is still a need to focus on how this practice can get deeper rooted in industry so that we can increase the likelihood of achieving the identified benefits of implementing S&OP. In other words, there is still a potential for implementing S&OP in Danish companies.

The respondents were also asked about the most important prerequisites for achieving successful implementation of S&OP. Figure 7 shows the respondents' perception about the different criteria for implementing S&OP and how far the current level of practice of S&OP is within the surveyed companies.

The success criterion that has received the highest rating is cross-functional involvement. This result clearly supports the message that S&OP is a business issue that focuses on creating a united approach across organizational silos. Clear ownership for S&OP and clear roles and responsibilities

Figure 6: S&OP practice

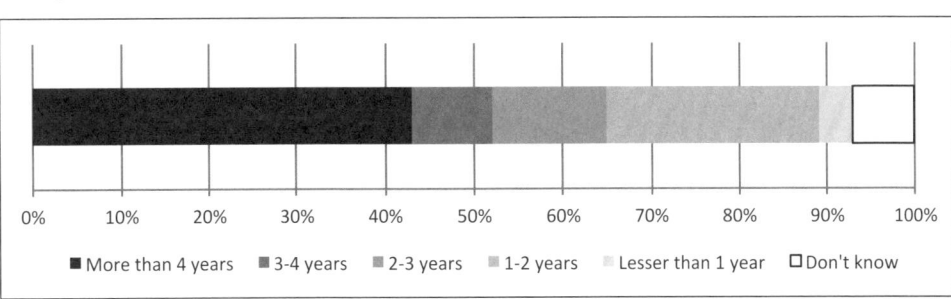

Figure 7: Success criteria for implementing S&OP

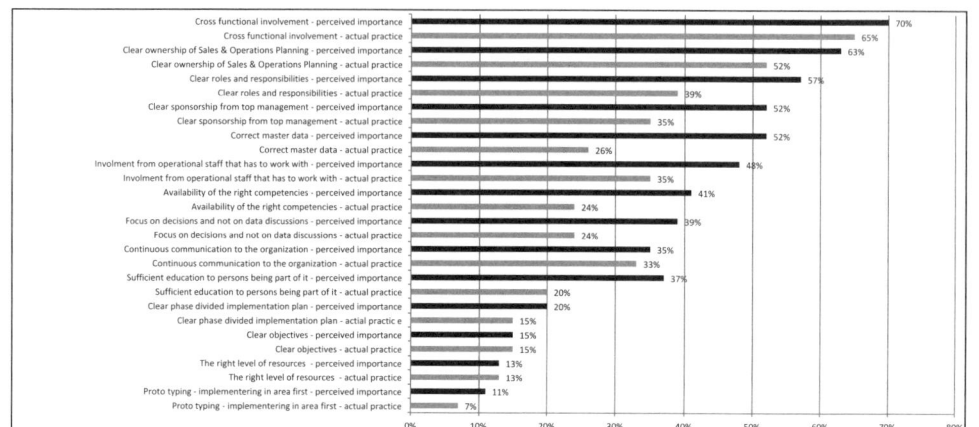

comes in as the second and third highest ranking success criteria respectively. It is interesting to notice that there is a big gap between the perceived importance on clear roles and responsibilities and the concrete practice of clear roles and responsibilities. It indicates that there is still a room for improvement in the organizational area regarding S&OP. Clear sponsorship from top management and correct master data ranks as the fourth and fifth highest success criteria respectively. Here too, there is relatively large gap between perceived importance about judgment of own practice and the concrete practice of judgment of own practice.

The respondents were also asked to evaluate the benefits achieved through implementing S&OP. It turns out that about half of the respondents believe that the introduction of S&OP has resulted in better management and leadership of the company (see Figure 8). Almost 30% of the respondents indicate that they have achieved benefits to some degree by implementing S&OP. Although there is an overall positive experience, there are still almost 40% who indicate that they benefit only to some extent, to a low degree or to a very low degree. This indicates that there is an opportunity for improvement with regard to both in preparing for S&OP and in the implementation processes as well as working according to the new procedures.

It is clear from Figure 9 that the topmost benefits of implementing S&OP are better capacity planning, improved transparency in plans, and better

Figure 8: Degree of better management and leadership due to S&OP

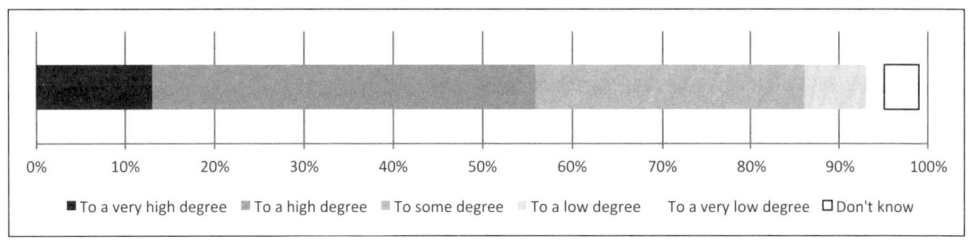

Figure 9: Perceived obtained benefits from S&OP implementation

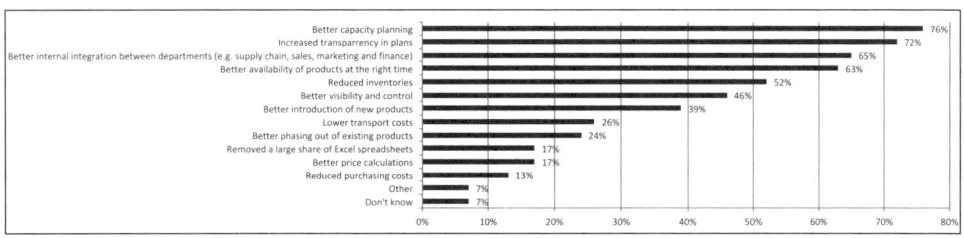

internal integration between the departments as well as improved availability of products at the right time. As shown in Figure 9, more than 60% of the respondents experience at least one of these top four benefits. This is in line with the observations in Figure 8, where management and leadership are expected to be improved when planning, transparency and integration is improved.

Summary

This mini-survey has focused on S&OP, which is an important integrative medium term planning process. The hope is that data from this survey can kick start discussions about S&OP in the company. How is the current practice? Is S&OP implemented? Why? Why not? And what are the explanations behind the current performance in this area? The survey indicates that the Danish companies are on their way to work with S&OP but it also reveals that there are still rooms for improvements. This potential for improvements exists in the companies that yet not have implemented S&OP and in the companies that are still in process of implementing S&OP; however there might be an additional need to ensure that the organizations actually pursue the new processes. The implementation of S&OP seems more to be about people and processes than about technique. A challenge with implementing S&OP seems also to be assuring and maintaining the right level of development-oriented competencies. We hope the future will bring new research on approaches to implement S&OP and a further diffusion of this important topic.

References

Barret, J. (2010), "Sales and operations planning maturity: What does it take to get and stay there?", Gartner RAS Core Research Note G00207249.

Feng, Y. and Sophie D'Amours, S. (2008), "The value of sales and operations planning in oriented strand board industry with make-to-order manufacturing system: Cross functional integration under deterministic demand and spot market recourse", *International Journal of Production Economics*, Vol. 115 No. 1, pp. 189-209.

Goodfellow, R. (2012), "Sales & Operations Planning, 1986-201: The story so far", *Operations Management*, Vol. 38 No. 4, pp. 18-26.

Grimson, J.A. and Pyke, D.F. (2007), "Sales and operations planning: An exploratory study and framework", *International Journal of Logistics Management*, Vol. 18 No. 3, pp. 322-46.

Thomé, A.M.T., Scavarda, L.F., Fernandez, N.S. and Scavarda, A.J. (2012), "Sales and operations planning and the firm performance", *International Journal of Productivity and Performance Management*, Vol. 61 No. 4, pp. 359-381.

The role of purchasing in open innovation: Fixed partners and flirts on new hunting grounds[1]

By: Thomas Johnsen and Ole Stegmann Mikkelsen

Introduction

To a greater extent companies are gradually looking at the purchasing function as an important player in the company, where focus not only is on cost minimization but also on value creation. One of the most important points where purchasing can contribute to value creation is by involving core suppliers in product development. Our experience from working with companies across Europe, for example within the automotive, aircraft, telecommunications and pharmaceutical industries, the best companies involve core suppliers both at the early stages of and last stages of product development projects. By working with selected suppliers, companies can reduce development costs and time-to-market, while improving product quality significantly. This is achieved by 'design-for-manufacture' i.e. by ensuring a development process that takes into account the production as well as sourcing right from the beginning of the product development process. One of the last decade latest buzzwords is 'open innovation', i.e. companies choose to involve external partners in the innovation process, rather than trying to manage the process internally: Do what you do best and connect to the rest.

However, there are some indications that the whole idea of supplier partnerships may not prove correct when companies face radical (also called

---

[1] This article is edited and translated to English from the Danish version: Johnsen, T. and Mikkelsen, O.S. (2013), "Indkøbets rolle i åben innovation: Faste partnere og flirts på nye jagtmarkeder", *DILF Orientering*, Vol. 50 No. 4, pp. 24-28.

disruptive or discontinuous) innovation. Such innovations involve either the development of brand new technology or the use of technology that has not previously been used in the company's industry. Think, for example, how cameras found their ways into mobile phones or how the development of new green products often requires new combinations of technology such as battery technology in cars. Here, the company's purchasing or sourcing function still plays an important role, but it often requires searches for opportunities beyond existing supply chains.

It is a new development that we are focusing on, but is it something that Danish companies have started to focus on? How good are Danish companies in involving their core suppliers in product development? What is the role of purchasing (or sourcing) in product development projects and how far are Danish companies in developing a procurement organization that deliberately seeks new technology outside the existing supply chain? These questions form the framework for the current mini-survey designed for *The Danish Supply Chain Panel*.

Results

The basis for this study includes the issue of how companies organize and utilize suppliers' knowledge as well as involve their suppliers' innovative capabilities. We started by asking whether the companies are working on innovation as a possible benefit from collaborating with suppliers? And, if they are not practicing, then we asked them whether they still believe they ought to do though they are not collaborating with suppliers.

As shown in Figure 1, 68% of the companies respond that they are working on innovation as a possible benefit from collaboration with suppliers.

Figure 1: Is innovation a possible outcome from collaboration with suppliers?

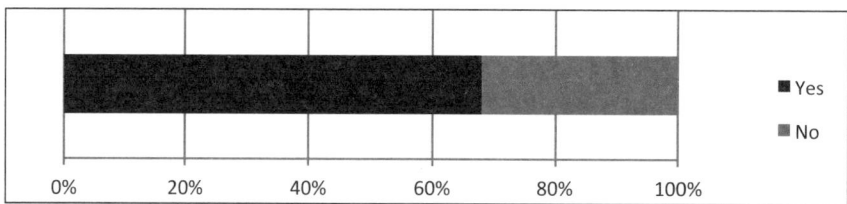

In addition, we asked the 32% of the companies who do not work with innovation as a possible benefit from supplier collaboration, if they think they should do that, and 62% of them answered that they work with innovation as a possible benefit from supplier collaboration.

Although 38% of the companies that does not work with innovation as a benefit of supplier collaboration do not consider it as relevant, the figures indicate that vendors as an innovative resource have some attention. But there is still a potential for improvement. Thus, only 12.2% of the surveyed companies believe that it should not be a topic for their business.

The next question focus on how much of the company's total supplier base is believed being capable to contribute with innovation as a part of the relationship. Our experience says that it is important to focus on selected core suppliers, so how is it reflected in the Danish companies?

As shown in Figure 2, 47% of the companies estimate that 0-20% of their supplier base is able to contribute with innovation. And, 21% of the respondents estimate that 21-40% of their supplier base is able to contribute with innovation, while a small proportion (13%) of the companies estimates that 41-60% of their suppliers can do this. Only 2% of the respondents indicate that over 60% of the suppliers can contribute with innovation as part of their collaboration. It is interesting that a relatively large proportion of the companies (18%) are not able to assess to what extent their supplier base is capable in contributing towards innovation. This can be due to several factors, including the fact that companies do not focus on suppliers' ability to contribute with innovation. However, it is also interesting that almost one fifth of the companies do not have a picture of the potential of their supplier base as a source of innovation.

Figure 2: Share of the supplier base being able to contribute with innovation

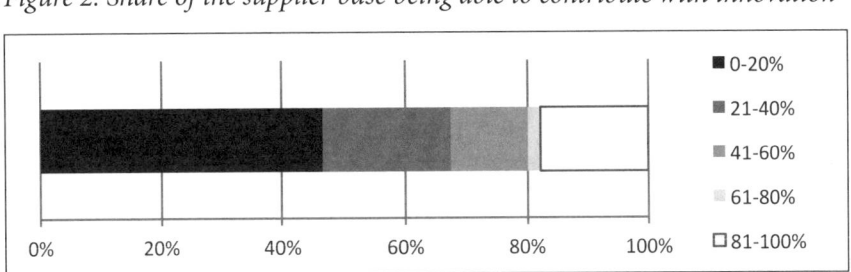

When are suppliers involved?

Early supplier involvement is one of the opportunities companies have for bringing suppliers' know-how into play. Traditionally, the idea is that the earlier the relevant suppliers are involved in the product development project, the better the performance can be achieved. It is in the early development stages where the most part of the overall cost structure of the product is being determined. The earlier changes in product design can be made for better and cheaper production, the less costly it is to make the changes. It is more costly to change a product that is already on the market than a product that is in the idea phase (in product development). With an early supplier involvement of selected suppliers, the supplier's knowledge and skills can easily come into play if the supplier first gets the opportunity to bring ideas to the table rather than giving an opportunity to bring ideas when the product is close to reach manufacturing. We therefore asked the panel a question about the involvement of suppliers in the phases from idea generation to ramp up in manufacturing.

As shown in Figure 3, most of the companies are good at early supplier involvement, although many find that their current practice is lagging behind from what it ought to be. In particular, companies consider that

Figure 3: Phases involving relevant suppliers (several marks are allowed; number are in percentages

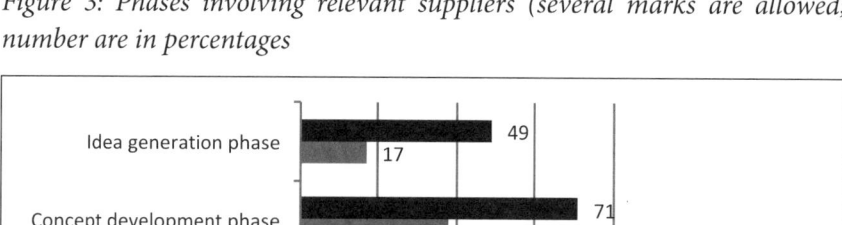

suppliers should be more closely involved in the idea generation phase and the conceptual development phase; wherein some companies consider that suppliers should be involved more in basic design and production planning phases, and some companies find that suppliers should be involved to a lesser degree when the product has entered manufacturing. This is in line with the above considerations that companies can achieve clear benefits from involving suppliers earlier in the processes.

Outsourcing versus insourcing

In order to determine whether suppliers should be integrated into product development and innovation projects, an important starting point is to conduct a make-or-buy analysis. This is a question about where company defines the line of what they are managing internally and what they choose to outsource. The tendency has been that many companies have chosen to focus on their core competencies, and therefore outsource everything that is not perceived as "core". But is this also a question that Danish companies are considering? We thus asked whether the companies are analyzing which competencies or technologies they want to maintain internally, which competencies or technologies they want to outsource or which competencies or technologies they want to insource or develop internally in the company. The responses are shown in Figure 4.

Only 24% of the companies conduct analyzes to a high or very high degree to determine which competencies and / or technologies should be handled in-house in the company and which ones are to be handled exter-

Figure 4: Does your company conduct technology, competence outsourcing and insourcing analyzes?

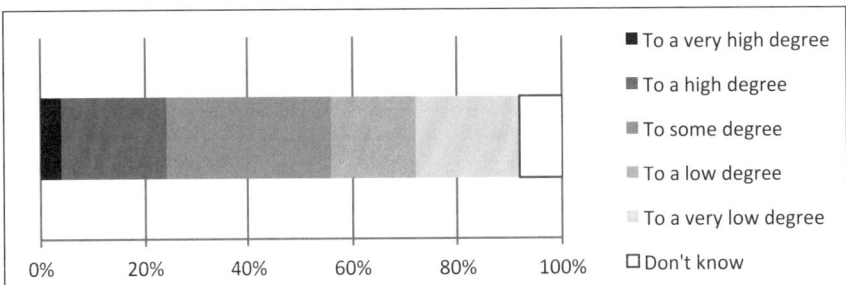

nally. One the other hand, it is surprising to notice that 36% of the companies are carrying out such analyzes only to a low or very low degree. We can also observe that more than 30% of the companies do respond that they are neither to a degree nor to a low degree carrying out such analyzes, which confirms our suspicion that there are relatively few companies who make decisions about out / insourcing on a well-analyzed strategic foundation.

Open innovation

The issue of open innovation lies in direct extension of the make-or-buy question. In an open innovation strategy, the company focuses on quite a few core competencies and seeks deliberately to open the process that was previously closed. Thus, the procurement function should play a key role in the sourcing of technologies and competencies adjacent to the core competences of company. We therefore asked the panel to which degree they do practice open innovation. The responses are shown in Figure 5.

Figure 5: Degree of practicing open innovation

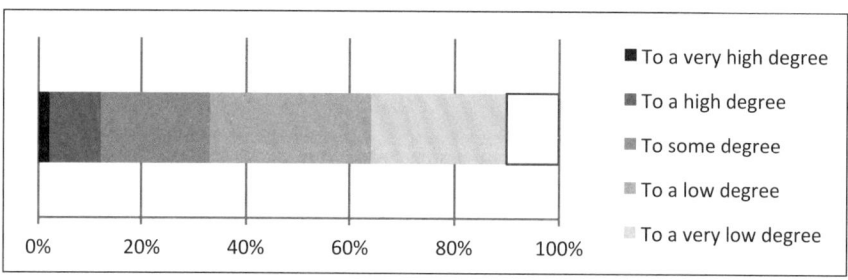

Figure 6: Degree to which companies are looking for new innovation opportunities in their supply markets

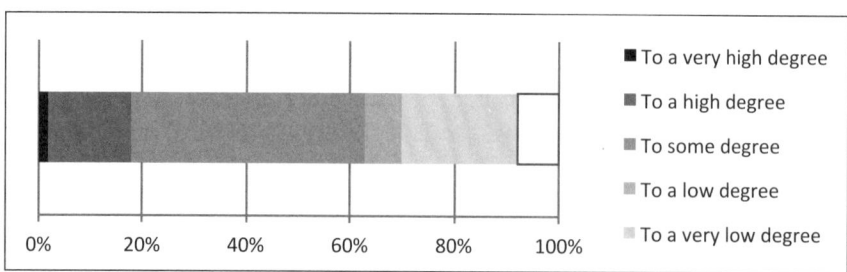

Figure 5 shows that open innovation is not very much prevalent. Only 12% of the companies are practicing open innovation to high or very high degree, while 57% of the companies indicate that they only practice open innovation to a low or very low degree. We asked further whether the companies are looking for new innovations/innovative technologies at their supply markets.

The picture here is almost the same as before. Only 18% of the companies argue that they are to a high or very high degree seeking for new innovation opportunities in their supply markets, while 29% of the companies indicate that they are only to a low or very low degree looking for such innovation opportunities. In a world where innovation is steadily nurturing, it might seem paradoxical that there is so little search for innovation opportunities in the supply markets.

The role of purchasing

We also asked whether seeking new innovations outside existing supply chains is a part of the purchasing's responsibility, and in addition, if it should be.

As shown in Figure 7, only 14% of the companies indicate that there to a high degree (0% indicates to a very high degree) is a defined task for corporate procurement, to seek new innovations outside the existing supply chain. However, 52% of the companies indicate that it to a high or very high degree should be defined as a part of the purchasing responsibility. Only 10% of the companies indicate that it to a low or very low degree

Figure 7: Degree to which seeking new innovations is part of purchasing's responsibility

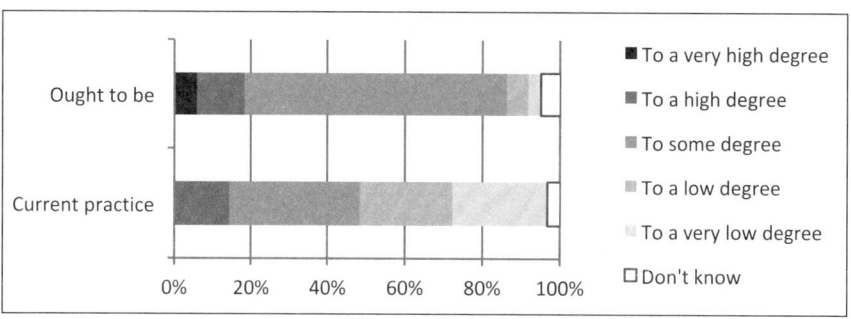

Figure 8: Dedicated group or department to identify new innovation opportunities in the supply chain?

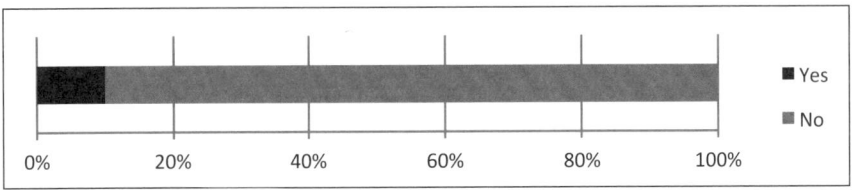

should be a part of the purchasing responsibility to seek new innovations outside the company's current supply chain. Thus, most of the respondents identify the potential in spite of them not yet having a system in place.

In connection with the above, it is interesting to investigate whether the companies have dedicated specific groups or departments whose primary task is to identify new innovation opportunities. Only 10% of the surveyed companies have dedicated a group or department with such tasks (see Figure 8).

And, of the 10% who have a dedicated group or department, where the primary task is to identify new innovation opportunities, we further asked them whether this group is separated from the general purchasing organization (see Figure 9). Here, 17% of them have chosen structurally to separate this function from the company's general purchasing organization. Most of the respondents did reply that they have chosen to integrate this activity as part of the company's general purchasing organization.

Figure 9: To which degree is the group/department separated from the general purchasing organization?

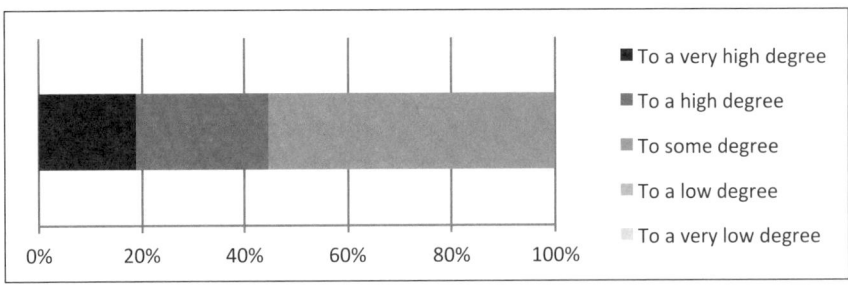

Supplier relations

Traditionally, many have considered supplier relationships as a continuum between two extremes – transaction-based versus relationship-based. Supplier involvement in connection with product development usually requires a form of strategic partnership where there is a close and trustworthy collaboration. However, recent research shows that when companies face radical innovation, it is necessary with short "flirts" with potential suppliers outside the company's existing supply chain. Flirts with suppliers outside of the existing supply chain might be necessary to access brand new technologies that the existing vendors are not able to offer. If you go to the usual suppliers you can end up in a competence trap. Often the time horizon for these strategic "flirts" is a single project, after which the collaboration is terminated. We therefore asked the panel whether they use such strategic "flirts". The first question concerns the application, while the second question deals with the degree to which such an application is a deliberate part of the company's strategy.

Figure 10 shows that 28% of the companies use strategic flirts to increase their innovation output whereas 50% of the companies do not use such flirts. Moreover, 22% of the respondents are not aware whether their company has this type of collaboration. Of the 28% who answered yes for using strategic flirts, we asked them whether it is a deliberate and explicit part of the company's strategy (see Figure 11).

Almost half of the respondents did answer that it to a high or very high degree is a conscious and explicit part of the company's strategy, while 19% of the respondents answered that it is not a conscious and explicit part of the company's strategy.

Figure 10: Does the company use strategic "flirts"?

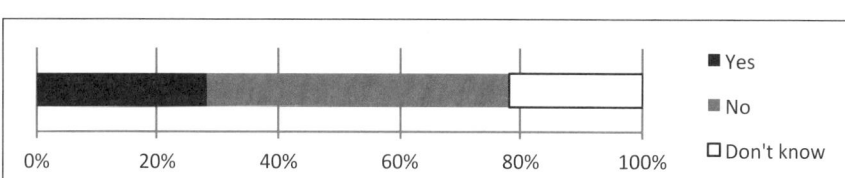

Figure 11: To which degree is strategic "flirts" a conscious and explicit part of the company's strategy?

- To a very high degree
- To a high degree
- To some degree
- To a low degree
- To a very low degree

Barriers for supplier innovation

The identification and exploitation of suppliers' innovation potential is not an easy and trivial task. Therefore we are interested to find out what are the various perceived essential barriers in identifying and absorbing innovations from the supplier base.

As shown in Figure 12, lack of time and human resources are in particular considered as great barriers. Lack of such scare resources is also reported as a barrier in other mini-surveys among *The Danish Supply Chain*

Figure 12: Barriers for identifying and absorbing innovations from the supplier base (numbers are percentages)

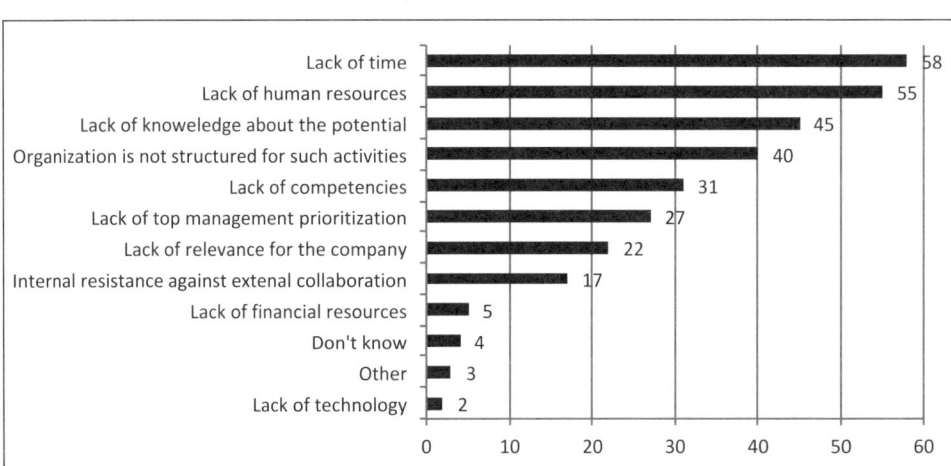

- Lack of time: 58
- Lack of human resources: 55
- Lack of knoweledge about the potential: 45
- Organization is not structured for such activities: 40
- Lack of competencies: 31
- Lack of top management prioritization: 27
- Lack of relevance for the company: 22
- Internal resistance against extenal collaboration: 17
- Lack of financial resources: 5
- Don't know: 4
- Other: 3
- Lack of technology: 2

Panel. Other central barriers are lack of knowledge about the potential of the supplier base which helps in bringing the suppliers innovation capabilities into play and the organization not is designed for such activities i.e. not having the right structure or the right skills. The lack of insight into the potential can be due to several things, including a too high focus on operation and "firefighting" rather than on focusing on the future.

We notice particularly the organizational barrier as interesting because it is linked to the fact that the company's structure and processes do not support the identification and absorption of the potential contribution of the supplier base. In spite of Danish companies have stopped some silo thinking, there still seems to be opportunities in implementing more cross-functional processes. It is interesting that 28% of the companies indicate lack of prioritization from top management as a barrier in identification and absorption of the potential contribution of the supplier base. It is strange that the companies in the light of the increasing competition still lack in prioritizing and utilizing suppliers' innovation capabilities.

Conclusion

This article has focused on the suppliers' potential contribution towards innovation. Early and close involvement of core suppliers in product development projects is gradually becoming an accepted "best practice" and being applied by many companies across the globe. This mini-survey confirm that many Danish companies have realized the effectiveness of this practice, although some companies acknowledge that they could be much better at involving core suppliers, both earlier and closer to the product development process.

It is surprising that only 24% of the companies perform analyzes to determine which competencies and/or technologies should be handled internally and which ones should be handled externally. It is not surprising that outsourcing decisions are taken on too fragile "cheaper price foundation" in many companies, but especially in the context of innovation, companies should analyze the opportunities and consequences of outsourcing core competencies and technologies.

In extension of the issue of outsourcing, this study has also focused on open innovation. This is a relatively new concept that has a direct impact for purchasing functions within the supply chain management in general.

Few (only 12%) of the companies who practice open innovation, indicates that it is an area that requires more attention. The last part of the survey focus on a new trend. The companies were asked if they were looking for more radical, or disruptive, innovations outside the existing supply chain. Research suggests that there might be a disadvantage of focusing more on incremental innovation and might be directly unsuitable for radical innovation while working closely with the existing suppliers within the current supply chain. Hence "flirts" with unknown suppliers beyond the existing supply chain might be a good idea. Therefore the respondents were asked if they use such strategic flirts, and 28% of the companies did report that they do strategic flirts. Over half of these respondents even reply, that is a conscious and explicit part of the company's strategy. It is very interesting and absolutely something new that other companies could learn from.

Organizational-wise the supply chain is a bag of mixed candies[1]

By: Jan Stentoft and Thomas Johnsen

Introduction

Since the introduction of Supply Chain Management (SCM) concepts in 1982, there have been found many discussions that were held about whether the SCM is just a new name for logistics or whether it has specific characteristics that goes beyond the logistics concept. Others even see SCM as an extension of the procurement function. The purpose of this article is not to open such discussions again. In this article, we consider SCM as a holistic concept to analyze, control and manage information, material and financial flows both in individual companies as well as in chains and networks of companies in order to meet customers' needs for goods and services. If SCM should play a role beyond just a broad definition of logistics or procurement, it must have an academic foundation in several functions that span both the upstream and downstream processes including logistics, purchasing (or sourcing), production, planning and distribution. The entire rationale for SCM is that companies cannot compete on their own, but need to interact with other resources and competencies in its value networks. SCM plays a pivotal role in business performance. If the supply chains not operates effectively, it may affect the cost consumption, product and service quality, and delivery performance negatively – i.e. the core competitive parameters.

SCM is becoming more important and complex with increasing and fluctuating price levels, transport and logistics costs, and with the movement

---

[1] This article is edited and translated to English from the Danish version Arlbjørn, J.S. and Johnsen, T. (2013), "Organisatorisk er supply chain området en pose blandet bolsjer", *DILF Orientering*, Vol. 50 No. 3, pp. 38-41.

of manufacturing to low wage countries. Some of these low-wage countries have experienced significant increases in wage levels, which have eroded some of the economic benefits along with a number of other indirect costs. Companies also experience increased supply risks (e.g. in terms of quality problems), longer lead times, and an inappropriate level of stock building which runs the risk to be obsolete). So there is a higher requirement than ever before to view SCM from an "end-to-end" perspective i.e. the flow from raw material suppliers through subcontractors over distribution to end customers. This can be achieved through an SCM organization that is both strategic and cross functional.

The issues of the SCM location in the company is the background for this study based on the responses from *The Danish Supply Chain Panel*. The interest is centered on to uncover whether Danish companies actually have an overlying and strategic SCM department, which includes the earlier individual and more operational oriented departments or whether Danish companies simply have renamed logistics departments to SCM departments? Additionally, to disclose how well equipped are Danish companies' supply chain organization to handle current and future challenges? This will be further explored in this article.

Supply chain vis-a-vis other functions

The Danish Supply Chain Panel was first asked to answer whether their company has a formal supply chain function/department. As shown in Figure 1, 84% of the respondents indicate that there is a formal supply chain function/department, which indicates that the area has gained organizational responsiveness.

SCM is a broad technical field. Therefore, it is of interest to look at the professional functions that are organized under SCM. Figure 2 reveals that the supply chain function primarily includes logistics (86%) and is followed by planning, inventory management and procurement. Only 29% of the surveyed companies consider production as a part of the supply chain function, which in turn indicates that production is usually not part of the supply chain function. IT does not seem particularly to be organized under the SCM. And, under "other" 31% of the surveyed companies indicate functions related to e.g.:

Figure 1: Does the company have a formal supply chain function/department?

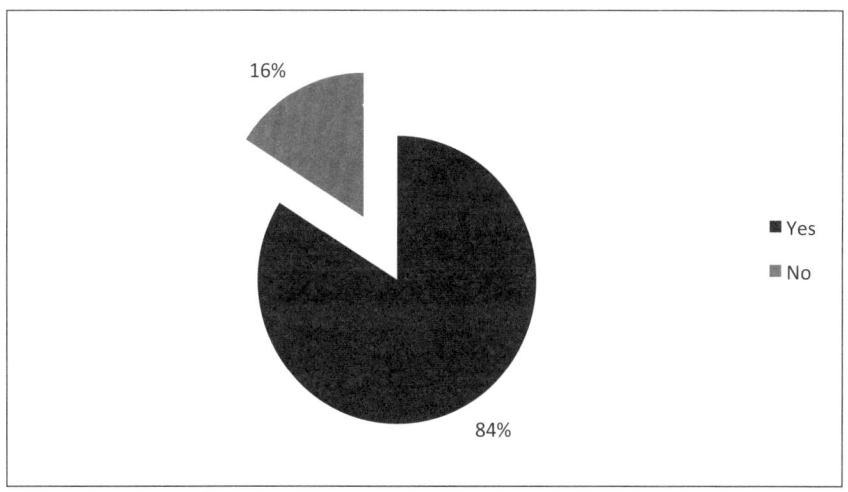

- Customer Service
- Controlling of cost to serve
- IT support of supply chain processes
- Project management (new products, implementation of IT systems, the establishment of new warehouse, etc.)
- Master Data
- Shipping and transportation
- Environment
- Legal work (licensing, tariffs etc.)

In order to investigate more concrete about the functional areas that belongs to their SCM department, the panel was respectively asked directly whether logistics or procurement act as the company's overall SCM department. These two areas were selected to have a representative of either an upstream or a downstream focus. According to Figure 3, 41% of the surveyed companies believe that the logistics department acts as the company's overall SCM department, which indicate an outgoing and customer oriented SCM focus. On the other hand, 55% of the surveyed companies think that logistics does not represent the company's overall SCM department. A reason for this might be that SCM in those companies is more represented by purchasing and /or other functions in an overall compre-

Figure 2: The supply chain function's content areas

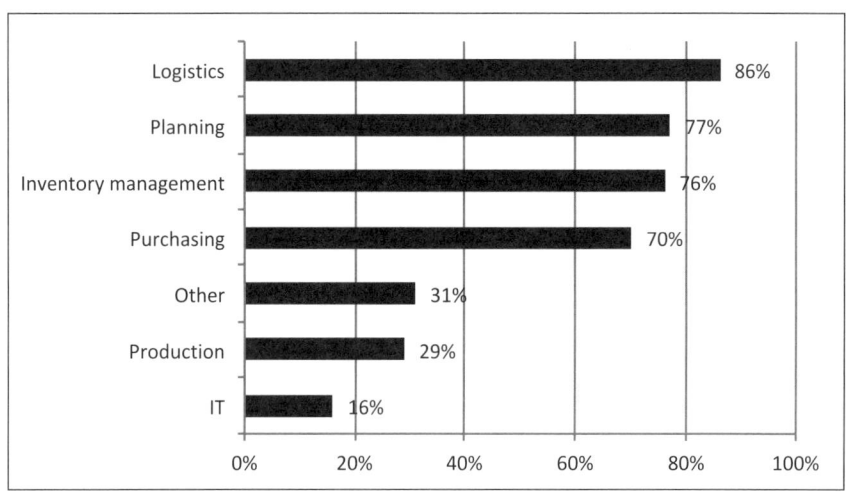

hensive SCM department (see Figure 2). Almost 27% of the respondents report that purchasing serves as the company's overall SCM department (see Figure 4) and 72% of the respondents report that purchasing does not represent the company's overall SCM department. This clearly indicates that SCM is broader than purchasing.

The Danish Supply Chain Panel was also asked about their practice concerning reporting structure between logistics and purchasing to SCM. As it

Figure 3: The logistics functions act as the SCM department

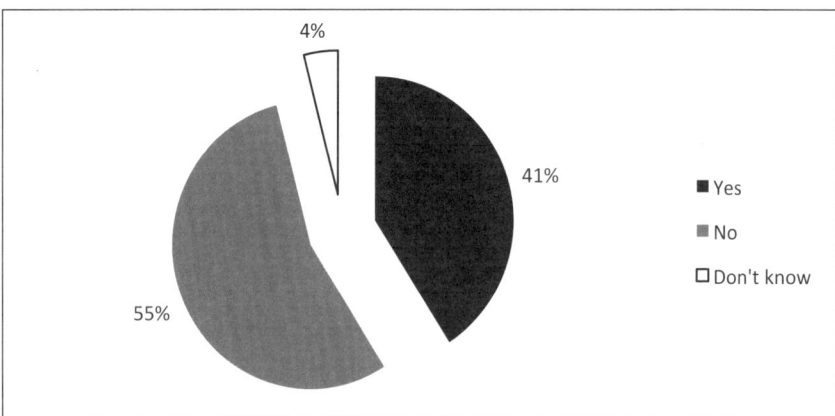

Figure 4: The sourcing/purchasing department act as the SCM department

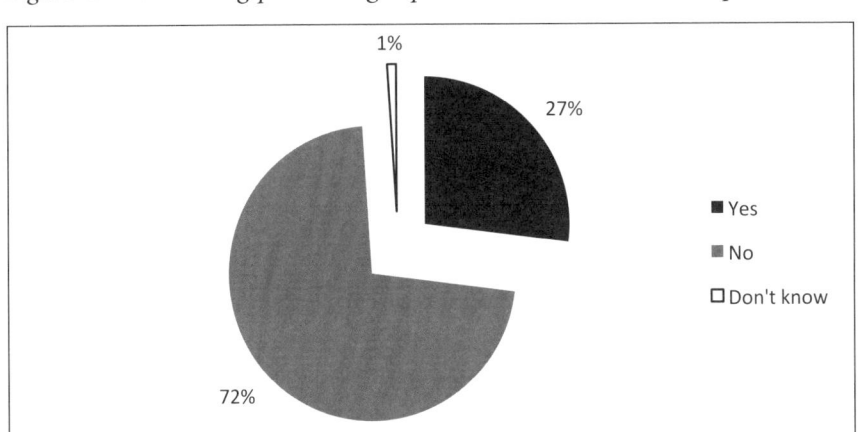

is clear from Figure 5, 53% of the respondents indicate that logistics reports to the SCM department. When compared with the answers in Figure 3 (in which 41% indicated that logistics acts as a company's SCM department), this may indicate that the SCM is a broader concept than logistics. Among the 43% of the respondents who answered that logistics does not refer to a SCM department, we found respondents who answered that their company does not have a SCM department (see Figure 1). On the other hand,

Figure 5: Reporting structure

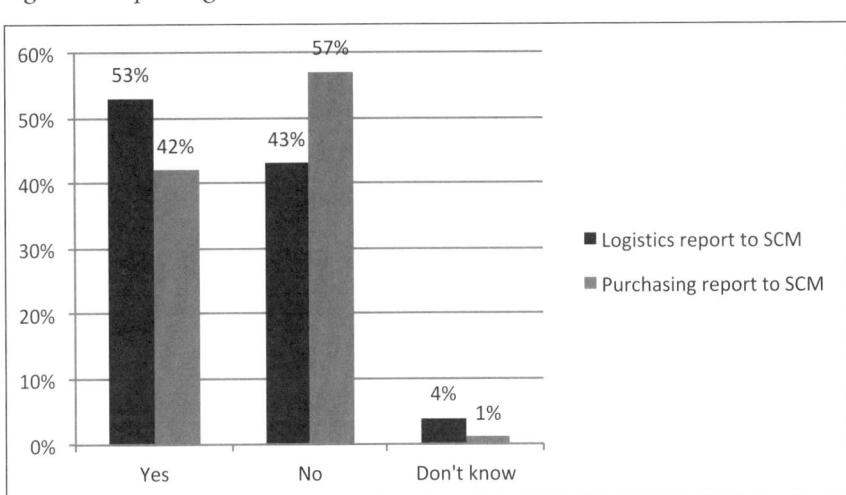

Figure 6: The integration role of the SCM department

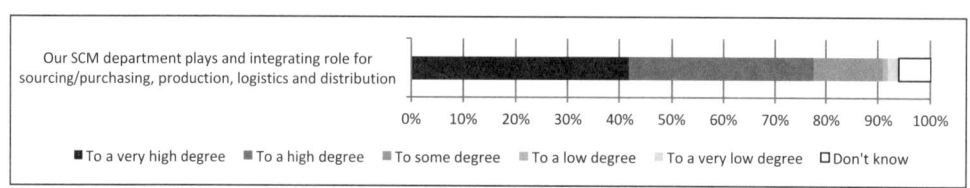

42% of respondents indicate that purchasing reports to SCM department, wherein 57% of the respondents indicate that purchasing does not report to SCM department. This clearly conveys that purchasing does not refer to company's overall SCM department. Thus, Figure 5 indicates that downstream and customer-oriented activities to a higher degree are organized under SCM than upstream related activities.

The respondents was asked to decide whether their internal SCM department plays an integration role for the functions like sourcing/procurement, operation /production, logistics and distribution (see Figure 6). It is clear that 76% of the respondents to a very high or to a high degree believe that their SCM department has this integration role across functions. This indicates an implicit message of SCM playing a central role in creating a cross-functional organization in order to break down sub-optimizations in traditional functional "silos". In practice, it can be recommended to determine what form of integration role SCM has to play; to which degree this actually takes place and which initiatives that must be started to close any gap between the desired and the actual level.

Is the SCM function really strategic?

Several strong arguments exists supporting that SCM should play a key strategic role in the company. Our experience shows that many have the perception that their SCM function is strategic, but in practice they actually have little influence on the company's strategic decisions. Therefore, *The Danish Supply Chain Panel* was also asked some questions related to their representation in their company's top management and their genuine participation in the company's strategic management process. Almost 61% of the respondents indicate that SCM is represented in the top management within the company (see Figure 7). This indicates that these companies

Figure 7: Representation of SCM in top management

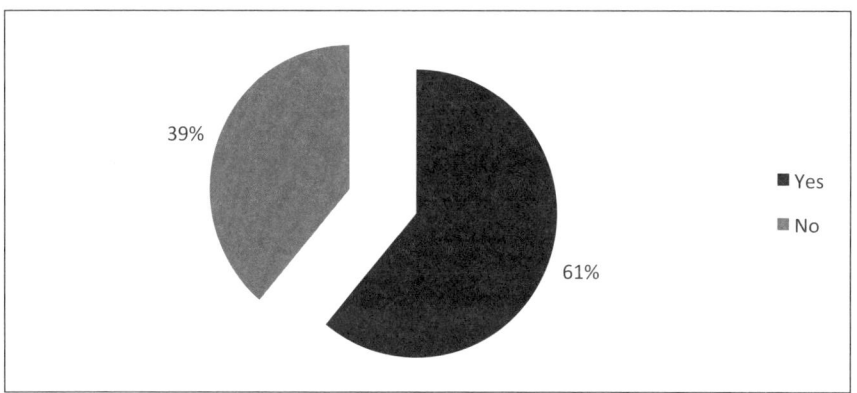

have recognized SCM as a strategic source for maintaining and developing competitive advantages (e.g. with a concurrent focus on both revenue enhancing and cost-minimizing activities). On the other hand, 39% of the respondents indicate that SCM is not represented in the top management within the company. In these companies, there may exists a need for internal sales efforts to market and create a greater understanding of what SCM really is about, and why it is important to consider SCM through strategic lenses.

Through this current mini-survey, it is possible to identify a strategic importance of SCM among the respondents, with 84% of the respondents acknowledging SCM as a part of their strategic planning process (see Figure 8). In other words, even if SCM is not directly represented in top management, for example with a supply chain director position, the main perception among the panel members is that SCM, after all, is part of the company's planning process. It is also supported by the results represented in Figure 9, where 77% of the respondents indicate that they, to a very high or to a high degree, are familiar with their company's strategic goals. Data in this mini-survey does not inform anything about the extent to which the respondents believe that SCM is contributing in achieving the strategic objectives.

The panel was also asked to consider whether their company's SCM department performance is measured by its contribution to the overall business success. And, 61% of the respondents consider (see Figure 10) that

Figure 8: Inclusion of supply chain in the strategic planning process

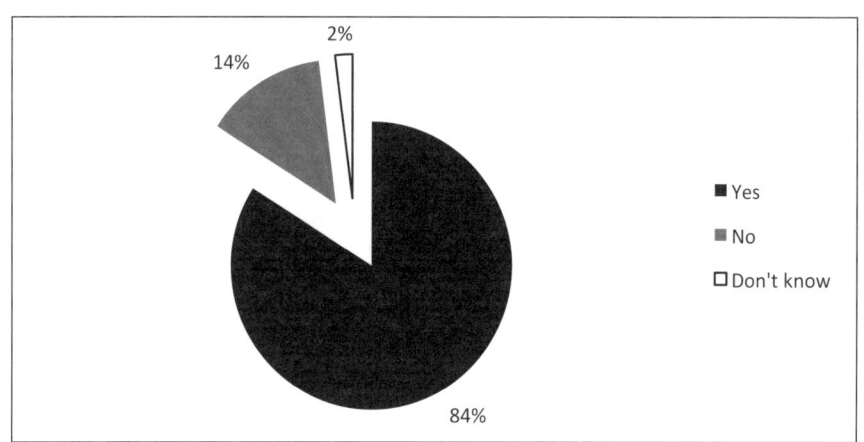

there are targets concerning the SCM department contribution to the company's overall performance. This indicates that there is some strategic link between the supply chain functions and the overall business strategy.

The results of this mini-survey has so far indicated that there appears to be an agreement on the importance of representing SCM in top management, and its contribution towards the company's overall strategic objec-

Figure 9: Familiarity to the company's strategic goals within supply chain

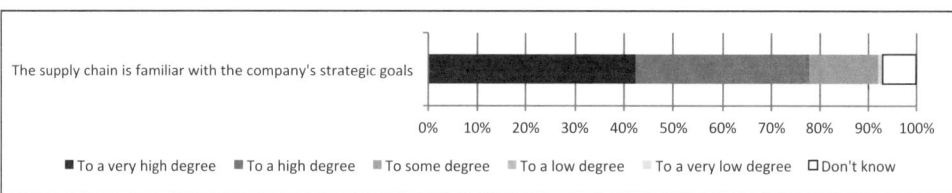

Figure 10: Performance measurement of the SCM department

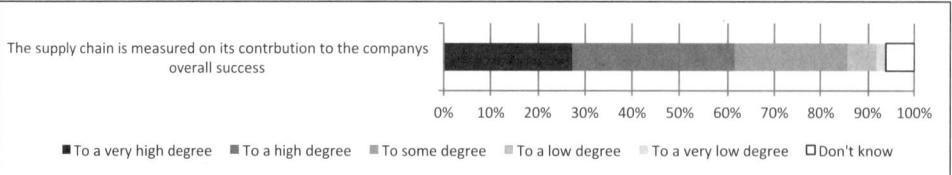

Figure 11: Level of a formal long-term plan for the supply chain

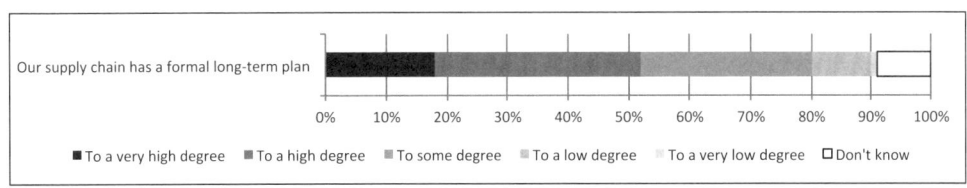

tives. Now we take a closer look at how many of the respondents do have a specific SCM strategy in the form of a long term plan. Although 52% of the respondents indicate that they to a very high or to a high degree have a long-term plan for SCM, it is remarkable that almost half of the respondents are less convinced about this fact (see Figure 11). There exists a task to develop a supply chain strategy and link it as well as interact with the corporate strategy.

Conclusion

This mini-survey has focused on the coordination of the SCM work. SCM seem to have found organizational foothold among the panel members. Though SCM is a broad academic area, why the organizational content of SCM functions seems to appear as a bag of mixed candies. One explanation for this may be that the supply chain functions among the respondents are responsible for solving different tasks. Some companies have, for example, many products and services (many variants) and some companies have many different types of customers and distribution channels. Some companies own large shares of their value chains and wherein other owns a minimal part. Some produce products and services with a relatively long life-cycle, others the opposite. Some companies have great complexity in their procurement tasks (many articles from many vendors) while others have more simple tasks. Likewise, we can continue with examples. The point here is that the actual organization of SCM must match both the operational as well as the strategic tasks. One possible application of the results of this mini-survey may be to evaluate how the SCM work is organized within a company? Are there "silo" problems that need to be addressed? What is the strategic importance of SCM in the company? Does the top management offer the necessary attention to SCM? How is SCM organized today in relation to the SCM tasks to be solved? What is the most efficient way to organize SCM in the company? SCM is not a static management, but on the other hand it is a dynamic management, therefore companies should continuously organize and adjust the issues in response to changes in both external conditions (such as market and competition) as well as in internal conditions such as (products, services and ownership structure).

Time-to-market: A cross-functional process with a gap between theory and practice[1]

By: Jan Stentoft

Introduction

This article focuses on the time, beginning from recognizing the need for a new product or a new service over the design phase, manufacturing and logistics, so it is ready for sale in the market. This is also called the time-to-market (T2M) process. An effective T2M process can increase competitiveness by launching products and services faster to markets than competitors. This enable firms to achieve faster break evens on investments in product and service development and a higher overall profit and return on investment as well as lower financial risk. T2M is a cross-functional process which requires project management skills and clearly defined roles and responsibilities shift. If such competencies are in shortage, the company runs the risk to operate with paralyzed decision-making processes, which in turn can lead to unclear defined specifications, delays in delivery and dearth in deliveries. This article encourages decision makers to evaluate the existing T2M processes in order to examine whether the processes need to be dusted off.

As shown in Figure 1, the understanding of T2M process begins in this article with an acknowledgment and understanding of market needs. Precisely, what are the markets and customers actual demands of products and services and at what time? To illustrate the practice in Power Point is often

---

[1] This article is edited and translated to English from the Danish version Arlbjørn, J.S. (2013), "Time-to-market: En tværorganisatorisk proces med et gab mellem teori og praksis", *DILF Orientering*, Vol. 50 No. 2, pp. 10-15.

Figure 1: Time-to-market

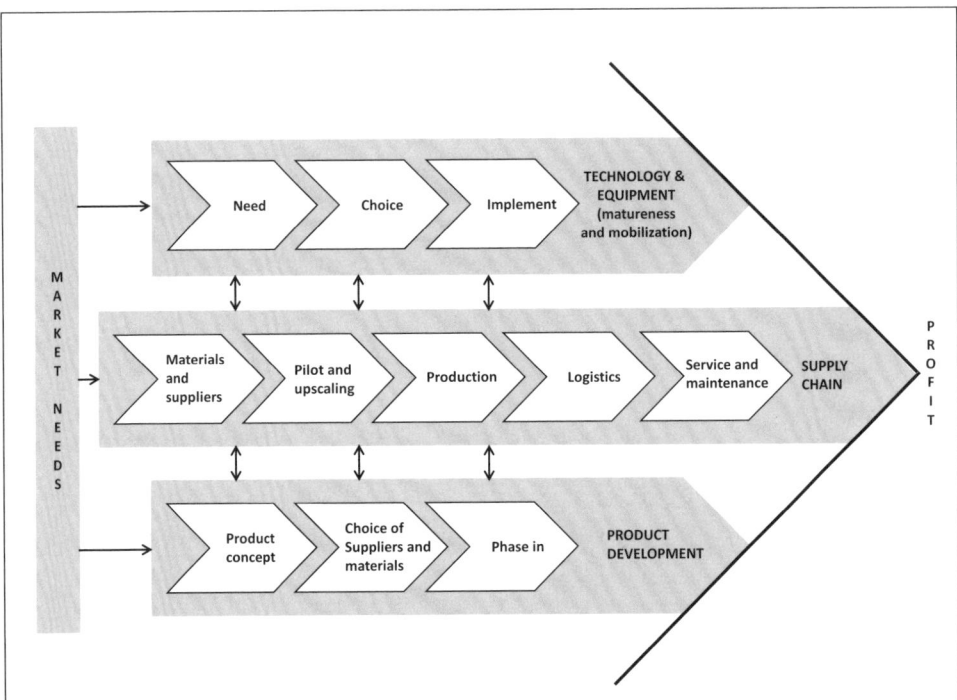

a simple and trivial task. However, the reality is often something different and far more complex than what can be illustrated.

The relatively linear approach, as shown in Figure 1, may well consist of a number of return flows to the previous sub-processes. The understanding of the market needs form the basis for initiating three parallel processes, respectively: 1) product development, 2) maturation and mobilization of technology and equipment and 3) the physical supply chain flow. Lack of focus on T2M can lead to delays in launching new products, loss of earnings and market shares and an unnecessary waste of resources (materials, equipment and working hours). Well-functioning T2M processes are typically characterized by:
- A clear understanding of market and customer needs
- A well-defined and optimized product development process with clear shifts in roles and responsibilities in the process flow

- A realistic development plan
- Availability of the appropriate financial and human resources
- Early involvement of supply chain incl. the Technical Department; support for parallel processes
- Reuse of design, materials and suppliers

In the following, we look closer to the answers from *The Danish Supply Chain Panel* on specific questions related to T2M.

Perceived importance and concrete practice

The Danish Supply Chain Panel has been asked to consider the extent to which the T2M process is perceived as a strategic competitive factor. As shown in Figure 2, almost 89% of the respondents indicate that, to a very high or to a high degree, T2M has perceived as an important strategic competitive parameter.

The respondents were also asked about the degree to which the companies are consciously working with T2M as a strategic competitive factor. It is clear from Figure 2, around 62% of the respondents believe that, to a very high degree or to a high degree, they put much focus on working with T2M. Thus, the actual practice seems to be lagging behind than the perceived importance, which might indicate an opportunity for new improvements within this area.

Figure 2: Perceived importance and concrete practice of the time-to-market

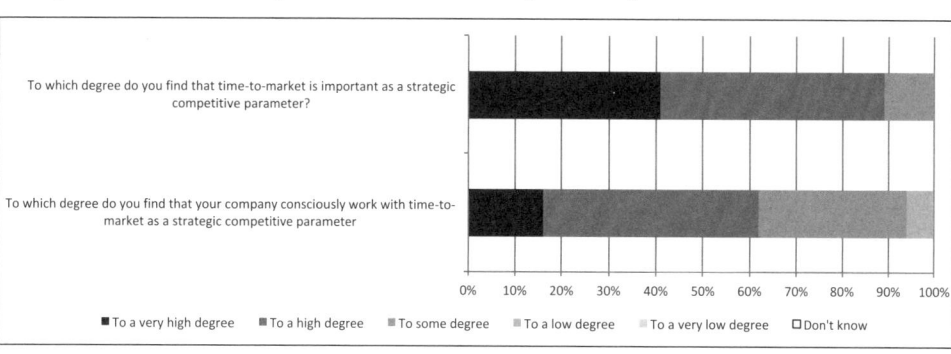

Cross-functional processes

As mentioned earlier T2M is a cross-functional matter and therefore, the panel was asked about their concrete practice of the processes between the three main functions – such as sales/marketing, product development and supply chain. Figure 3 shows that 35% of the respondents to a very high degree or to a high degree find that their T2M processes are well established between the product and supply chain. Almost 61% of the respondents to some degree or to a very low degree indicate there is a room for improvement. Approximately 34% of the respondents to a very high degree or to a high degree believe that there are well established processes between sales/marketing and supply chain; whereas 63% of the respondents only to some degree to a very low degree believe that there are well established processes between sales/marketing and supply chain. This also indicates that there is a need for improved processes. Finally, 33% of the respondents indicate to a very high or a high degree that there are well established processes between sales/marketing and product development; wherein 61% of the respondents only to some degree to a very low degree believe that this is happening.

Measuring Time-to-Market

"What gets measured gets done" is a saying in business environment. This is one of the principles underlying the overall performance management. Measurements can help the companies to monitor whether they develop in

Figure 3: Time-to-market processes between sales marketing, supply chain and product development

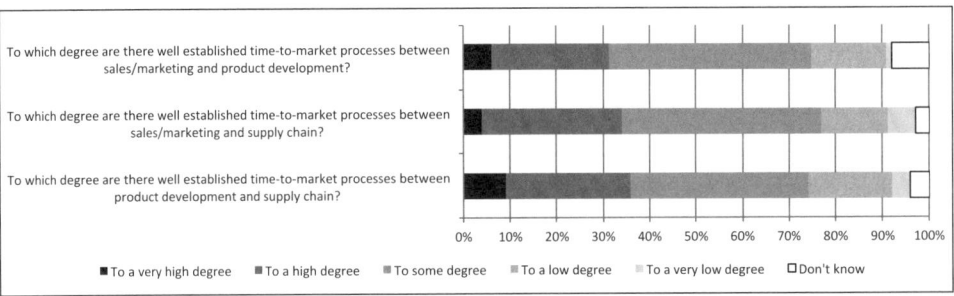

Figure 4: Performance management of the time-to-market processes

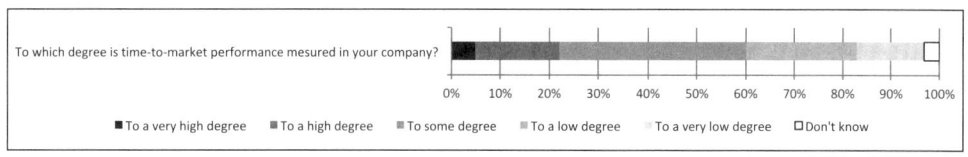

the right direction and in the right pace. Therefore, it is interesting to ask *The Danish Supply Chain Panel* about the degree to which the companies are having concrete measures on T2M processes. Figure 4 reveals that only 22% of the respondents believe that the performance management of T2M takes place to a very high or to a high degree. Whereas, 38% of the respondents indicate that the performance management of T2M takes place only to some degree. Moreover, 37% of the respondents consider that the performance management of T2M merely takes place to a low or very low degree. If improvements required in this area, then the companies better have to initiate an active measurement practice on this T2M process.

Barriers for effective time-to-market processes

T2M processes can at first glance look quite affordable and straightforward to implement. However, actual practice often shows a different picture. Therefore, the panel members were asked about the main barriers to implement effective T2M processes from their perspective.

As shown in Figure 5, the highest ranked barrier is "too much silo mentality". We have now worked, in more than 30 years in the Supply Chain Management discipline, to tear down the silos within the companies, thus promoting cross-functional business processes. In spite of massive messages to avoid silo thinking, it seems that these efforts have still not broken the walls. The second highest scoring barrier is "missing target management of the time-to-market". As discussed in the previous section, the performance management can help to ensure attention and management focuses. Then follows the barriers such as lack of a project model with clear go/no go gates; too much focus on operational task at the expense of development tasks in cross-functional T2M processes and staff from product development and sales are the kings – supply chain staff just has to deliver. Under "other", respondents indicate further potential barriers like a lack of under-

Figure 5: Barriers to time-to-market processes (several marks allowed)

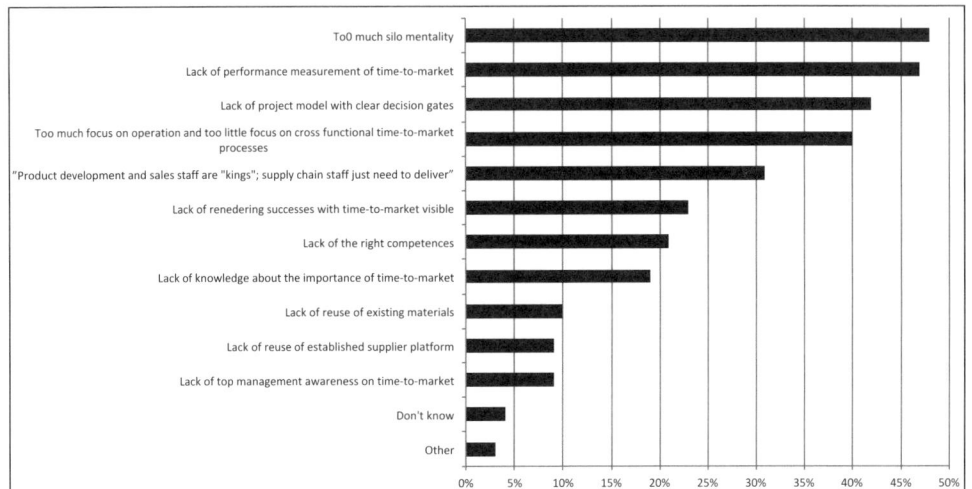

standing for closing the projects in the right way (including follow-up and contacts with product managers and project managers in case of challenges with the new products and services); lost support when the novelty of product and service fade; constant changes of performance specifications; too high requirements on low cost prices; deadlines are too often through from top management; and suppliers that do not deliver to the specified quality level.

T2M processes are concerned with delivering new products and services to the market and thus establishing them into the company's existing product and service program. In practice, there is often a lack of management focus on phasing in new products. In general, introducing something new is now receiving much attention. In contrast, this does not apply, at the other end with phasing products and services out. Often there are considerable opportunities for improvement in optimizing processes with phasing products and services in and out. A lack of managerial attention might lead to an unintended increase in the number of items, some of which even have very low inventory turnover rates and other being obsolete. The number of stock storage units is often a major cost driver. Figure 6 shows that 31% of the respondents to a very high degree or to a high degree have the necessary focus on phasing in and out of goods and services. This in turn

Figure 6: Focus on in and out phasing

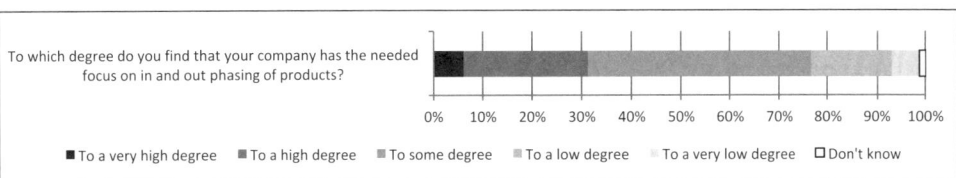

indicates some positive signs. However, greater number of respondents (45%) believes that only to some degree there is a focus on phasing in and out of goods and services and 22% of the respondents indicate that the focus on phasing in and out of goods and services is only at a lesser extent. These figures indicate an obvious need for improvements, which in turn also can lead to more strategic work on pruning customers and products and services.

Closing

This article has primarily focused on T2M process. T2M is a cross-functional process, or should be, that among others binds the main functions sales / marketing, product development and supply chain together. As shown in this article, there seems to be a potential for development in Danish companies towards improving T2M processes. It is the hope that this article can serve as an inspiration for dialogues on T2M processes in order to maintain and further develop competitiveness. A focus on T2M includes improved workflows in both production and supply chain as well as in administrative functions. It is recommended that practitioners create consciousness about the actual T2M performance in order to compare this with targets for the area. If gaps are identified then this may initiate concrete cross-functional developments projects that can help to break down the silos.

Section 5 – Panel articles in 2012

Working with sustainability is primarily driven by financial savings[1]

By: Jan Stentoft and Ole Stegmann Mikkelsen

Introduction

Sustainability has received considerable attention in the past years. There has emerged a much greater awareness around it to be environmentally responsible. The reasons include media, politicians and interest groups focus on CO^2 emissions as well as global warming. Thus, there is an increased wave of initiatives focused on sustainable business solutions. For many companies, it has become a part of the overall competitiveness in offering sustainable solutions and on the other hand, for some companies the situation is even harder. Sustainability is not the most important criteria however considered as a demanding qualifier among others with regard to customer demand. The increased attention around the sustainability of the supply chain has helped to initiate the development new supply chain management solutions. Increased fuel taxes, forced industry to develop new forms of distribution to ensure competitiveness. Similarly, taxes on waste, increased focus on material recycling in order to reduce costs. Despite the good intentions with sustainability, it is not that easy job to drive it equally at all circumstances. It is not possible working with sustainability and in several areas it is a challenge to make visible what is actually achieved by concrete action. Accordingly, this article aims in processing the results of a mini-survey on sustainability – a mini survey that is answered by *The Danish Supply Chain Panel*.

---

1 This article is edited and translated to English from the Danish version Arlbjørn, J.S. and Mikkelsen, O.S. (2012), "Arbejde med sustainability er primært drevet af økonomiske besparelser", *DILF Orientering*, Vol. 49 No. 6, pp. 10-14.

Strategy and organization

To uncover the spread of sustainability in Danish supply chains, the respondents were asked whether sustainability has gained an increased focus in supply chain strategy. The responses are shown in Figure 1.

From Figure 1 it is clear that only 24% consider focusing on sustainability in their supply chain strategy to high extent, and none of the respondents consider sustainability in their supply chain strategy to a very high extent. And, around 42% of the respondents indicate that they only to some extent focus on sustainability in their supply chain strategy. Furthermore, 34% of the respondents indicate that they have lesser focus on sustainability in their supply chain strategy. Thus, there seem to be a gap between society's general perception about the development of potential sustainability and corporate understanding of supply chains' impact on the area.

The respondents were also asked 'where the organizational responsibility for sustainability is anchored in their organizations?' The results are presented in Figure 2.

From Figure 2, it is apparent that approximately 30% of the respondents believe that the control of sustainability, to a great extent, is distributed within the organization. In addition, 15% of the respondents believe that supply chain takes the control of sustainability. Then, followed by purchasing and "other place" (e.g. Corporate Social Responsibility (CSR), Sales & Marketing and Health, Safety, environment & Quality). The responsibility seems to be logical because purchasing typically responsible for external relations often represents a relatively large part of the company's total costs and hence, it is a potential Sustainability footprint. On the contrary, the location in purchasing/procurement might lead to over-consideration of sustainability to external relationships and activities and the company

Figure 1: Degree of sustainability focus in supply chain strategy

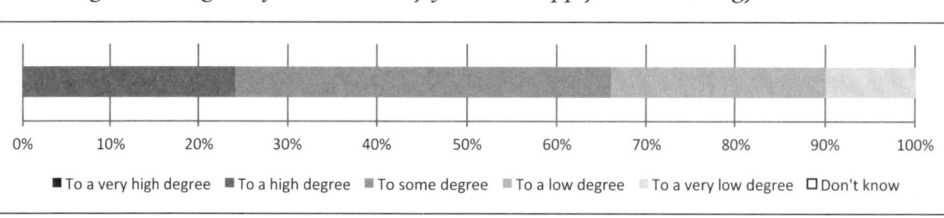

Figure 2: Organizational anchoring of sustainability

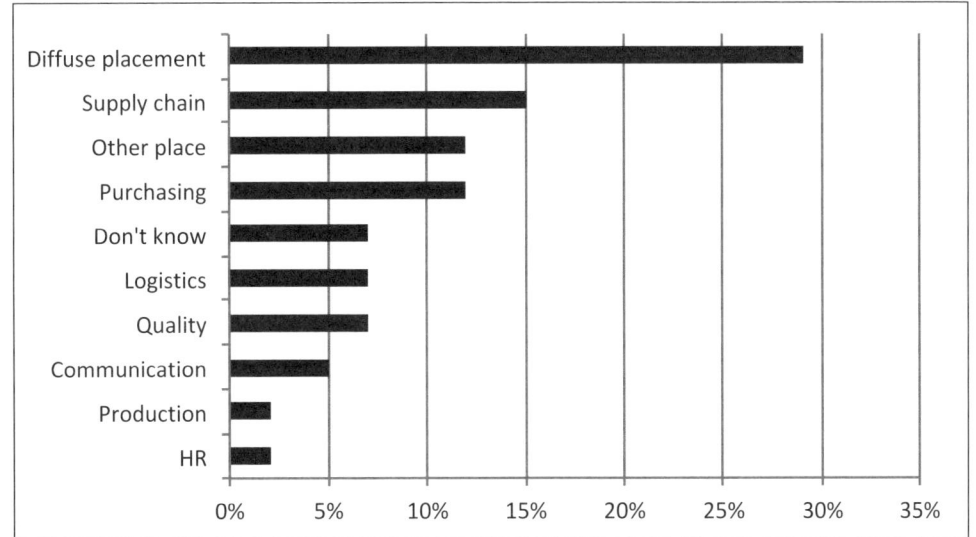

should overlook the impact the company has on downstream customers. A potential disadvantage of anchoring sustainability work in one or more operational functions can be that it may soon become a feature project (both perceptually and practice) and not a business strategic activity.

Driving forces and barriers

The Danish Supply Chain Panel was asked about the driving forces behind businesses' sustainability. It is apparent from Figure 3 that the most common driving force was to obtain financial savings. In other words, it can be inferred that it is not expensive to behave spot-on environmentally and the liabilities such as fuel tax, waste tax and electricity has forced the companies to think different for new sustainable solutions. It is also not surprising to notice customer demand being an essential driver for sustainability and of course, customers also can claim for sustainability. In fact, customer requirements can be seen as an additional desire that propagates sustainability further important for the overall supply chain and to achieve sustainable competitive advantage. In other words, the most common driving forces in this mini-survey are concerned with a classical economic focus (bot-

Figure 3: Driving forces for sustainability

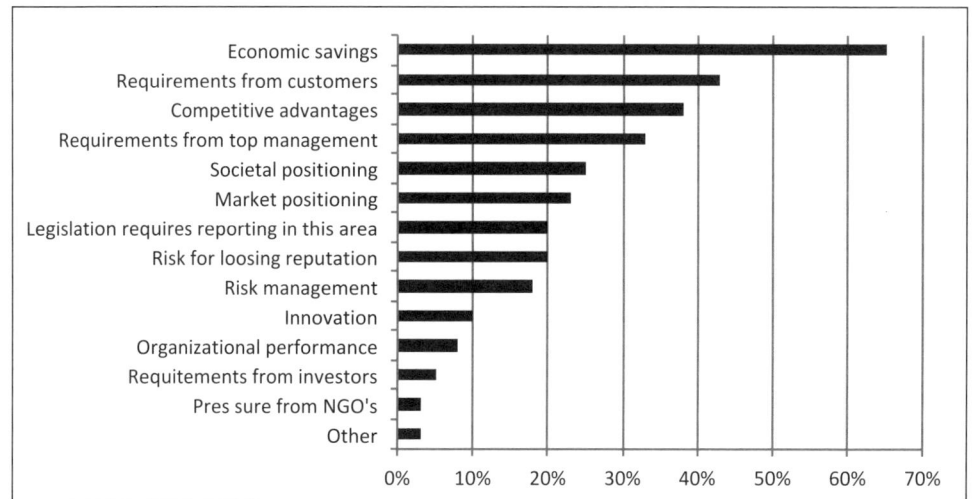

tom line, customers and competitive advantages). Other important driving forces are requirements from the top management and societal/market positioning (reputation).

For several companies, sustainability is not a simple and manageable task to put into practice. Working with sustainability is a process in which there are many stakeholders associated. It is a task that requires top management's full support. It can be a hard job to succeed with sustainability and several barriers can be met in this process (see Figure 4).

The majority of the respondents believe that the predominant barrier for implementing sustainability is the difficulty of visualizing the benefits of the concrete efforts taken (see Figure 4). When it comes to daily operations, the companies might develop an attitude that sustainability is merely an additional burden and not actually contributing in any ways. Another key barrier for implementing sustainability is that customers will not pay for it. This is in contrast to the previously mentioned drivers, where precisely the customers listed as a driving force to get sustainability implemented (because they require it). The major challenge is that customers, in general, demand sustainability; however they will not pay for it. This broadcasts sustainability more as a moderate qualifier rather than broadcasting it as the most significant in business contexts. The third barrier in

Figure 4: Barriers for implementing sustainability

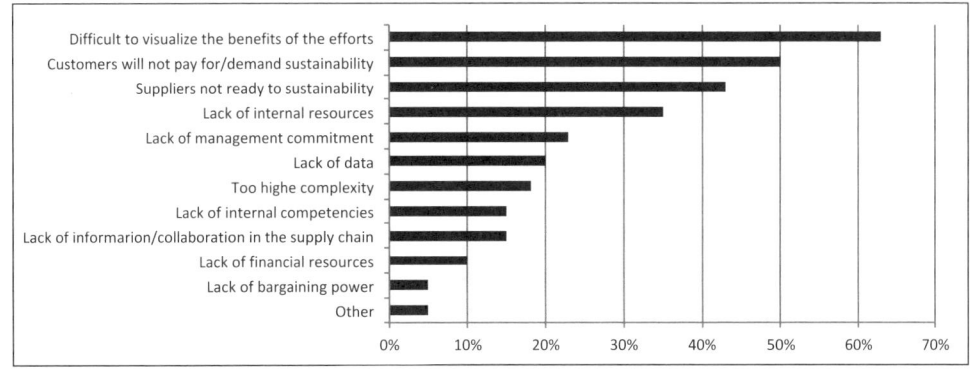

implementing sustainability appears to be the suppliers who are not ready to work with sustainability. Hence, the participants of the supply chain panel indicate demand of their suppliers for sustainability as a significant barrier and also claim that this is merely because of lack of understanding regarding sustainability. This can be explained with a skewed strength ratio where suppliers, based on the company size, are forced to prioritize other things higher than living up to demands for sustainability from a Danish customer. Another explanation may be that the supplier is aware that the products delivered are in scarce supply, so the motivation to prioritize sustainability could be negligible.

Focus areas and performance

As shown in Figure 5, the main focus of the work with sustainability is centered around reduction of energy consumption and waste (waste), which supports the high focus on cost reductions (see Figure 3). The focus is therefore primarily on simple and tangible actions immediately that can be implemented and which have a potential for visualization of an impact. Initiatives that are more knowledgeable and process oriented and which perhaps have an impact only in the long run seems to be more difficult to communicate internally.

The supply chain panel was also asked to consider the extent of concrete performance measurements of their efforts with sustainability. Only 11%

Figure 5: Forms of sustainability

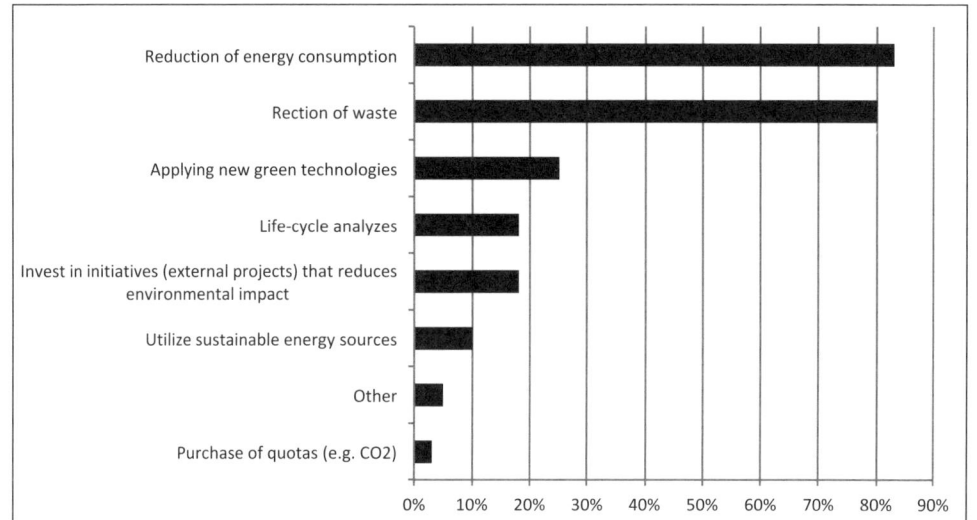

specify that they, to very high or high extent, measure sustainability performance in their supply chain (cf. Figure 6).

On the other hand, 65% indicate that the measure on sustainability performance is either less interesting or it is not at all interesting. At the same time, respondents indicate that it is hard to visualize what is actually gained from the work (see Figure 4). The challenge is that if the work is not done systematic and focused then the performance goals of sustainability in supply chain still remains invisible. Monitoring and visibility go hand in hand.

Respondents were also asked on the extent to which their work with sustainability in the supply chain has given financial savings and increased revenue. As shown in Figure 7, almost only 8% of the respondents indicate that their work with sustainability provides an opportunity for financial savings and increased revenue (to a high extent or very high extent). However, majority of the respondents (63%) indicate that it only to some extent provides an opportunity for financial savings and increased revenue. Comparing this with the main driver (i.e. cost savings); it shows an interesting discrepancy between driving force and goal achievement. There seems to be an outstanding strategic effort to create coherence between goal and result performance and thus the visibility of sustainability in the supply chains.

Figure 6: Degree of measuring sustainability performance

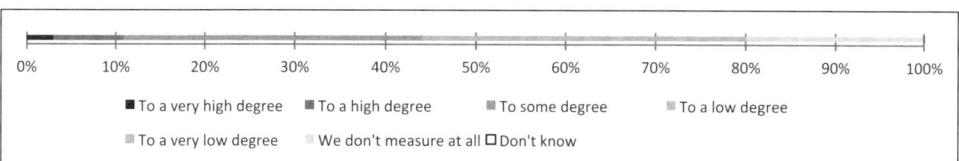

Figure 7: Achievement of economic savings

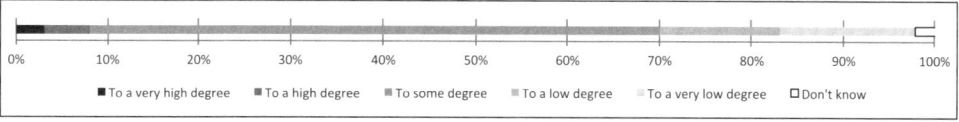

Figure 8: Improved earnings

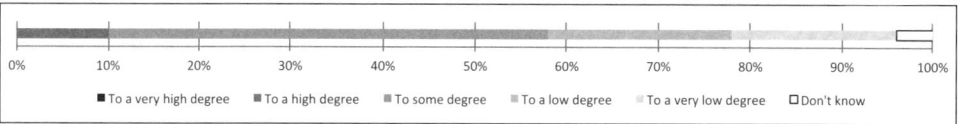

As shown in Figure 8, only 10% believe that working with sustainability in supply chains greatly increases the earnings. Then, 48% of the respondents agree that only to some extent it increases the earnings, whereas 38% of the respondents indicate that it is only to a lesser degree increases the earnings. Again, this shows that the customers are on one hand consider sustainability as a requirement (see Figure 3), wherein on the other hand they are not will willing for it (see Figure 4). This in turn moves sustainability from being the most significant indicator to a normal/moderate qualifier.

Sustainability is also interesting to study in a supply chain perspective, as intelligent solutions and performance improvement is also stored in, and is dependent of cooperation between partners from up and down the supply chains. Therefore it is interesting to ask the panel about their practice of cooperation on sustainability with external stakeholders. As shown in Figure 9, the practice of collaboration on sustainability is carried out mainly with the upstream suppliers (18% corresponds to a high degree or very high degree, while 48% corresponds to some degree). With regard to the collaboration with customers, only 15% of the respondents believe that the practice of collaboration on sustainability with customers takes place

Figure 9: Collaboration about sustainability

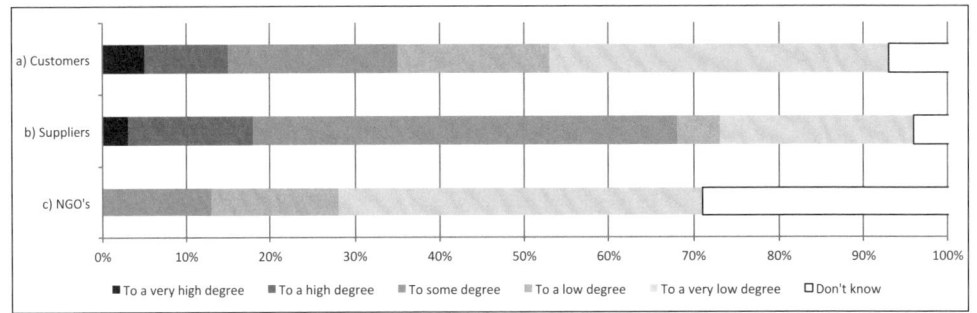

to a high degree or very high degree. In addition, 20% consider that the collaboration on sustainability with customers takes place only to some extent. The major difference between the collaboration on sustainability with customers and suppliers exists in 'collaboration on sustainability to some degree'. It indicates a greater consumption of resources for collaboration activities against suppliers than against customers, which is in line with customers' lack of willingness to pay for Sustainability (for instance, expressed through collaboration, cf. Figure 4). Non-Governmental Organizations (NGOs) are often significant stakeholders and agenda administrators in public. Therefore, it is normal for companies to a certain extent establish collaboration with them. However, the responses from the supply chain panel indicate that only few companies (13%) have established some form of collaboration with NGOs in the field of sustainability. It seems that there is a potential possibility for developing collaboration, including managing on how sustainability performance can be measured and implemented.

This mini survey examined the various practices with sustainability in supply chains and identifies a number of areas where there is still a room for improvement. There is no doubt that sustainability has come to stay, and it will be like fighting against the law of gravity. It is thus important to create awareness about the potential that lies in supply chain to support the company's sustainability objectives.

"Home knitted" approaches to measuring supply chain performance[1]

By: Jan Stentoft and Ole Stegmann Mikkelsen

Introduction

"Difficult and boring – my favorite combination". This is not a rare comment from senior executives who work to improve corporate performance measurement systems (Likierman, 2009). Many managers find it cumbersome and downright threatening. This work is therefore being assigned to the personnel, who are not the most experienced in measuring performance. Such a practice leads to lot of comparison and often provides limited information about the companies' real performance. It could also lead to decisions affecting the company. The objective of performance measurements include:

- To look back and thus create the basis, for example, bonus
- To look forward, for example, to motivate a common direction
- To compare historical targets with current target figures
- Break down the goal to share goals and vice versa

Performance measurement is an important approach to ensure the supply of resources in order to continuously monitor the companies' competitiveness. Today numerous supply chain activities are carried out in both private and public organizations often in situations of resource scarcity. This article has set out to investigate the practice of performance measurement among the members of *The Danish Supply Chain Panel*.

---

1 This article is edited and translated to English from the Danish version Arlbjørn, J.S. and Mikkelsen, O.S. (2012), "Det danske supply chain panel: Supply chain strategi er prioriteret i topledelsen", *DILF Orientering*, Vol. 49 No. 5, pp. 10-16.

Table 1: The seven deadly sins of performance measurement

Sin	Description
Vanity	Performances measures are made-up to look good.
Provincialism	Performance measures are not aligned across functions leading to su-optimization
Narcissism	Performance measures with a strong internal focus at the expense of the customers perspectives
Laizness	Inappropriate performance measures due to inadequate thought processes and efforts to define the measure.
Pettiness	Performance measures do only a focus on fraction of what really matters.
Inanity	Performance measures may have negative consequences on human behavior and on the enterprise performance.
Frivolity	Performance measures are not taken seriously – a flow of excuses of poor performance instead of tracking the root causes of the poor performance.

Source: Based on Hammer (2007)

As shown in Figure 1, almost 36%, to a high or very high degree, has implemented performance management in their supply chains. And, nearly 44%, to some extent, have implemented performance management to manage and follow up on supply chains. Moreover, approximately only 20%, to a low or very low degree, have implemented performance measuring systems.

Figure 1: Implementation of performance management in supply chains

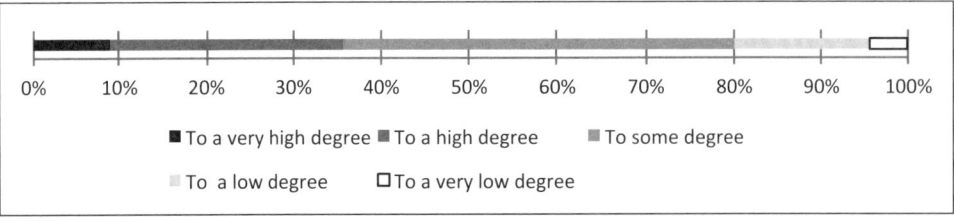

It is surprising that most of the surveyed firms have not completely implemented performance measuring systems, in spite of the increased pressure in the supply chain to deliver faster, more accurate and so on. How would you optimize unless you know where you stand, and in what direction things are moving? It seems that the untapped potentials exist here.

Performance management systems

In both theoretical and practical contexts, there are several different performance management systems (see Table 1). It is therefore interesting to see the systems that are most used for supply chain performance management in companies. The results are shown in Figure 2.

As shown in Figure 2, the majority of the performance management systems used in businesses is home-made; on the other hand, it is clear that "clean" performance programs are not used as widely. Balanced scorecard has its supporters, whereas, the earlier hyped applications such as EFQM are not much used to certain extent. It would be interesting to see to which extent companies rely on the known performance systems in relation to their own performance measurements systems. However, the available data material does not offer an opportunity to execute such an analysis. Similarly, it could be assumed that the resources spent on development and oper-

Figure 2: Used supply chain performance management systems

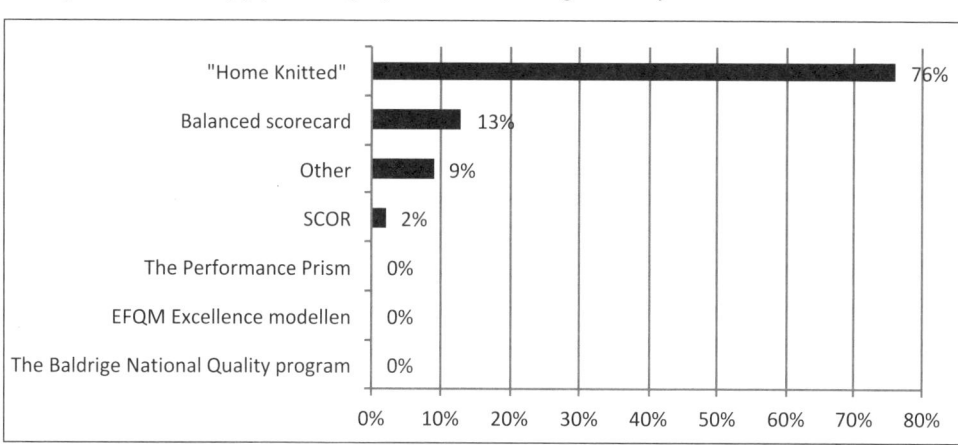

ation of the performance systems (e.g. the balanced scorecard) completely depends on the size of the company as well as its implementation. But the underlying fact cannot be inferred significantly regarding the relationship between the size of the company and usage of the performance system.

Table 2: Some performance management systems

Performance system	Short description
Balanced scorecard	Focuses on business performance areas from four perspectives with the aim to answer four basic questions: How do the customers look at us? (The customer perspective What must we excel at? (The internal business perspective Can we continue to improve and create value? (The innovation and learning perspective) How do our shareholders look at us? (The financial perspective)
Baldrige Criteria for Performance Management (www.nist.gov/baldrige/publications)	Works with the following seven areas of performance goals: Leadership Strategic planning customer and market focus Measurement, analysis and knowledge management Human Resource Management Process management Results
The EFQM Excellence model (http://www.efqm.org/en)	The EFQM Excellence Model is used as a basis for self-assessment, where one is evaluated against nine criteria. With this case, an effective relationship can be analyzed between what the organization does and the results obtained. Five of the nine criteria are enablers and the other four are focused on results. Enabler criteria cover what the organization does and how it does. The performance (result) criteria cover what are the organizations' tangible achievements.

The Performance Prism	The Performance Prism contains five consecutive perspectives. The first perspective is the satisfaction of stakeholders when asked about whom they are and what they want. The second perspective is about the contribution from the stakeholders – what can they deliver? The third perspective focuses on strategy. Here the question is 'To what strategies are needed to meet stakeholder needs vessel?' The fourth perspective deals with processes that are necessary to deliver the strategies. The fifth perspective is about capabilities needed to run the processes.
SCOR (http://supply-chain.org/scor/)	The Supply-Chain Operations Reference model (SCOR) is developed under the auspices of The Supply-Chain Council (SCC), which is an independent, global SCM organization. The SCOR model captures the organization's vision of SCM. The model's content has been used in practice for several years and provide a framework for connecting business processes, metrics, best practices and technology into a unified structure. This makes it easier to communicate the SCOR model for supply chain partners with the aim of improving efficiency. The SCOR model is divided into five major elements: Plan, Source, Make, Deliver and Return.

The practice of supply chain performance metrics

The purpose of performance measurements is to ensure that activities and actions move the company in the desired direction. Therefore, it is important that companies monitor the right relative to the company strategies. Respondents have therefore been asked the extent to which they use the measurements in supporting the company's overall strategy. It appears that 60% of the companies believe that they, to a very high degree or to a high degree, use performance systems and measurements in the supply chain to support the company's overall strategy. However, it is important to measure the right things and to confirm whether the measurements are reliable. Therefore, respondents were asked about the extent to which they consider the measurements used as reliable. The responses appear in Figure 3.

It is clear from Figure 3 that 73% of the respondents consider their performance measures, to a very high or high degree, as reliable. In contrast, it means that 27% of the respondents consider their measurements as reliable only to some extent or less. Such companies run the risk of making

Figure 3: Perceived reliability of the performance measurers

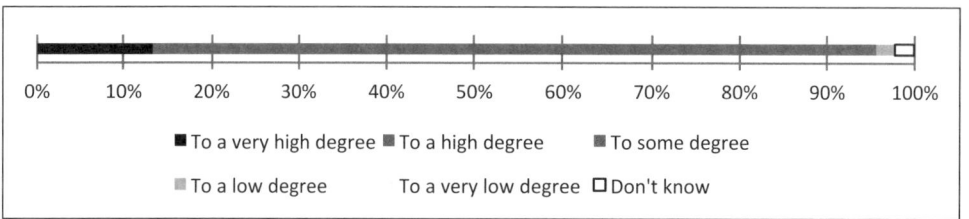

decisions on an unreliable basis. Therefore, there seem to be a potential for improvements.

Although the measurements are reliable and measuring on the appropriate criteria, it helps not much, if the measurements take too long time to collect; the world has changed its focus from measurement aspect to real-time aspect and thus made the decision obsolete and worthless. The respondents were therefore asked to what extent they used the performance data in real time. In other words, the measurements are an expression of the real picture of the current situation, during which you have to make decisions? The survey shows that only slightly less than half (48%), has real-time measurements of their supply chain performance, but 42% believe that their measurements to some degree is in real time.

Reconciling supply chain measures

A common problem is that the individual departments' goal, and in this manner performance indicators, not always matched internally – even within the supply chain. A classic example of conflict is that the logistics department is measured on the stock rotation, the natural push for low inventory levels while purchasing department is measured on the purchase price development, often leads to demands for large purchases to get volume discount from the suppliers. Figure 4 shows to which extent the respondents consider their key performance indicators being reconciled internally and externally.

It is clear from Figure 4 that there is a great difference in the extent of internal and external reconciliation of corporate supply chain performance indicators. In Table 1, one of the seven deadly sins is sub-optimization – measurements must be coordinated across within the organization. Figure

Figure 4: Degree of internal and external alignment of key performance indicators

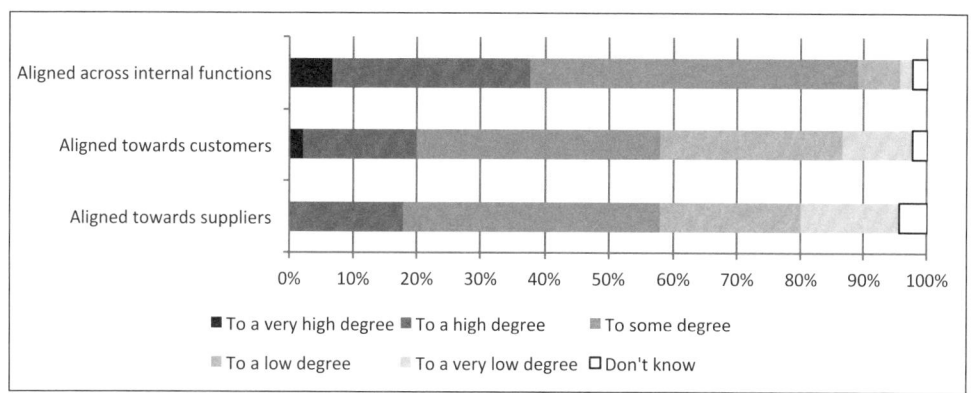

4 shows that only 38% of the respondents believe that their supply chain performance indicators, to a very high degree or high degree, tuned across functions within the organization. This allows, as mentioned earlier, some potential challenges for the remaining companies, since such reconciliation across functions may lead to conflict with performance measurements and thus result in misalignment with the corporate strategy.

No company can stand alone. Companies are part of increasingly complex supply chains and networks, where it is imperative that end customers are presented the best value propositions in terms of product attributes, quality, price, delivery, etc. Otherwise, customers may invest their money in other chains or networks. Thus, companies become increasingly dependent of these chains and network performance. It is therefore surprising that only about 18-20% of the respondents to a very high or a high degree has aligned their performance management indicators with their customers and suppliers.

Responsibility for performance measurements

The respondents were also asked 'who in the company is responsible for the development of performance measurements that follow up / monitor the measurements as well as to ensure the quality of the data in the measurements?' The results appear in Figure 5.

Figure 5: Responsible for supply chain performance measures

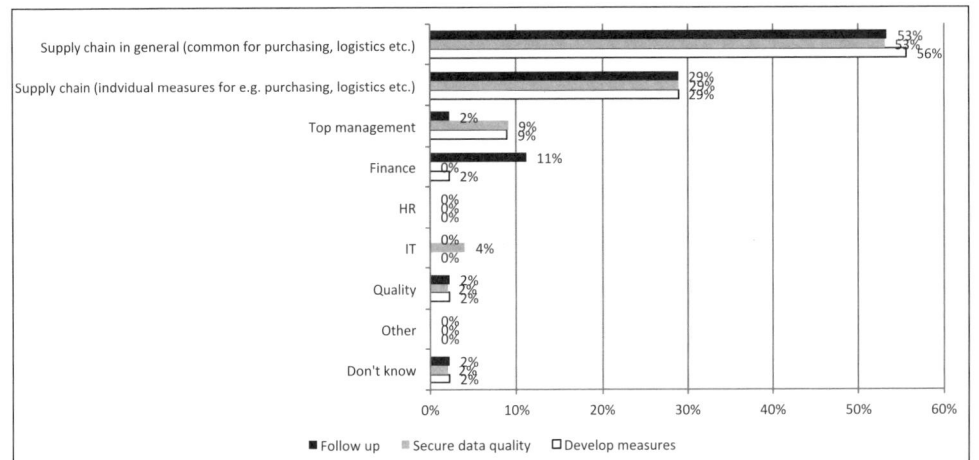

Figure 5 shows that it is predominantly a shared responsibility in the supply chain to develop as well as to follow up the secured data and to ensure the quality of the measurements. This result indicates a positive direction towards the alignment across performance metrics. In contrast, almost 29% of the respondents indicate that the measures of supply chain functions (for instance, procurement, production, logistics, etc.) are independently followed up and ensured for data quality measurements. Therefore, as mentioned earlier, there might be a potential risk that the individual functions performance goals pulls in different directions and even perhaps in a different direction than the company's overall strategy.

Management review of supply chain performance

The respondents were also asked 'how often the performance measures are followed up and what their perceived optimal interval is?' The data shows that the majority of the respondents do follow up on a weekly or monthly basis. And, about 5% of the respondents do follow up on a daily, quarterly or yearly basis. Therefore it is clear that there is a lesser tendency towards daily or weekly follow-up cycles than the tendency towards the follow-up on a weekly or monthly basis.

Data foundation for supply chain performance measurements

Developing supply chain performance measurements is not a trivial task that can be solved with a quick-fix guide. There is often a major task in collecting, collating and presenting the data for the measurements in order to monitor performances. The respondents have been asked on how data is collected, combined and presented in order to get an insight to the degree of automation in these tasks. The results are shown in Figure 6. Although spreadsheets are still well represented in the enterprises (about 20% – semi-manual and manual), it is surprising to see that the automatic data capture is far the predominant method.

Challenges with performance management in supply chains

Although many companies have automatic data capture and with varying degree of finishing, there are still some challenges experienced in regard to corporate supply chain performance measurements. Figure 7 display the reported challenges.

Figure 6: Degree of automation: Data capture, consolidation and presentation

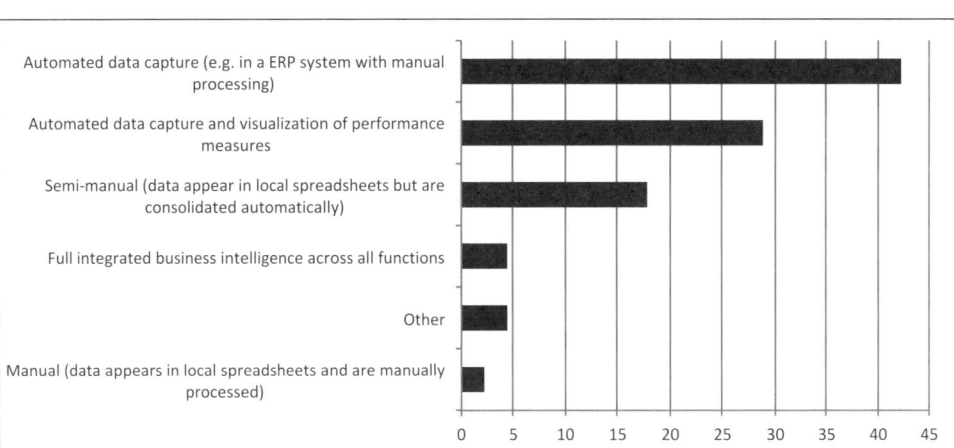

Figure 7: Challenges with supply chain performance measurements

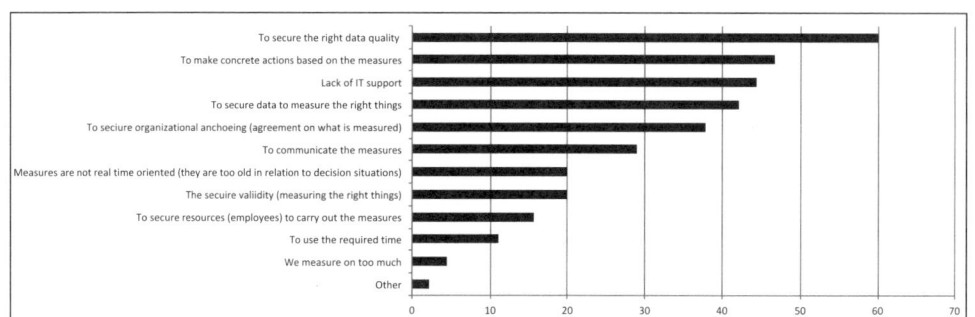

The challenge that most companies points out, is to ensure the right data quality. This corresponds well with others studies, which show that the quality of the, for example, master data is a major challenge for businesses (Schlichter et al., 2011). Another major challenge is to secure data to measure the right thing and around 73% of the respondents, to a very high degree or to a high degree, consider supply chain performance measurement as reliable; it may indicate that a large part of companies are very much focused on ensuring data quality.

There is obviously also a challenge in undertaking concrete actions based on the measures. Lack of IT support is also a high reported challenge, so in spite of companies indicate a relatively high degree of automation in data acquisition and consolidation; they desire an increased degree of automation, which is not surprising.

It is interesting that the "classic" challenges, such as resources and time, appear relatively far down the list which goes against previous mini surveys. Likewise, it seems that companies have managed to increase the focus on to the most necessary measurements, and on the other hand, only a minority believes that they measure on too much. In contrast, 20% of the respondents believe that they do not measure on the right things. Unfortunately we cannot observe in the material if companies believe that they measure everything too little.

References

Hammer, M. (2007), "The seven deadly sins of performance measurement [and how to avoid them]", *MIT Sloan Management Review*, Vol. 48 No. 3, pp. 19-28.

Likierman, A. (2009),"The five traps of performance measurement", *Harvard Business Review*, Vol. 87 No. 10, pp. 96-101.

Schlichter, J., Arlbjørn, J.S., Haug, A. and Zachariassen, F. (2011), *En analyse af stamdatakvaliteten i danske produktionsvirksomheder*, Institut for Entreprenørskab og Relationsledelse, Syddansk Universitet.

Cost-focused supply chain innovation[1]

By: Jan Stentoft and Ole Stegmann Mikkelsen

Introduction

Supply chain management (SCM) contains important areas for creating competitive advantages via its simultaneous focus on both revenue enhancing and cost-reducing activities. The importance of SCM is not of less relevant as globalization of trade continuous to expand. Raw materials, components and finished goods are purchased in a region and further processed in a different region, then sold at another third region. A major part of the product's total value is, in general, now added outside the focal company, explicitly in its supply network. Thus, it is not unusual that a company's supply chain represents 60-70% of the total cost-consuming, which means that SCM as a discipline is of high strategic importance.

As a result of increased globalization, supply chains have also become more complex and SCM executives must continuously be aware of a number of key issues such as:
- Where will the production take place (local vs. global?)
- How should risk management be handled?
- How do we achieve the supply chain performance objectives?
- With whom should we integrate and on what in the supply chain?
- How do we exploit the latest technology in the supply chain?
- Are we doing enough in Corporate Social Responsibility and sustainability?

---

[1] This article is edited and translated to English from the Danish version Arlbjørn, J.S. and Mikkelsen, O.S. (2012), "Omkostningsfokuseret supply chain innovation", *DILF Orientering*, Vol. 49 No. 4, pp. 22-26.

Such issues are examples of areas that can foster supply chain innovations; accordingly, this is the focus of this article. The presentation of the mini-survey results can be used as discussion points in the organization.

Supply Chain Innovation

In order to give a deeper understanding of issues related to supply chain innovation, we will first introduce a conceptual framework for understanding supply chain innovation. The questions in this mini-survey were formulated based on this conceptual framework. Supply chain innovation can be defined as:

> "Supply chain innovation is a change (incremental or radical) within a supply chain network, supply chain technology, or supply chain process (or a combination of these) that can take place in a company function, within a company, in an industry or in a supply chain in order to enhance new value creation for the stakeholder." Arlbjørn et al. (2011)

This definition of supply chain innovation includes five key characteristics. Firstly, supply chain innovation expresses a change and is thus a dynamic phenomenon. Secondly, supply chain innovation varies along a continuum from small incremental to the major radical changes. Thirdly, supply chain innovations take place both inside a company and among companies. Fourthly, supply chain innovations are more than the invention of something new, as it also includes the process of commercializing. Finally, a supply chain innovation must prove its commercial value to a partner, end customer or other stakeholders in the supply chain. A model for showing the components in supply chain innovation appear in Figure 1 and the three components are briefly described in Table 1.

Figure 1: Supply chain innovation

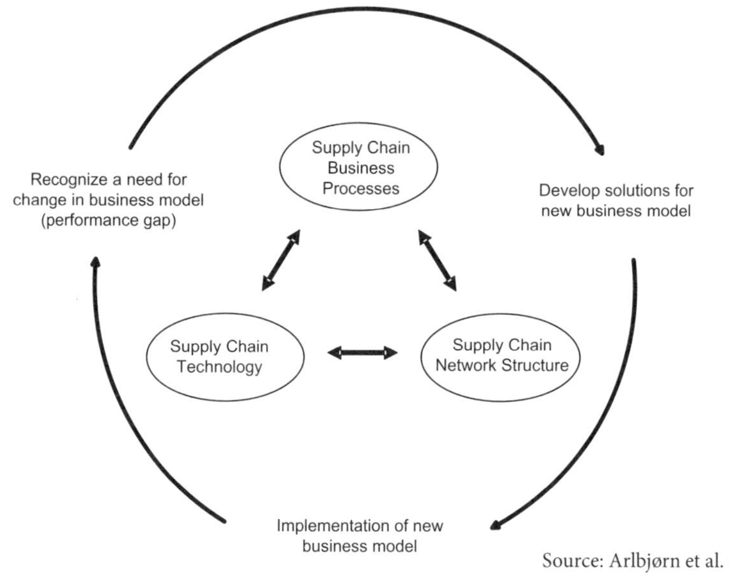

```
                    Supply Chain
                     Business
                     Processes
  Recognize a need for                    Develop solutions for
  change in business model                new business model
  (performance gap)
              Supply Chain  ←→  Supply Chain
              Technology        Network Structure

                  Implementation of new
                     business model
                                    Source: Arlbjørn et al. (2011)
```

Table 1: Supply chain innovation components

Supply chain business processes	Structured set of activities that provide a measurable output. Business processes cut across traditional functional "silos" in a company such as sales, warehousing, production and purchasing.
Supply chain technology	IT technology related to the management of materials and information within companies and across partners in supply chains (i.e. global position system (GPS), radio frequency identification (RFID), electronic data interchange (EDI), cloud and grid computing and enterprise resource planning (ERP).
Supply chain network structure	Concerns both depth and breadth of upstream and downstream relationships.

Developing the supply chain as a source of competitive advantage

Data from this mini-survey reveals that all respondents within the past two years has worked with supply chain innovation, of which two-thirds mainly have been incremental in nature, while one-third predominantly has been radical innovations.

The respondents have been asked whether they consider development of their company's supply chain as a source of competitive advantage; whether they consciously develop their supply chains to achieve competitiveness; and whether they believe that innovation is a component of the company's supply chain strategy. The respondents' answers are shown in Figure 2.

In Figure 2, 74% indicates to high or very high degree that the development of the company's supply chain is considered as a source of competitiveness. Then, 57% does to a high or very high degree indicate that their business consciously develops their supply chains in order to increase competitiveness. Also 57% does to a high or very high degree indicates that they have innovation as a conscious part of their supply chain strategy. However, only 13% responded that they to a very high degree believe that their company consciously develop the supply chain to increase competitiveness and 17% state that they to a very high degree believe that supply chain innovation is a part of the overall supply chain strategy. This should be compared with the 33% that to a very high degree consider supply chain area as a source of competitiveness. Thus, there seems to be a gap between

Figure 2: Supply chain management and competitiveness

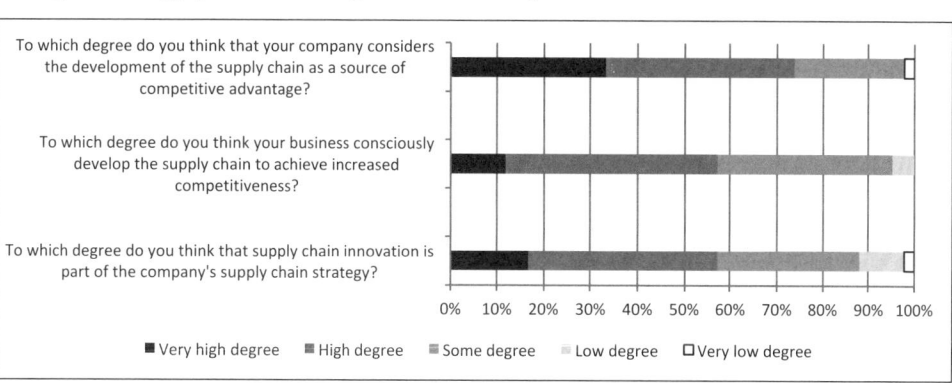

the perception of importance and a deliberate execution of supply chain innovation. Later in this article we will discuss the results of the respondents' perceived barriers with this issue.

Supply chain innovation focus

The respondents were asked of which supply chain components, the respective supply chain innovations have been focused on (see Figure 1 and Table 1). The responses are shown in Figure 3.

As shown in Figure 3, 95% of the respondents have focus on business processes in their supply chain innovations, while a small part has been focused on the network (41% of respondents). Technology has been the focus among 57% of the respondents. It is not surprising that the processes are the main focus, as supply chain management precisely deals with both internal and external business processes. In contrast, we are surprised that so few of the respondents have worked with innovations related to the company's business network, because supply chain management, in fact, is an inter-organizational discipline. A possible explanation may be that innovations related to processes and technology usually is an internal matter whereas innovations in network requires the involvement of external parties, which can make it more difficult. Another possible explanation can be

Figure 3: The focus of supply chain innovation

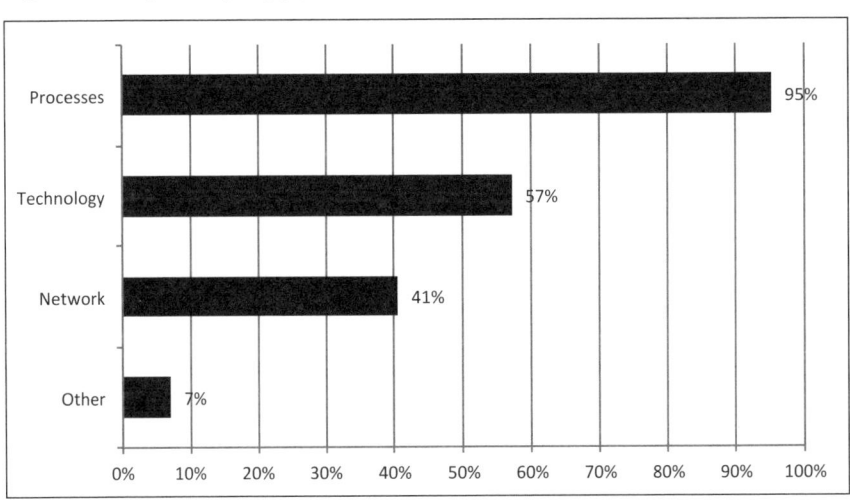

Figure 4: The supply chain components importance for supply chain innovation

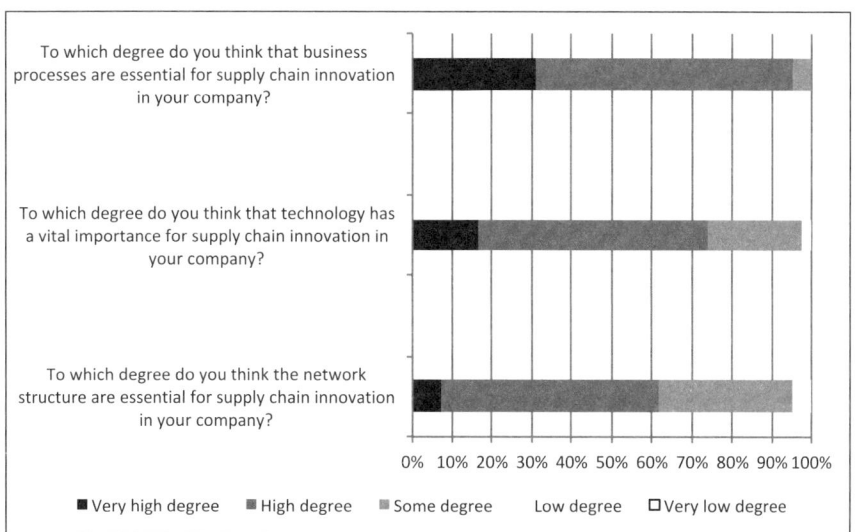

found in the context of respondents' answers to the importance of the three components of supply chain innovation as shown in Figure 4.

Figure 4 shows that respondents predominantly consider that business processes are essential for supply chain innovation (95% in high and very high level), while the network structure to a lesser degree is considered to have a major role (62% in high and very greatly). Thus, perhaps not surprisingly, this indicates an interrelationship between the perceived importance of supply chain innovation and the companies' specific focus.

Driving forces of supply chain innovation

A special interest has been to investigate what the respondents find to be the driving forces for supply chain innovation. The respondents' answers are shown in Figure 5.

As shown in Figure 5, the need for cost reductions by far the biggest driver to work with supply chain innovation (79% of respondents). Intensified global competition leads to greater demand to drive costs out of the supply chains. Such cost reductions are, for instance related to inventory, transport, handling and purchasing. The need to provide better services is

Figure 5: Driving forces for supply chain innovation

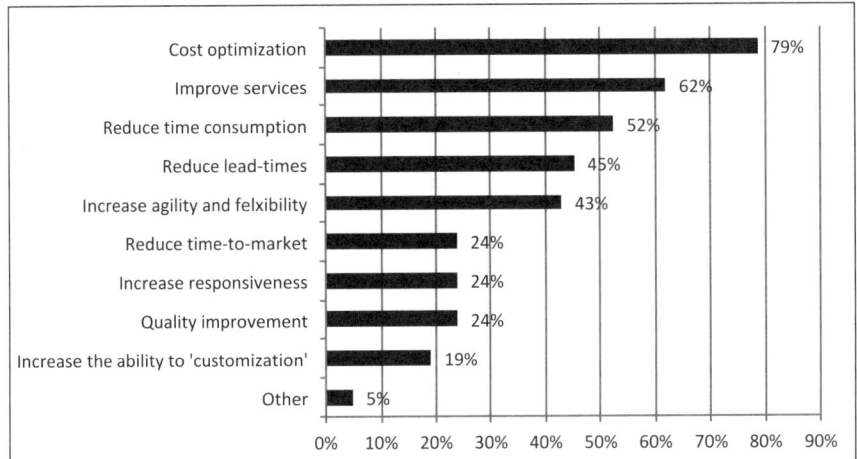

also a key driver of supply chain innovation. It may be parameters such as order status visibility, delivery reliability and follow up on supplies. It is important periodically to perform a service check of the supply chain in order to ensure that the control parameters are in line with the fundamental supply chain design. Several companies have examples of those customers with the lowest profit margin actually the best service and vice versa. A third driving force is the need to reduce the time consumption – be it in both physical and administrative processes.

Initiators of supply chain innovation

Respondents were asked to specify who in the respective organizations have initiated the supply chain innovations. Improvement measures can be caused by several factors at the same time; it is because the respondents have been able to select multiple options (see Figure 6). Not surprisingly, over 70% of the supply chain innovations have been initiated by the person being responsible for the supply chain. The daily top management team is also a source of commencement of supply chain innovation initiatives, suggesting that the company management have recognized supply chain area's importance to the company's overall competitiveness. It is gratifying to see that employees in 50% of the respondents have been the initiators of the

Figure 6: Initiators of supply chain innovation

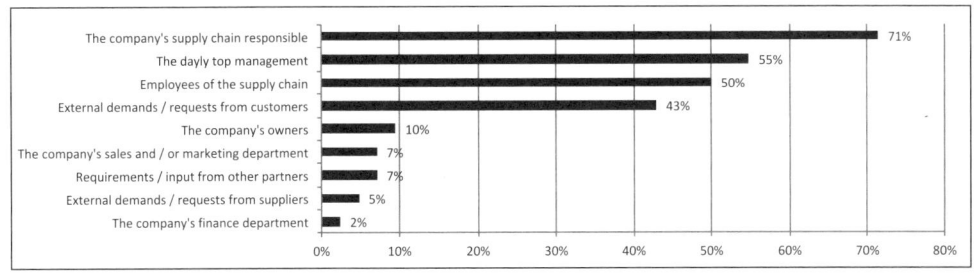

supply chain innovations. This indicates an increased acknowledgement of the valuable knowledge that employees hold. And, 43% of the respondents state that supply chain innovations have been initiated by "requirements/wishes from customers". Thus, the voice of the customer is a source for supply chain innovation (e.g. through customer-oriented projects such as the reduction of lead times, increased delivery flexibility and vendor managed inventory).

Barriers to the development of supply chains

Change management in global supply chains can be both complicated and resource demanding. When asked about the barriers that the respondents considered as important, there were two distinct answers. The first is lack of time to implement supply chain innovation projects (64% indicate that as a major barrier cf. Figure 7). More specifically, operation wins over development. If one continues with such a practice over a longer period, there is an increased risk for that the need for innovation increases relatively more than the time that is put into operation. Furthermore, the presence of the appropriate resources is also listed as a significant change barrier. This indicates a gap in skills among the surveyed companies. "A too high degree of silo mentality", "lack of managerial anchoring/focus", "lack of internal development-oriented skills", "lack of economic resources" and "supply chain complexity" is indicated as barriers by approximately 30% of the respondents.

Figure 7: Barriers for supply chain innovation

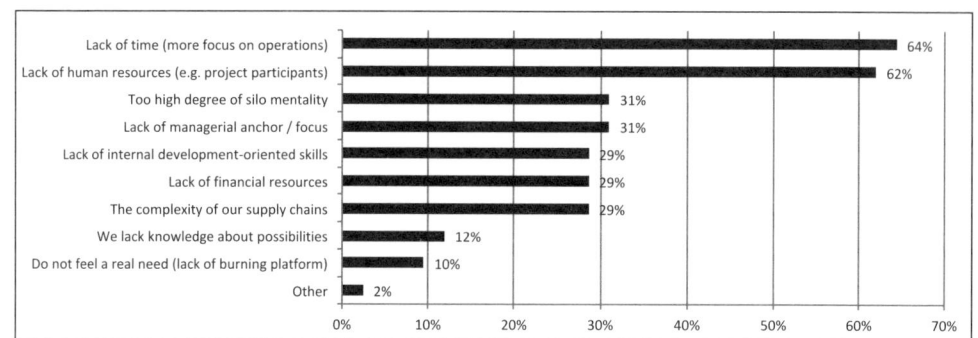

Conclusion

This mini-survey has focused on the need for and the actual implementation of supply chain innovation. The results indicate that they do acknowledge the importance of supply chain innovation. The companies state that they have started with this supply chain innovation strategy. It is primarily the reduction of costs is the driving force for innovations. Main barriers for supply chain innovations are listed as "lack of time" and "lack of the right human resources". An explanation of the listed gap between the perceived importance of supply chain innovation and the conscious work on it can be that the companies being part of this survey are pursuing very much performance-driven behaviors. Thus, one can question whether the companies lack specific performance targets for the development of the supply chain in line with operational performance goals in order to create focus and direction.

In light of the results presented in this mini-survey, it is recommended that companies work more consciously with supply chain strategy, including specific performance requirements for the company's supply chains. Next, working with analyzes of the gap between the current performance and its objectives and to map the improvement projects that contribute to specific strategic objectives. It is not unknown that such work may reveal a lack of consistency between the ongoing projects and strategic objectives. Such an approach can help to foster the right level of energy to complete the supply chain innovations that companies needs most to ensure continued competitiveness.

Reference

Arlbjørn, J.S., de Haas, H. and Munksgaard, K.B. (2011), "Exploring supply chain innovation", *Logistics Research*, Vol. 3 No. 1, pp. 3-18.

Supply chain strategy is prioritized in top management[1]

By: Jan Stentoft and Ole Stegmann Mikkelsen

Introduction

In April 2012, *The Danish Supply Chain Panel* was established through invitations to Danish supply chain executives. The panel did consist of 56 active supply chain management (SCM) executives who want to give their opinions on various SCM related issues. This article is the first in a series that addresses these issues. The participants in the supply chain panel were from different industries, however, majority of the participants were from stock and order-producing (43%), followed by order-producing (27%), stock producing (16%) and in addition, there were participants from other industries (14%), for instance service. The distribution of companies in terms of size, 38% of the companies have less than 200 employees, while 62% have 200 or more employees. The panelists were from The Capital Region of Denmark (33%), The Region of Southern Denmark (31%), The Central Region of Denmark (25%), The North Region of Denmark (8%), and The Region Zealand (2%). The mini survey shows that 74% of the panelists have an opinion that senior management in their companies consider SCM as an important or very important contributor to the company's competitiveness. And, 80% definitely have a SCM strategy, but only 49% have it on paper. In addition, 59%, to a greater extent, have a SCM strategy, which is anchored in the top management. The following gives an overview of the short-term issues related to supply chain strategy. The presentation of the results may be used for discussion points on the same topics in the company.

---

1   This article is edited and translated to English from the Danish version Arlbjørn, J.S. and Mikkelsen, O.S. (2012), "Det danske supply chain panel: Supply chain strategi er prioriteret i topledelsen", *DILF Orientering*, Vol. 49 No. 3, pp. 40-44.

Basic competitive parameters

Panelists were asked to rate the importance of cost control, service levels, quality and time as the elements of a supply chain strategy and to what extent these elements are of concrete part of supply chain strategy from their companies' perspective. The results are shown in Figure 1.

The elements of supply chain strategy are ordered descending in terms of importance. From figure 1, it is clear that companies lag in using these elements their own businesses though they understand the importance of supply chain strategy elements. Especially, concerning service levels and quality there is a gap in implementing compared to the perceived importance (51% and 41% respectively, which includes both very high degree and high degree of implementation of service and quality). Wherein, the cost control is internally focused (92%, which includes both very high degree and high degree of importance in a supply chain) and it is same as service and quality which particularly affect customers. The lack of implementation may be because companies might find it difficult to define the right level, or they are constantly exposed to pressure from customers for improvements. Therefore they end up in a situation where they constantly feel that they are lagging behind.

Figure 1: Cost control, service level, quality and time

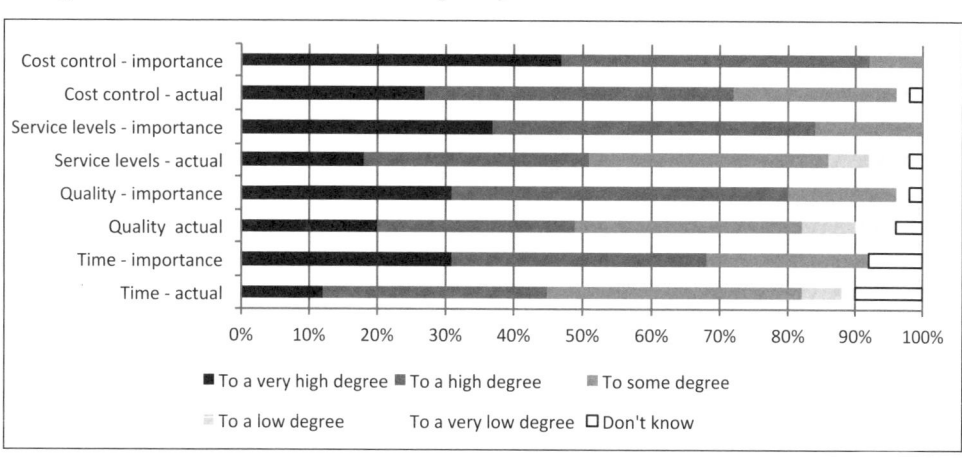

Integration and cooperation

The panelists were asked about the importance and actual practice of integration and cooperation with external partners. The results are shown in Figure 2.

It appears that especially integration with suppliers and customers is considered as important components of a supply chain strategy (78% and 68% respectively, which includes both very high degree and high degree). However, it also appears that there is a huge gap in relation to the implementation of the activities in the companies and thereby, appears to be a significant potential for improvement in both areas. On the other hand, the collaboration with competitors looks as if it is not important to supply chain strategy and this could be the reason for not implementing it.

Make or buy, offshoring and outsourcing

The panelists were asked whether offshoring, outsourcing and make or buy decisions are important elements in a supply chain strategy. The results are shown in Figure 3.

It can be noted that there is a gap in the implementation compared to the perceived importance of offshoring, outsourcing and make or buy deci-

Figure 2: Integration and cooperation

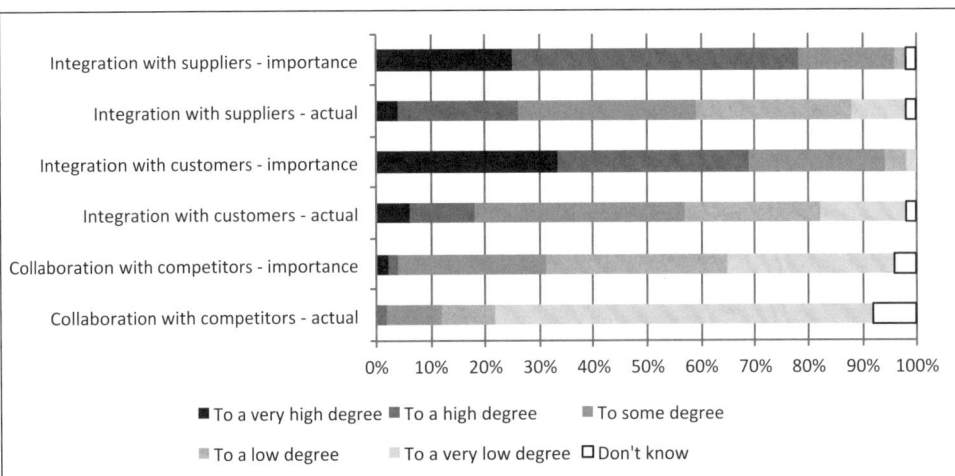

Figure 3: Make or buy, offshoring and outsourcing

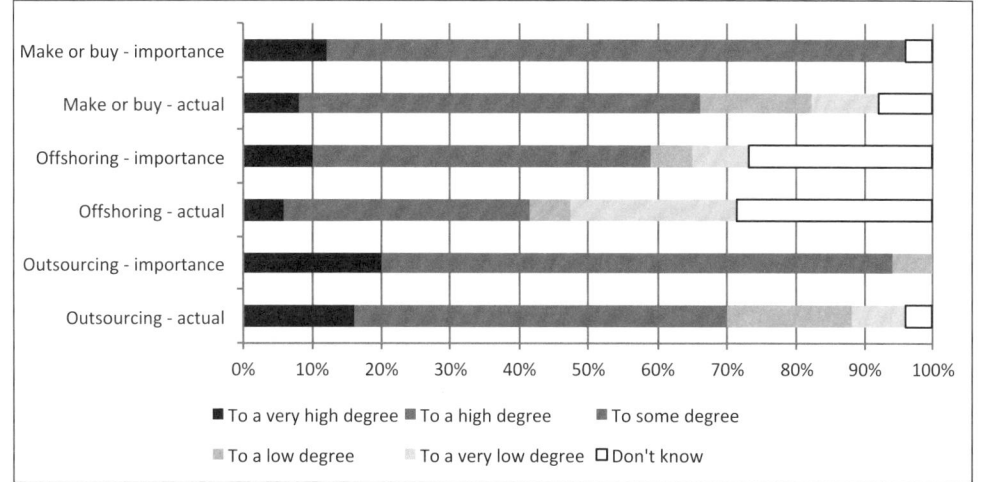

sions. The respondents realize issues and decisions on company boundaries – what should be created within the company, and what should be left to external parties – as important in a supply chain strategy, which is perhaps not so surprising. However, the more surprising point is that less than one third of the panelists find offshore decisions as important in a supply chain strategy (30%, which includes both very high degree and high degree). The reason for this might be that such decisions have not yet considered supply chain related. On the other hand, it also appears that there is very less gap between importance and implementation (24%, which includes both very high degree and high degree).

Performance management and risk management

Within the areas of performance management and risk management, it is obvious from the result that there is also a room for improvement with respect to importance and concrete implementation (see Figure 4).

It is evident from the results that companies do consider both performance management and risk management as important components of a supply chain strategy (86% and 81% respectively, which includes both very high degree and high degree). Considering the existence time of performance management on the agenda, it is surprising that only about 40% of

Figure 4: Performance management and risk management

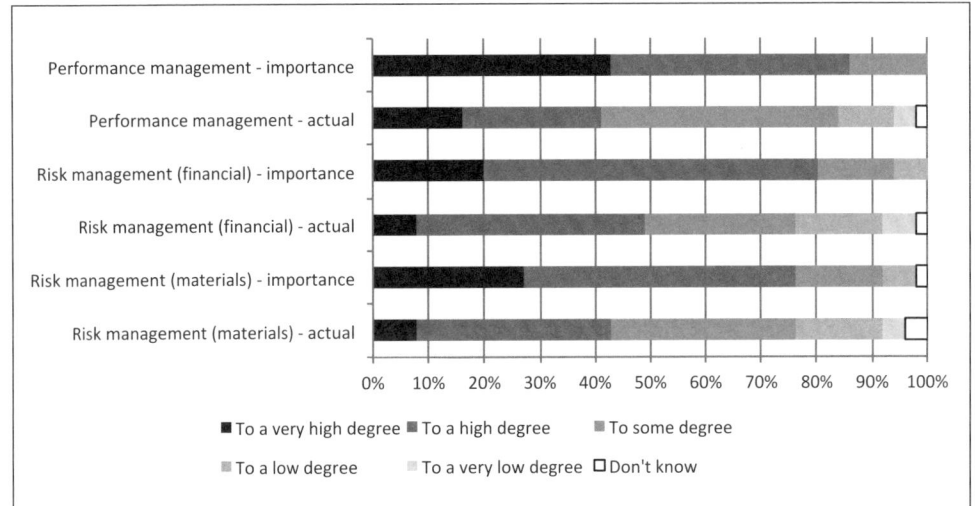

panelists indicate the implementation to a high or very high degree. With recent years of large fluctuations in the availability and pricing of raw materials, risk management has been made available on the strategic agenda. Both types of risk (financial and materials) are considered as important (81% and 76%, which includes both very high degree and high degree). And, when it comes to the usage of both risks (financial and materials), it is slightly higher than that of performance management.

Data quality and information technology

In order to control and maneuver in todays' complex world, companies need to have data. Therefore, the panelists were asked about the importance of data quality and information technology, in a broad sense, in a supply chain strategy. The results are shown in Figure 5.

It appears that both data quality and use of information technology are observed, to a high degree or very high degree, as important elements, however with regards to implementation, they are, to some extent, lagging behind. The result shows that 92% considers, to a high extent or very high extent, data quality as an important element. However, concerning the status of implementation of data quality in practice, it seems only 45%

Figure 5: Data Quality and information technology

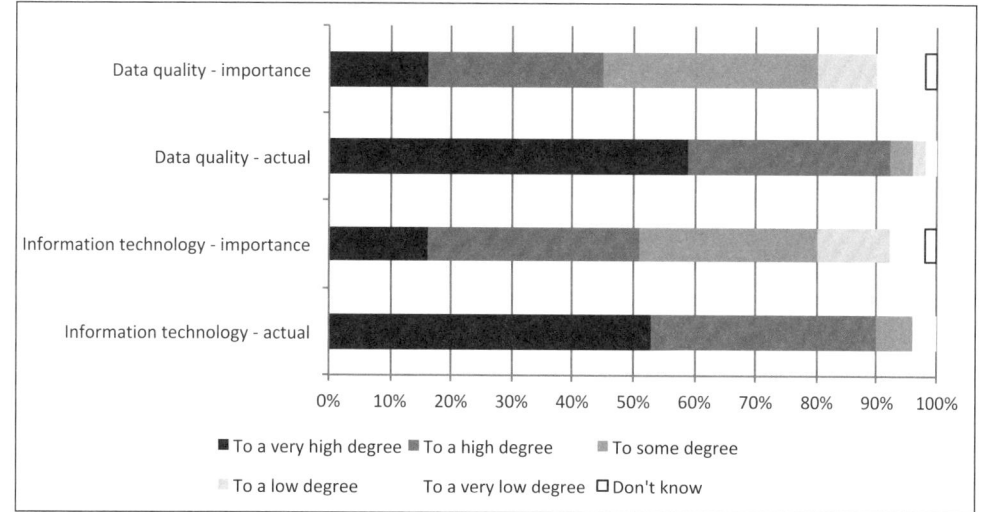

(including both very high and high degree) of the companies are actually practicing data quality. On the other hand, 90% believes that information technology, to a high degree or very high degree, is an important element. Again, when it comes to implementation of information technology in practice, only 51% of the companies, to a very high degree or to a high degree, are actually practicing information technology.

Organization, competence and innovation

This mini survey also includes other elements such as organization, competence and supply chain innovation and identified relatively large gap between the perceived importance and actual practice. The results are shown in Figure 6.

It is clear from the result that 84% of the companies acknowledge the definition of organizational roles and responsibilities, to a very high degree or high degree, as an important element. However, in practice, only 49% of the companies are, to a very high degree or high degree, actually implementing this element in the supply chain strategy. Lack of roles and responsibilities can lead to silo thinking, which can be a major barrier to the implementation of the company's supply chain strategy. Almost 74%

Figure 6: Organization, competence and innovation

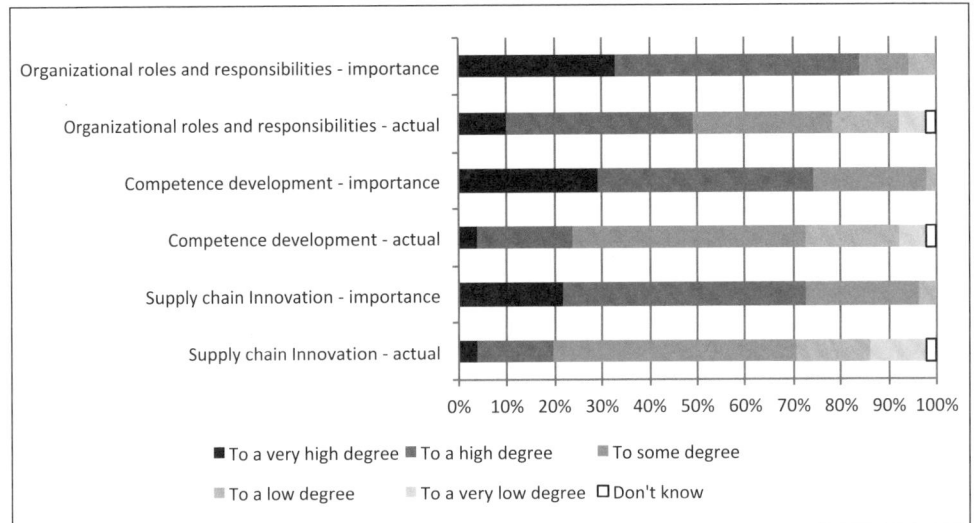

of the companies have an opinion that competence development is, to a very high degree or high degree, an important element in a supply chain strategy, however; only 24% thinks that this competence development is, to a very high degree or high degree, implemented or reflected in the supply chain strategy. And, on the element of supply chain innovation, 73% of the companies believe that this element is to a very high degree or high degree important in a supply chain strategy. Still, in practice, only 20% of the companies, to a very high or high degree, are actually practicing supply chain innovation.

Sustainability and Corporate Social Responsibility

Sustainability and Corporate Social Responsibility (CSR) are some of today's hot topics in relation to corporate behavior – not least in relation to environmental impact and the supplier base. The panelists were asked questions pertaining to these topics and the results are shown in Figure 7.

Given the great attention that the subjects have achieved, it is surprising that less than 50% of the companies consider sustainability and CSR as essential components of a supply chain strategy. Regarding sustainability,

Figure 7: Sustainability of Corporate Social Responsibility

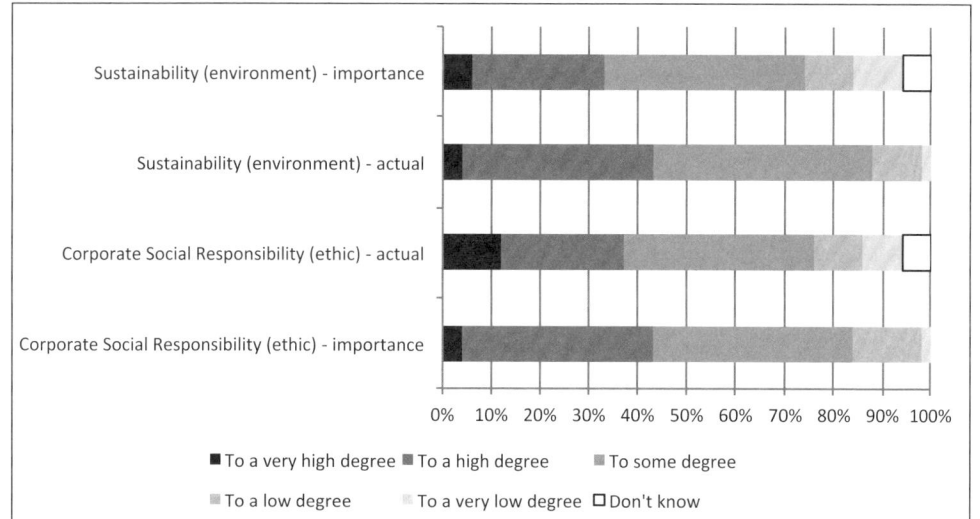

43% of the companies believe that sustainability, to a very high or high degree, is an important content element. And, in practice, only 33% of the companies, to a very high degree or high degree are implementing it. With regards to corporate social responsibility (CSR), 43% of the companies believe that it is, to a very high or high degree, an important element in a supply chain strategy. In practice, only 37% of the companies, to a very high degree or high degree, are implementing it.

Barriers to implementation of supply chain strategy

In summary, the supply chain strategy elements including the gap between perceived importance and the actual practice are shown in Table 1.

PRACTITIONERS PERSPECTIVES

Table 1: Supply chain strategy elements – the importance and concrete practice

Topic	Importance	Practice	Gap
Cost control, service, quality and time			
Cost control	92%	72%	20%
Service	84%	51%	33%
Quality	80%	49%	31%
Time	68%	45%	23%
Integration and collaboration			
Integration with suppliers	78%	26%	**52%**
Integration with customers	68%	18%	**50%**
Collaboration with competitors	4%	2%	2%
Make or buy, offshoring and outsourcing			
Make or buy	61%	26%	35%
Offshoring	30%	24%	6%
Outsourcing	69%	43%	26%
Performance management and risk management			
Performance management	86%	41%	**45%**
Risk management (financial)	81%	49%	32%
Risk management (materials)	76%	43%	33%
Data quality and information technology			
Data quality	92%	45%	**47%**
Information technology	90%	51%	**49%**
Organization, competence development and innovation			
Organizational roles and responsibility	84%	49%	35%
Competence development	74%	24%	**50%**
Supply Chain Innovation	73%	20%	**53%**
Sustainability and Corporate Social Responsibility			
Sustainability	43%	33%	10%
Corporate Social Responsibility	43%	37%	6%

As clearly shown in Table 1, there are areas where there is significant gap between perceived importance and actual implementation degree. The largest gaps are identified for integration with customers and suppliers, performance management, data quality and information technology, com-

Figure 8: Barriers to implementing a supply chain strategy

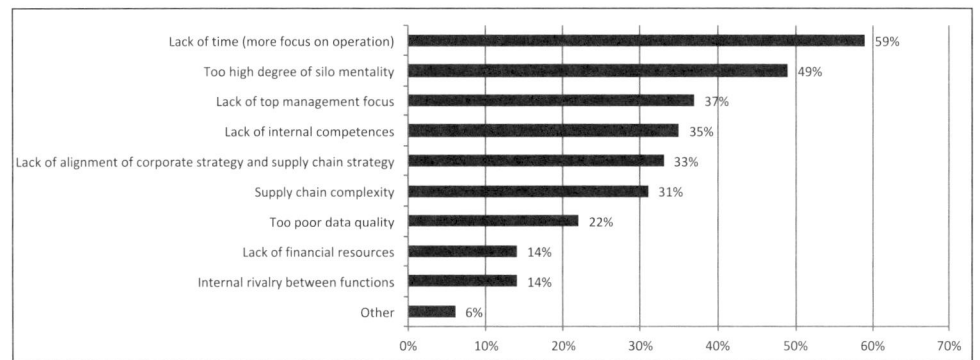

petence development and supply chain innovation. Respondents were therefore asked to select the three barriers that are considered significant for the implementation of supply chain strategy. The results are shown in Figure 8.

The option "other" includes "lack of alignment with IT" and "constant monitoring of all SC functions". It is evident from the results that among barriers for the implementation of supply chain strategy, lack of time and silo mentality seems to be much prevalent in the companies.

About the contributors

Jan Stentoft is a Professor of Supply Chain Management at the Department of Entrepreneurship and Relationship Management at the University of Southern Denmark in Kolding. He holds a PhD in Logistics and Supply Chain Management. He is Head of a strategic research program focusing of supply chain innovation in the offshore wind energy sector (ReCoE) (www.recoe.dk). He also lead a research project focusing on Sales & Operations Planning with a special emphasis on small and medium-sized enterprises and the human aspect in business processes as a mean to tear down the functional silos (www.salesandoperationsplanning.dk). His research and teaching interests are within supply chain management, supply chain innovation and operations management. He has published research articles in journals such as *International Journal of Physical Distribution & Logistics Management, Journal of Supply Chain Management, Supply Chain Management: An International Journal, Journal of Operations Management, International Journal of Production Research, Supply Chain Forum: An International Journal, Journal of Purchasing & Supply Management, International Journal of Energy Sector Management, Journal of Cleaner Production, Operations Management Research, Industrial Management & Data Systems, Journal of Enterprise Information Management, International Journal of Production Economics, Logistics Research, International Journal of Integrated Supply Management, Journal of Agile Systems and Management*, and *European Business Review*. He primarily instructs MSc, PhD and MBA students in supply chain management, operations management and administrative information systems. He has practical industry experience from positions as Director (Programme Management Office) at LEGO System A/S, ERP Project Manager at Gumlink A/S, and as management consultant in a wide number of industrial enterprises. From 2017 he has become associated partner at 4IMPROVE.

Ole Stegmann Mikkelsen is a Associate professor of Supply Chain Management at the Department of Entrepreneurship and Relationship Management at the University of Southern Denmark in Kolding. He holds a

PhD in Business Administration. His research and teaching interests are concentrated on globalization, supply chain management, strategic sourcing and supply chain innovation and operations management. He has published research articles in journals such as *Journal of Purchasing & Supply Management, International Journal of Procurement Management, Journal of Business & Industrial Marketing* and *Supply Chain Forum: An International Journal, Operations Management Research*. He primarily instructs MSc and PhD students in supply chain management, operations management and strategic sourcing. He has practical industry experience from positions as purchaser and planner at Milliken Denmark A/S, internal senior consultant, and director within strategy and business development, BI-implementation, and sourcing development & controlling within Danfoss A/S. Before that he served 10+ years as (Staff) Sergeant in the Royal Danish Army.

Thomas E. Johnsen is the Gianluca Spina Professor of Supply Chain Management at Politecnico di Milano School of Management in Italy, a Chair created in the honour of the past President of MIP. Prior to this role he was Professor of Purchasing and Supply Management at Audencia Nantes School of Management, where he was Head of the research axis: 'Organisation & Value Chain Management' and, most recently, at ESC-Rennes School of Business. Before joining Audencia, he was Lecturer (Assistant Professor) in Purchasing and Supply Management at the University of Bath and part of the Centre for Research in Strategic Purchasing and Supply (CRiSPS). He has held Part-Time Professorships at Jönköping International Business School in Sweden and University of Southern Denmark, and he is currently Associate Editor of the *Journal of Purchasing & Supply Management* and Associate Partner of Aperitas: a Danish start-up company offering a sustainable supply chain management platform. He has been executive board member of the International Purchasing & Supply Education & Research Association (IPSERA) and was Chair of the IPSERA 2013 conference at Audencia. His research has been cited over 2500 times; recent publications have appeared in leading international journals and his book (with M. Howard and J. Miemczyk) Purchasing and Supply Chain Management: a Sustainability Perspective was published by Routledge in April 2014 and awarded the ACA-Bruel coup de coeur prize. Thomas currently focuses on two issues: Purchasing involvement in discontinuous innovation and sustainable purchasing and supply chain management. He has worked with a large number of companies including Nokia, QinetiQ, UK

NHS, UN, Valmet, OP Financial Group, Metsa, Dyson, Airbus, Unipart, Filtronics, Land Rover, Nestle, TWR, Man Diesel, PA Consulting, Deloitte Touche and Viking Life.

Morten Munkgaard Møller is Associate Professor at Aalborg University. He has been active in the Danish purchasing and logistics community as a consultant and teacher and has helped numerous companies develop their sourcing strategies, implement supplier relationship management and worked with supplier segmentation in both theory and practice. Previously, Morten Munkgaard Møller, was Director for Global Procurement, LEGO System A/S. He took an active role in setting up e-procurement for LEGO, developing a new global purchasing strategy and implemented a HR-Competence Assessment system. Prior to that, Munkgaard Møller has worked as an Assistant Professor at Aarhus University. Preceding this, Morten Munkgaard Møller has spent 10 years in various purchasing and business development positions with Bang & Olufsen and Arla Foods. He holds a Ph.D. in Supply Chain Management from Aalborg University and a M.Sc. in Strategy from Aarhus School of Business/Aarhus University. Morten Munkgaard Møller is also a part-time, Associate Professor at Aarhus School of Business where he teaches industrial marketing, sourcing management and logistics management.

Jesper Kronborg Jensen is an economist at Energinet.dk. Before this position, he was an assistant professor of Supply Chain Management at the Department of Entrepreneurship and Relationship Management at the University of Southern Denmark in Kolding. He holds a PhD in Green Supply Chain Management with a focus on development of environmentally sustainable food supply chains and participated in a number of research projects including a strategic research program focusing of supply chain innovation in the offshore wind energy sector (ReCoE) (www.recoe.dk). He also participated in a research project focusing on developing sustainable transportation through improved actor interfaces. His research and teaching interests are within supply chain management, supply chain innovation and operations management. He published research papers in journals such as *Journal of Cleaner Production*, *International Journal of Physical Distribution & Logistics Management*, *Operations Management Research*, *Supply Chain Forum: An International Journal* and *European Business Review*. At that time, he primarily instructed Master of Science (MSc), Bachelor (BSc) and Graduate Diploma (HD) students in supply chain management, operations management and innovation management. He also has practical industry experience from positions as project employee at Kohberg Bread A/S.

Morten Brinch is an industrial PhD student employed at Siemens Gamesa and enrolled at the Department of Entrepreneurship and Relationship Management at the University of Southern Denmark in Kolding. Mortens is M.Sc. in Economics and Business Administration: Management and Leadership and former work has been as a business development consultant for SME's. The PhD project is embedded within supply chain management with a focus on understanding, conceptualizing and creating value from big data. To date, an in-depth literature review and an explorative Delphi study have been conducted, which have been published in conferences and business magazines. Future work will include case studies on how business processes can create value using big data. The PhD thesis is to be complete in 2019 and aims at disseminating research results in peer-reviewed journals.

Antony Paulraj is a Professor of Operations and Supply Chain Management at the Alliance Manchester Business School, The University of Manchester, UK. He completed his PhD in Operations Management from the Cleveland State University, Ohio, USA. His research interests are within operations management, supply chain management, strategic sourcing, sustainable supply chains and supply chain innovation. He has published over 40 research articles in operations and supply chain management journals including *Journal of Operations Management, International Journal of Operations and Production Management, Journal of Supply Chain Management, Journal of Business Logistics, International Journal of Production Research, Journal of Business Ethics*, among others. He has taught courses at undergraduate, masters, doctorate, and executive MBA programs. Among others, the courses that he has taught includes operations management, supply chain management, strategic sourcing, logistics management, sustainable supply chain management, service operations, research methodology, multivariate statistics, and structural equation modelling. He has been involved in numerous executive education as well as executive training programs in the USA, Europe and India. He has worked as an information technology consultant for over ten years. His consulting experience includes a range of organizations such as the State of Ohio, Global Energy Services (Emerson), Nationwide Insurance and the Children's Research Institute.